T3-BOE-229

Expans'd Hieroglyphicks

A CRITICAL EDITION

OF SIR JOHN DENHAM'S

COOPERS HILL

BY BRENDAN O HEHIR

UNIVERSITY OF CALIFORNIA PRESS

BERKELEY AND LOS ANGELES 1969

BRESCIA COLLEGE
LIBRARY
35117

University of California Press
Berkeley and Los Angeles, California
University of California Press, Ltd.
London, England

© 1969 by The Regents of the University of California
Library of Congress Catalog Card Number: 68-27163
Designed by Wolfgang Lederer
Printed in the United States of America

COPYRIGHT RESERVED. (PAINTING REPRODUCED BY PERMISSION.)

"Nor doth he need those Emblemes which we paint,
But is himself the Souldier and the Saint"
(Coopers Hill, "B" 109–110).

Rubens' "St. George and the Dragon"
(now in Buckingham Palace), commissioned by Charles I;
the saint wears the features of Charles himself,
the rescued princess those of Queen Henrietta Maria.
The scene is the right bank of the Thames near
the site of the Southwark end of Blackfriars Bridge.
Across the river lies an imagined early medieval
London: the square church tower (left) probably represents
St. Paul's; the fortress (center background,
above the king's head) is the Tower.

Expans'd
Hieroglyphicks

Dianae Venerique: Vivamus atque amemus . . .

Preface

"Sir *John Denham*, in his *Coopers Hill* [has written] a Poem which your Lordship knows for the Majesty of the Style is, and ever will be the exact Standard of good Writing." So wrote John Dryden in 1664, near the beginning of his career. At the end, in 1700, he expressed yet once more the undeviating admiration for Denham and his poem which he had also voiced several times in the interim. To Dryden's admiration for the poem may be added that of Herrick (the first to praise it), of Addison, Garth, Goldsmith, and Johnson. Pope and his antagonist Dennis disagreed over *Coopers Hill* only as rivals in lauding its beauties. These are names only of the better known today of countless admirers of Denham's poem. Perhaps hundreds of obscurer men committed their adulation to writing, while thousands were content to marvel in silence. For two centuries, Pope's prophecy seemed only a truism: "On Cooper's Hill eternal Wreaths shall grow, / While lasts the Mountain, or while Thames shall flow." [1]

Now once more, although *Coopers Hill* may have lost its fame as the exact standard of good writing, a new edition of the poem fortunately need not be a feeble voice in a dismal wilderness vainly calling scholarship to attend to it. Several recent scholars have already shown that *Coopers Hill* is a prime document for the study of English Augustan poetics, canons of taste, and even cosmology and social doctrines. [2] Additionally, a sympathetic reading can still elicit some-

---

1. The irony of history has begun to deplete Pope's lines of their intended salutation to Denham's poem. In 1953 H.M. Queen Elizabeth unveiled the Runnymede Commonwealth Air Force Memorial, on the brow of Cooper's Hill in Surrey, thereby, according to one booklet, "fulfilling the prophecy of Pope that — 'On Cooper's Hill eternal wreaths shall grow. . . .'"

2. I have in mind especially Rufus Putney ("The View from Cooper's Hill," *University of Colorado Studies*, Studies in Language and Literature, no. 6 [1957],

thing of the genuine charm that for more than a century enchanted readers of the poem. My work is intended as a contribution to this body of scholarship, and is not without hope even of reviving the possibility of aesthetic appreciation of the poem. But it is the work of modern scholars which justifies and requires the *edition* of the poem which constitutes the foundation of the present book. Obviously these scholars have all accomplished their studies of *Coopers Hill* without benefit of this edition; but this edition has been undertaken on the premise that even the best of those works might have profited from its prior existence, and that future serious attempts to study the poem without such an edition as that included here are foredoomed to futility.

An ideal universe would have no place for an editor. The literary critic could simply pick up the text of his author, assured of its veracity, and proceed to the immediate exercise of his trade. But in this imperfect world the author's holographs are usually unavailable and contemporary editions of his work scarce and available only in the collections of great libraries. A critical edition then becomes a necessity to both the critic and his reader. The critic must be assured that he has, as far as diligence and labor can attain it, a veritable text together with all its significant variations, and with the relationships among its exemplars clearly set forth. The reader needs the same material as common ground on which to follow the intricacies of the critic's argument. A "critical edition" of *Coopers Hill* already exists, in *The Poetical Works of Sir John Denham* (1928), edited by T. H. Banks, Jr. Therefore my edition cannot pretend to meet an explicit demand; it must show that it fills a need unrecognized. It is to the scholar who believes he can find all he requires for the study of *Coopers Hill* in the accepted edition that the present edition must jus-

---

pp. 13–22); Earl R. Wasserman (*The Subtler Language* [Baltimore, 1959], pp. 35–88); Aubrey Williams (edition of *Windsor Forest* in Alexander Pope, *Pastoral Poetry and An Essay on Criticism*, Twickenham Edition of the Poems of Alexander Pope, I [London and New Haven, 1961], 125–194); and Ruth Nevo (*The Dial of Virtue* [Princeton, 1963], pp. 30–37).

tify itself. The only justification upon which the present edition can rely, of course, is such justification as arises from whatever merits it may possess. Nevertheless without undue cautiousness the fundamentals of its dissent from its predecessor may be set forth: very bluntly, the preceding edition commences from a false premise and proceeds by an unsound method.

In stating the essential textual problem of *Coopers Hill* all subsidiary dispute may for the moment be set aside. It has never been a secret that *Coopers Hill* exists in at least two quite distinct versions, yet for some reason the implications of the fact have never been squarely faced; one modern scholar has even deliberately sought to avoid facing them. Yet about the poem this much at least is unquestionable: it was first printed in 1642, and reprinted in 1643 and 1650. Except for minor differences, those three editions contain the same text. In the present work that text is called the "A" text. In 1655 the poem was published again, but the text of that edition differed drastically from the "A" text. Once again in Denham's lifetime *Coopers Hill* was published: near the end of his career, in 1668, he brought out his collected *Poems and Translations*. The text of *Coopers Hill* in that volume is substantially the same as that of 1655, but with four lines added and some divergence in the readings of isolated lines. (Subsequently he added still another six lines, but these have only recently been recovered, and have never hitherto been incorporated in the text of the poem.) The 1655–1668 text in the present work is called the "B" text. Moreover, several manuscript copies of the poem survive, all containing texts more nearly resembling the "A" text than the "B" text.

In the face of this evidence Banks adopted the premise that in effect there is only one "real" text of *Coopers Hill*, namely the "B" text of 1668. Accordingly that is presented as the text of the poem, and all the other versions are compelled into a procrustean *apparatus criticus* in the guise of "variant readings." A predictable result is that the text must be confined only to the recto of the pages, the verso being reserved for the "variants." The pattern is set on the first page, where

twenty lines of text are confronted by thirty-four lines in the apparatus. So cumbersome a method virtually enjoins inequity and insuffi-
ciency of representation. As a consequence, the "B" text edition of
1655 is allowed a fairly free voice, and the manuscripts (of which only
two were known to Banks) a sporadic independence, but the three
editions of the "A" text are arbitrarily leveled to a single representative, the edition of 1642. Therefore the fact, for instance, that 1643
corrects a number of false readings in 1642 never comes to light.

At its most accurate this system grossly misrepresents the textual
facts, for there is virtually no line correspondence between the "B"
text and either the "A" text or the text contained in any of the
manuscripts. Therefore to be offered what purports to be the "A"
text variant reading of (say) line 115 of the "B" text is thoroughly
misleading unless the fact is made clear that the "variant" is actually
the reading of line 149 of the "A" text. Similarly to be told that a
manuscript contains a unique couplet occurring "after line 188" is
nearly meaningless. No exemplar of the "B" text contains the couplet;
the manuscript in question embodies a text much nearer to the "A"
text than to the "B" (although identical with neither), and in the "A"
text the equivalent place is after line 218. In the manuscript itself,
however, the unique couplet occurs as lines 209–210, and consequently comes after line 208.

The system also compounds the confusion attendant upon failure
to discriminate among the texts. Instead of only one real text of
Coopers Hill, there are two main texts revealing a succession of at
least four distinct drafts of the poem. The manuscripts represent not
a "variant" intermediate between the "A" and the "B" texts; they
represent rather two separate texts, both earlier than the "A" text.
I am fortunate in having three newly uncovered manuscripts upon
which to base my argument, which serve to sharpen the delineation
of the texts represented by the two manuscripts previously known.

In my edition of Coopers Hill I have recognized the fact that the
"A" text and the "B" text are products of two distinct periods and
sets of circumstances in Denham's life, set apart by more than a

decade. The "A" text has accordingly been edited separately from the "B" text, as an autonomous version of the poem. Since the manuscripts represent stages in the evolution of the "A" text, they have been introduced into the critical apparatus of that text, although the two drafts they represent have also been presented separately. The "B" text did not "evolve" out of the "A" text, but was basically the product of a single drastic and radical revision, designed to alter fundamentally the tenor of the poem. The separate editing of the "B" text offers sufficient complexities without introducing irrelevancies from the "A" text, which is best construed as a single totally variant reading. Additional material to the central presentation of texts includes an attempted analysis of the development of the poem through its stages, incorporated in critical interpretations of the principal texts.

Acknowledgments

Only when faced with the actuality of attempting to return some crumbs of gratitude for the banquets of help of which I have been the beneficiary am I made aware of the inevitable perfunctoriness of all such listings as this. The people who have helped me, at any rate, are almost too numerous to name, and the help they have given too vast to specify. Of some of those who have contributed materially to this book I do not even know the names: without, for instance, the friendly and intelligent staffs of the Bodleian Library, the British Museum Library (especially the Manuscripts Room), the Public Record Office, the Henry E. Huntington Library, and the William Andrews Clark Memorial Library, I might still be hopelessly embogged in books and documents; certainly the work would have been much less pleasurable without those gracious and busy people. Other names I have doubtless forgotten or overlooked, but to everyone so slighted I can only add my sincerest apology to my equal gratitude. Nor, though certain persons are named only in this present list, others only in the companion biography of Denham, would I willingly imply that anyone's contributions can be arbitrarily isolated within a single one of the two books.

For the present book, however, the aid I have received has been so particularly generous and profuse that I can merely list here, alphabetically, the more prominent in my memory of those to whom I am gratefully indebted. Some receive specific acknowledgment also within the body of this work; some, whose generosity is so catholic that few practicing scholars can have escaped indebtedness to them, will perhaps not recall the help they have extended. But I assure all that I retain a lively sense of their kindnesses although for economy of space I merely list their names without attempting the monumental task of specifying the often innumerable ways in which each has been helpful. My heartfelt thanks, then, to Professor R. C. Bald, Department of English, University of Chicago; Professor Thomas G. Barnes, Department of History, University of California, Berkeley; Mr. Carey S. Bliss, curator of rare books, Henry E. Huntington Library; Mr. Kenneth E. Carpenter, assistant to the librarian, Library of Harvard University; Dr. Giles Dawson, curator of books and manuscripts, The Folger Shakespeare Library; Mrs. S. M. Foster, reference librarian, Union Theological Seminary Library, New York; Miss Mary Isabel Fry, librarian, Henry E. Huntington Library; Mr. C. J. Hindle, former assistant librarian, Department of Printed Books, Bodleian Library; Professor F. D. Hoeniger, Department of English, Victoria College, Toronto; Michael B. Hutchinson, Esq., Caux, Vaud, Switzerland; Professor Robert L. McNulty, Department of English, University of California, Berkeley; Mr. D. G. Neill, assistant librarian, Department of Printed Books, Bodleian Library; Mr. James M. Osborn, Department of English, Yale University; Dr. M. Poch-Kalous, Direktor, Gemäldegalerie der Akademie der Bildenden Künste, Vienna; Miss M. Pollard, library assistant, The Library, Trinity College, Dublin; Mr. M. Randall, Publications Department, The National Gallery, London; Dr. Allen H. Stevenson, bibliographer, Chicago; Professor Stanley Stewart, Department of English, University of California, Riverside; Mr. F. C. Tighe, city librarian, City of Nottingham Public Libraries; Professor Ernest Tuveson, Department of English, University of California, Berkeley; Mr. R. J. B. Walker, curator of pictures, H.M. Ministry of Works, London; Professor Earl R. Wasserman, Department of English, The Johns Hopkins University; Mr. James M. Wells, custodian, The Rare Book Room, The Newberry Library; Mr. A. W. Wheen, keeper of the library, Victoria and Albert Museum; Professor Aubrey Williams, Department of English, University of Florida; Miss Marjorie G. Wynne, librarian, Rare Book Room, Yale University Library; and two final persons, most regrettably to be set apart — the late Professor William A. Jackson, librarian of the Library of Harvard University, and the late Mr. A. E. Villars, clerk of the Egham Urban District Council, Egham, Surrey.

Two others require special notice even among so many: my stepson, Michael Farnham Fiske, whose unjaded eyes caught many a textual variant invisible to me; and my good friend, Professor Ralph W. Rader of the Department of English, University of California, Berkeley, without whose critical and practical aid and advice completion and publication of this work might have been long delayed.

B. O H.

Contents

A Chronology
OF DENHAM'S LIFE
RELATIVE TO THE COMPOSITION
AND REVISION OF *COOPERS HILL*

1615		Born, Dublin
1617		Removes to Egham, Surrey (location of Cooper's Hill), where he grows up
1631		Enters Trinity College, Oxford
1634		Marries; begins law study at Lincoln's Inn
1636		Translates *Aeneid* II–VI
1639		Inherits estates on death of his father; is admitted to the bar
1641	March	Trial of Strafford begins; Denham a witness for defense
	May	Execution of Strafford; "On the Earl of Strafford's Tryal and Death"; *Coopers Hill*, Draft I?
	Later	*The Sophy*?
1642	February	"Elegy on the Death of Judge Crooke" *Coopers Hill*, Draft II?
	August	*The Sophy* and *Coopers Hill*, Draft III ("A" text), published in London
	October	Takes up arms for the King
	December	Prisoner of war in London
1643	March?	Released; joins King at Oxford
	April?	*Coopers Hill*, corrected, republished in Oxford

1647	Wife dies; estates sequestered
1648	Flees to Continent
1649 January	Charles I executed
1650	1642 *Coopers Hill* republished in London
1651–52	Satirical poems on Davenant's *Gondibert*
1653 March	Returns to England; harbored at Wilton by Earl of Pembroke, member of Council of State
April	Cromwell's coup d'état expels Rump
December	*Instrument of Government* names Cromwell lord protector
1653–54	At Wilton revises *Coopers Hill* and *Aeneid* translations
1655	*Coopers Hill*, Draft IV ("B" text), published in London
1656	*The Destruction of Troy* (*Aeneid* II) published in London
1660	Restoration of Charles II; Denham appointed surveyor general
1661	Knighted (Order of the Bath)
1665	Remarries
1666 April	Suffers brief attack of madness; quickly recovers
June	Lady Denham the Duke of York's mistress
November	Lady Denham complains of poisoning
1667 January	Lady Denham dies; autopsy reveals no trace of poison Burst of renewed poetic activity
1668 Spring	*Poems and Translations* published, including revised version of 1655 *Coopers Hill*, containing four new lines;

also partial translation of *Aeneid* IV
Subsequent to publication of
Poems and Translations adds six new
lines to *Coopers Hill*
Additional new poetic composition continues

1669 March   Dies; is buried in Westminster Abbey

Topographical Note

COOPER'S HILL / EGHAM, SURREY

Cooper's Hill, the "auspicious height" of Denham's famous poem, rises in the northern part of the present Egham Urban District, closely adjacent to the village of Egham proper, Denham's childhood home. Therefore the hill must have occupied a prominent place in his awareness from infancy to manhood. Although the hill, in fact a ridge of what is called Bagshot sand, rises a mere 220 feet above the surrounding land, its value as a viewpoint is out of all proportion to its height, for the land lying north and east of it is absolutely flat. A spot on the hill known as "The Lookout" has always been frequented by local people for the views that can be obtained from it.

Since Denham grew up in Egham it is unlikely that any one survey of the view from Cooper's Hill provided the occasion or the inspiration of his poem. Yet tradition assigns his poetical survey to one particular spot in the grounds of Kingswood Lodge, an eighteenth-century residence that occupies part of the ridge of Cooper's Hill. One of the earlier owners of the lodge erected a seat on the spot, to commemorate the poem, and the seat is unfailingly mentioned in nineteenth-century guidebooks. From that spot, or from any other viewpoint on the hill, the view to the west and north must still closely resemble what Denham saw, but the view to the east has been radically altered. Egham itself is in the extreme northwest corner of Surrey, immediately adjacent to Windsor Great Park and Windsor Forest in Berkshire to the west and north, and separated by the Thames from Buckinghamshire to the north and from Middlesex to the immediate east. Therefore the view from Cooper's Hill readily embraces four counties (including Surrey), and is said to extend over seven counties in all.

To the west of Cooper's Hill, only a few miles away in Berkshire, the towers of Windsor Castle rise impressively above a landscape of trees. Only five miles to the east, in Chertsey, St. Anne's Hill, also a steep ridge of Bagshot sand, thrusts up abruptly from the river plain to a height of 240 feet, and from some points of view appears almost conical. No trace remains of St. Anne's Chapel (built in 1334) but in 1858 apparently a small pile of stones remained, close behind the St. Anne's "View-point." Directly below Cooper's Hill the Thames and the meadows, retained undeveloped as washland for the river, remain much as Denham saw them. These features provided not merely specific associations and settings for incidents of his poem, but also for his more general imagery of river floods and flood control.

Directly below Cooper's Hill, "Between the mountain and the stream embrac't," the grassy meadow still exists which served as locus for Denham's allegorical stag hunt, and also, as he specifies in the poem, as the meeting place of King John and his barons at which Magna Charta was first issued. The memorial to Magna Charta erected by the American Bar Association in 1957 in fact stands on the lower slopes of Cooper's Hill. Aside from historical piety, what has preserved the meadows at Egham from development is the periodic overflowings of the Thames. The limitations of feasible flood controls "When a calm River rais'd with sudden rains, / Or Snows dissolv'd, oreflows th'adjoyning Plaines," which Denham employs symbolically in *Coopers Hill*, are based on the realities of dealing with the Thames in the vicinity of Egham. The words of the late Mr. A. E. Villars, clerk of the Egham Urban District Council (in a letter to me), provide in fact a very cogent commentary on much of the imagery of Denham's poem:

Much of the land adjoining the River Thames is open to provide wash land for the flood waters, but further down stream there is quite a lot of development which is now regretted because of its spoliation of the riverside and the problem it creates in times of flooding because land covered by buildings to longer can perform its function of wash land.

There is no question of trying to control the flooding; although the Thames has a number of locks and weirs and adjustment of these takes place when the river is in full spate, if there is abnormal rainfall or a very quick thaw after heavy snowfall the river is not big enough to take all the water, and flooding is inevitable. The length of banks involved, apart from other considerations, makes it impossible physically or economically to contemplate trying to contain the river to prevent flooding.

At the same time, as Denham also makes clear, sane and judicious defenses against flooding are not merely desirable but practical: "The Husbandmen with high-rais'd banks secure / Their greedy hopes, and this he can endure." The floodplain below Cooper's Hill provided in Denham's time, as it still does, one example of such a "high-rais'd bank": the causeway constructed in the reign of Henry III to protect low-lying parts of the town and to facilitate passage between Egham and Staines during floodtimes. Mr. Villars reported that the causeway even yet performs well its old function:

It now takes the form of a raised bank which constitutes the footpath adjacent to the main road (which bears the name "The Causeway"), but, by reason of development and alteration in the connecting highways, as well as the construction of new motorways, it has been somewhat cut about. However, it has proved a staunch barrier against flooding from the River Thames. Although the District suffered its worst flooding for over fifty years in 1947 this was due to infiltration, and not direct assault from the River. However, most road works carried out adjoining or across or interfering with the causeway have been executed with due regard for the function it performed, so that in most cases the new works replace, in an entirely different form, the old causeway. A certain amount of flooding is experienced on average every three years but, with the improvements made to the lower reaches of the River Thames which have resulted in the more rapid passage of the waters, the tendency for flooding has diminished, and it is interesting to record that although [in 1962–63] we have suffered the heaviest snowfall and coldest weather within living memory and the conditions were not dissimilar to 1947, no flooding whatsoever has been experienced.

From the washlands of Runnymede and Long Meadow below Cooper's Hill it was probably less hyperbolic in 1642 than it is today to describe the hill as an "aery Mountain." At that time, it is pretty certain, much of the approach and the slope was grass covered and would therefore give the impression of greater height into misty loftiness, whereas this now is minimized by hedges, trees, and development. In Denham's time the hill was probably unbuilt upon, whereas now it bears not only the eighteenth-century Kingswood Lodge, but also the nineteenth-century former Cooper's Hill Royal Engineering College, now used by the London County Council as Shoreditch Teachers' Training College. Most recently considerable additional building has risen in association with the college, for living and working accommodations for the students. Between Kingswood Lodge and the college, on what was formerly waste ground, an elaborate memorial to the airmen of the Commonwealth who lost their lives in World War II, and who have no known graves, was dedicated in 1953. These three constructions now entirely occupy the summit of the ridge, yet without diminishing its advantages as a viewpoint.

Exactly how clearly Denham could distinguish St. Paul's in London from Cooper's Hill the poem leaves open to conjecture. Certainly all versions of the poem strongly suggest that London was chiefly discernible as a smoky cloud, although they disagree somewhat among themselves as to the visibility of the cathedral — whether Denham could actually see it, or merely knew that it was there. Obviously the landscape in that direction from Cooper's Hill has been altered so drastically since the seventeenth century — by the enormous growth of London, by the erection of tall buildings, by such developments as factories, powerhouses, railways, motor roads, and bridges undreamed of in Denham's time — that it is almost impossible to recapture what the scene was like which presented itself to his eyes. Without question London, just to the north of east, in the seventeenth century was already wrapped in a pall of coal smoke (the commissions established by James I and Charles I to investigate the fabric of St. Paul's note the corrosion of stone caused by the smoky atmosphere). Still, in a booklet published in Egham about 1840, it was asserted that from the grounds of Kingswood Lodge "the hour and minute hands of St. Paul's Clock, have, by the aid of a telescope been distinctly seen." Mr. Villars, who communicated this information, added that "it came as news to the present occupier [of the lodge] that it had been possible to see" St. Paul's clock from the place. A certain apocryphal quality in the assertion may be felt, however, when it is discovered that precisely the same claim was made for St. Anne's Hill in 1858. John Murray, publisher and possibly author of *A Handbook for Travellers in Surrey, Hampshire, and the Isle of Wight* (London, 1858), offers this information to the prospective tourist on St. Anne's Hill: "A deep pall hovers over London, but you can see the dome of St. Paul's looming through the mist; nay, we have heard of those who have told the hour of the day upon its broad-faced clock with the assistance of a good glass" (p. 102).

Although Murray also guides the traveler to Cooper's Hill, he apparently has no tales of clocks or telescopes pertaining to it. Nonetheless he may be allowed here the final word on that hill:

From the ancient residence of Denham the tourist may proceed to Cooper's Hill, the famous scene of his poem. This is a long ridge of the "Bagshot sand," stretching away toward the N.W., and rising abruptly from the plashy meadows which adjoin Runnimede. Its elevation is not great, but the prospect might well inspire a far worse poet than Denham. It embraces nearly every point that has been already noticed at St. Anne's Hill; but the towers of Windsor here confer an additional grandeur, and the river still glides below us as in the days when the poet desired to make it "his great example, as it was his theme" (p. 105).

xxvii

Abbreviations

For sources cited repeatedly in this work I have habitually used the following abbreviations and short titles:

Banks, *Poetical Works* Theodore Howard Banks, Jr., *The Poetical Works of Sir John Denham*. New Haven, 1928.

Dugdale, *History of St. Paul's* Sir William Dugdale, *The History of St. Paul's Cathedral in London, from its Foundation.* 2d ed. London, 1716.

Harmony from Discords Brendan O Hehir, *Harmony from Discords: A Life of Sir John Denham*. Berkeley and Los Angeles, 1968.

Heylyn, *Historie of St. George* Peter Heylyn, *The Historie of . . . St. George . . . The Institution of the most Noble Order of . . . the Garter.* 1631; 1633.

JEGP *Journal of English and Germanic Philology*

Johnson, *Lives of the Poets* Samuel Johnson, *The Lives of the Most Eminent English Poets.* London, 1781. 4 vols. Frequently republished.

MLQ *Modern Language Quarterly*

PMLA *Publications of the Modern Language Association*

PQ *Philological Quarterly*

Wood, *Athenae Oxonienses*   Anthony Wood, *Athenae Oxoni-enses: An Exact History of all the Writers and Bishops Who have had their Education in the most Antient and Famous University of Oxford . . . The Second Edition, very much Corrected and En-larged.* London, 1721. 2 vols. in 1.

Thus there are two bookes
from whence I collect my Divinity;
besides that written one of God,
another of his servant Nature,
that universall and publik Manuscript,
that lies expans'd unto the eyes of all . . .
surely the Heathens knew better how
to joyne and reade these mysticall letters,
than wee Christians, who cast
a more carelesse eye on those
common Hieroglyphicks . . .

Sir Thomas Browne / *Religio Medici*

INTRODUCTION TO *COOPERS HILL*

Coopers Hill
and "Local Poetry"

Cooper's Hill is the work that confers upon [Denham] the rank and dignity of an original author. He seems to have been, at least among us, the author of a species of composition that may be denominated local poetry, of which the fundamental subject is some particular landscape, to be poetically described, with the addition of such embellishments as may be supplied by historical retrospection or incidental meditation.

To trace a new scheme of poetry has in itself a very high claim to praise, and its praise is yet more when it is apparently copied by Garth and Pope, after whose names little will be gained by an enumeration of smaller poets, that have left scarcely a corner of the island not dignified either by rhyme or blank verse.

So wrote Samuel Johnson in his life of Sir John Denham.[1]

As is true of most of what Dr. Johnson ever has had to say, there is in these remarks a great deal of truthful perception, a certain amount of judgment couched in terms that must be interpreted if they are not to mislead, and a small share of inaccuracy. For instance, it is not quite true that no poem like *Coopers Hill* had ever before been written in English, though exactly which poems are selected as its antecedents depends upon the definition of the kind it itself exemplifies. Moreover, to be an accurate evaluation of what actually takes place in *Coopers Hill*, each of Johnson's phrases in definition of its genre requires careful qualification. The poem's "fundamental subject" is the "particular landscape" of the Thames Valley as seen from Cooper's

---

1. *Lives of the Poets*, "Denham."

Hill only if the phrase "fundamental subject" is understood to have a meaning such as "substructure of the discourse." That is, *Coopers Hill* is not *about* the landscape: the landscape underlies and contains what it is about. The real "subject" of the poem is what Johnson calls the "embellishments . . . supplied by historical retrospection or incidental meditation," and here "incidental" must not be understood to mean merely fortuitous, but instead *dependent upon* or naturally *arising out of* some feature of the scene. Johnson's most unfortunate inexactitude is his statement that these embellishments are an "addition" to the poetical description of the landscape: on the contrary, they derive from the landscape. Historical retrospection and incidental meditation upon the landscape in fact yield and embody the real substance and "subject" of the poem. Johnson's description, in other words, takes account of the realities of the situation, but formulates them with a false placing of emphasis.

Alexander Pope's analysis of *Coopers Hill* and its kind superficially resembles what Johnson says. In Denham's poem "the descriptions of places and images raised by the poet are still tending to some hint, or leading into some reflection upon moral life or political institution, much in the same manner as the real sight of such scenes and prospects is apt to give the mind a composed turn, and incline it to thoughts and contemplations that have a relation to the object."[2] Pope's statement has led to as much mistaken thinking about the genre of *Coopers Hill* as has Johnson's, though perhaps with less reason. In the century and more of literary nature worshiping which followed the ages of Pope and Johnson, the chief virtue of any poem that resembled *Coopers Hill* would be taken to be the verisimilitude of the described landscape, its resemblance to "the real sight of such scenes and prospects." But Pope's statement, it will be noticed, does not stress the description of the landscape as the essence of the poem: his focus is upon the "tending to some hint, or leading into some reflection upon moral life or political institution." To Pope, in other words, it is the

---

2. Pope, *The Iliad of Homer* (London, 1763), III, 169n.

historical retrospection and incidental meditation that appeal, and the landscape of the poem, like the landscapes of nature, is of importance for the thoughts and contemplations to which it inclines the mind rather than for its passive values as an object of sight or as a pleasure to the senses. In this view of the nature of *Coopers Hill* Pope is at unison with Denham who in all four drafts of the poem tries to make clear that the apprehension of the scenery by the mind takes preeminence over mere sense perception: "More boundlesse in my Fancy then myne Eye." At the same time Denham through all drafts also tries to emphasize the active rather than the passive role of the landscape itself in initiating cognition: "Windsore . . . above the Valley Swells, into myne Eye . . . her gentle Bosome doth present" in the earliest draft of the poem becomes in the final draft "*Windsor* . . . above the Valley swells / Into my eye, and doth it self present."

Pope's own practice shows how thoroughly in reality he understood the true nature of *Coopers Hill,* for not merely does *Windsor Forest* stand self-confessed as a poem inspired by *Coopers Hill,* but a careful analysis shows it to conform to the precedents of Denham's piece in every significant detail.[3] Accordingly, one part of Johnson's remarks on *Windsor Forest* can usefully be brought to bear on his definition of the poetic kind of *Coopers Hill:* "The design of *Windsor Forest* is evidently derived from *Cooper's Hill,* with some attention to Waller's poem on *The Park.*"[4] This remark reveals that Johnson's instincts are brilliantly superior to his verbal formulations. On the one hand he has categorized *Coopers Hill* as the initial English specimen of "local poetry"; on the other hand he has associated it specifically with *Windsor Forest* and Waller's *On St. James's Park, as lately improv'd by his Majesty.* And certainly it is true that *Windsor Forest* borrows some details from Waller's poem, so that Pope also acknowledges, tacitly,

---

3. For an elaborate analysis of *Windsor Forest* in the light of *Coopers Hill* see Earl R. Wasserman, *The Subtler Language* (Baltimore, 1959), pp. 89–168. The two poems had been earlier compared in some detail, though with a demented bias against Pope's work, by John Dennis (*The Critical Works,* ed. E. N. Hooker [Baltimore, 1943], II, 116–137).

4. Johnson, *Lives of the Poets,* "Pope."

both *Coopers Hill* and *St. James's Park* as progenitors of *Windsor Forest*, and so, implicitly, precursors in the same genre. To elaborate, then, Pope and Johnson between them have established *Coopers Hill* as an early specimen of a genre that includes also *St. James's Park* and *Windsor Forest*; while Johnson also has denominated the kind "local poetry" and indicated a proliferation of the kind through the work of "smaller poets" who, as a writer in the *Gentleman's Magazine* complained in 1788, since *Coopers Hill* might be found "reclining on almost every mole-hill." [5] Although in his remarks specifically directed at *Coopers Hill* Johnson names Samuel Garth rather than Edmund Waller as a noteworthy later practitioner of the kind, it is perhaps significant that he does not name Garth in connection with *Windsor Forest*, and if, as seems probable, it is Garth's *Claremont* he had in mind, he fails to mention that poem whatsoever in his life of Garth.

Because *Coopers Hill*, *St. James's Park*, and *Windsor Forest* are all poems concerned with geographical places, Johnson's term, "local poetry," may seem to cover their common kind adequately enough, and my attempt to insinuate an unconscious distinction on his part between the poems he names and the other specimens of "local poetry" he feels there would be little value in enumerating is merely farfetched. But whether or not Johnson felt a real distinction between these three poems and the perhaps hundreds of topographical poems in a succession commencing, it may be, with Fage's *St. Leonard's Hill*, and including Dyer's *Grongar Hill*, a real distinction does exist. For, although all these poems — hill poems, estate poems, town poems, building poems, region poems, river poems, and park poems — share with the poems of Denham, Waller, and Pope a topographical focus, the latter three share many other more important attributes not characteristic of their lesser imitations. [6]

5. Quoted by R. D. Havens, *The Influence of Milton on English Poetry* (1922), p. 248, cited by Banks, *Poetical Works*, pp. 56–57.

6. R. A. Aubin, *Topographical Poetry in XVIII-Century England* (New York, 1936), provides an extensive bibliography of "Hill-Poems, Sea-Poems, Mine- (and Cave-) Poems, Estate-Poems, Town-Poems, Building-Poems, Region-Poems, River-Poems, Journey-Poems."

Whenever a literary work of a new kind achieves a critical or popular success, as *Coopers Hill* did in the seventeenth century, it is almost certain to give rise not merely to the continuation of its own proper kind, but to pseudogenres as well. Since by virtue of the very novelty of the new work its essential nature may not be understood even by its creator, prominent superficial characteristics are almost inevitably seized upon as definitive of the new kind, and spurious new genres then arise based upon imitation of the accidents rather than the essence. *Coopers Hill* has at least three obvious characteristics that, either singly or in combination, enter into all its successors so far mentioned: (1) it is named after a hill, which in some sense it is "about"; (2) it describes a specific landscape — the Thames Valley as viewed from Cooper's Hill; and (3) apart from landscape description, it narrates a stag hunt that seems to be in some sense "allegorical." From the first characteristic derive the forty-six "hill" poems up to 1821 which Raymond D. Havens counted.[7] From the second characteristic, more important, derive not only the "hill" poems but the general body of "local poetry." Under this heading it is of course also possible to include both *St. James's Park* and *Windsor Forest*. The third characteristic is also frequently repeated. *Windsor Forest* contains an almanac of hunting scenes, and in *St. James's Park* a mutation of the stag hunt may be recognized in the angling practiced on the lake as well as in the king's sport of *paille-maille*. *St. Leonard's Hill* (1666) contains a stag hunt, and the hunt in *Coopers Hill* may probably claim a separate offspring in Sir Robert Howard's *The Dewell of the Staggs*. That poem conforms to the description by the 1655 editor of *Coopers Hill* of the hunt in Denham's poem as an "Allegory of the *Royall Stag*." The setting for Howard's poem is Windsor Forest, and the contending stags are described as rivals for a monarchy; the poem is obscurely about the falls and the succession of princes, and overt allusion to the recent civil wars strengthens the impression that in some way it is topical or allegorical. Yet any attempt to apply the details of the poem

---

7. *The Influence of Milton*, App. C.

to the details of the succession from Charles I to Cromwell, for instance, or from Cromwell to Charles II, runs at once into irresolvable difficulties. Nonetheless, *The Dewell of the Staggs* may properly be regarded as a sterile offshoot of *Coopers Hill*, an instructive instance of a pseudogenre.

But poems that share with *Coopers Hill* no more than some combination of its three obvious characteristics are all merely representatives of pseudogenres. Which is to say that Johnson's denomination of *Coopers Hill* as local poetry is a merely superficial denomination, a placing of the poem in one of the pseudogenres it generated. All the same, both *St. James's Park* and *Windsor Forest* really do belong to the same essential genre as *Coopers Hill*. Among these three poems even further superficial common traits may be instanced which distinguish them from the mass of topographical poems, even from Garth's *Claremont*. All three, for instance, deal with the Thames, and with its importance to British commerce and for Britain's power and prestige in the world. *Windsor Forest* deals not only with the forest, which was part of the view from Cooper's Hill, but reciprocally with Cooper's Hill, and with essentially the same landscape as that of Denham's poem: the Thames Valley from Windsor to London. Waller's poem, though narrower in scope and on the whole more trivial than the other two, is set in part of the same scene: the royal city of Westminster. It views St. James's Park as a microcosm of all England, and indeed of the world, and there is no difficulty recognizing in it a minuscule model of the landscape of *Coopers Hill*. Whereas Denham had set the King's Windsor at one end of his panorama, the turbulent people's London at the other, with St. Paul's Cathedral as a token of the royal presence among the Londoners, Waller is able to see from the King's St. James's Park both the Parliament building and, "Hard by that House where all our ills were shap'd," the one church edifice in England most closely associated with royalty, Westminster Abbey. The special structurings of the landscapes described in all three poems, distinctive as they are of these poems from most other examples of local poetry, do not in themselves constitute the specific differentiation of the kind to which these poems really belong. The shared landscape is technically accidental, but it does point to where the real differentia lies. It is not the landscape that counts, so much as the use made of it. Each poem meditates upon a landscape that it specifically associates with a monarch. Each poem is concerned primarily with the question of monarchy — the nature of princes, the place of the monarch in a commonwealth, reciprocal duties of subjects and rulers, and, above all, the harmony and balance of a well-constituted state.[8] The poems are primarily political in subject and intent, and are therefore poles apart from their scores of superficial imitations dealing with the grandeur of Welsh hills and Irish parks, and the amenities of private gentlemen's estates.

Another road to true understanding of the intent of these poems is opened through the direct classical connections established clearly by Pope, less obviously by Denham. It has long been recognized that Pope, playing what may be viewed as a childish if harmless game, labeled *Windsor Forest* a "georgic" poem, in association with his *Pastorals*, by imitating the association that Vergil made between his *Bucolics* and his *Georgics*. That is, Vergil repeated, in the last line of his last *Georgic*, the first line of his first *Eclogue*, and Pope repeated, in the last line of *Windsor Forest*, the first line of "Spring," his first *Pastoral*.[9] Consequently, it appears, Pope found no incongruity in an "imitation" of *Coopers Hill* being at the same time an "imitation" of Vergil's *Georgics*; therefore he presumably thought of *Coopers Hill* and the *Georgics* as being separate representatives of the same poetic kind. Of ultimately greater significance is the fact that Sir John Denham seems also to have been under the same impression. Denham had written no obvious pastoral poetry by means of which he could work the Vergilean labeling trick worked by Pope, but another method of

---

8. Wasserman discusses *Coopers Hill* and *Windsor Forest* in this light in *The Subtler Language*, pp. 35–168. His otherwise perceptive study of *Coopers Hill* is sadly marred, however, by his attempt to evade the problem presented by the several discrepant texts of the poem (p. 48 n. 2).

9. See, e.g., E. Audra and Aubrey Williams, eds., *Pastoral Poetry and An Essay on Criticism*, Twickenham Edition of the Poems of Alexander Pope, I (London, 1961), 194.

Vergilean labeling came to his hand. At *Aeneid* II.306, Vergil repeats a phrase from *Georgic* I.325–326; when Denham in 1656 published *The Destruction of Troy*, a translation of part of *Aeneid* II, he used for his equivalent of line 306 a phrase borrowed from *Coopers Hill*, a phrase that conveyed the same general sense as the Latin but did not literally translate it. That Denham's intention of thereby labeling *Coopers Hill* as his georgic did not fail of notice is evidenced by Moses Pengry's 1676 translation of *Coopers Hill* into Latin, which renders the *Coopers Hill* phrase by the equivalent phrase in *Georgic* I (and *Aeneid* II), even though the respective English and Latin phrases are not true translations of each other.[10] Whether or not Denham, Pope, and Pengry are correct in identifying *Coopers Hill* (and *Windsor Forest*) with the genre of Vergil's *Georgics*, it seems fairly clear that they did make the identification. If *Coopers Hill*, *Windsor Forest*, and the *Georgics* are all viewed synoptically with a late-Renaissance eye, it is also relatively easy to see certain large resemblances among them which might account for that identification. To state the matter as simply as possible, all are poems ostensibly *de re rustica* which really deal with imperial themes.

No species of classical poetry has been so ill understood by later times as has the georgic. The Renaissance tendency to divide the world of men into only three spheres, rustic, urban, and courtly, tended to confound the georgic with the pastoral; in most of the sixteenth- and seventeenth-century systems of classifying the various "kinds" of poems it is impossible to find any category that will satisfactorily separate the two. The fact is highly ironic, for the Renaissance in general also accepted the Vergilean career as the model for any poet who aspired ultimately to write a great epic, doctrinal to a nation: he must apprentice himself first to the writing of epic meters in the conventional, simple form of the pastoral, for which relatively little learning was required. With growing maturity he would proceed to the georgic

---

10. See App. A, below, *Coopers Hill Latine Redditum*, note to line 174; B. O Hehir, "Vergil's First *Georgic* and Denham's *Coopers Hill*," *PQ*, XLII (1963), 542–547.

and thence, having wandered long enough in fancy's maze, go on at last to soar into the epic air above Helicon. Milton's pastoral beginnings, for instance, are as readily discernible as his epic climax, but whether or not he passed through an intermediary georgic stage is a question at best only moot. Pope, on the other hand, has clearly denoted the first two stages of the *Imitatio Vergilii* in his own career (although the disintegration of the third stage in fact constitutes the profoundest and most fascinating part of his poetic life), and *Windsor Forest* is his georgic work. For still later critical tastes the world of men was further narrowed to two spheres, city and country, and the attention of poetry largely directed only to the latter. In such a critical ambience both pastoral and georgic were represented as poems concerned with the description of nature, or poems that ought to be so concerned, and because of the manifest artificiality of most specimens of both classes, both in time fell out of favor. The same critical fate overtook *Coopers Hill* and *Windsor Forest*. Pope's poem, for instance, in postromantic academic appreciation was accepted as a saving poetic token from that classic of our prose, because of its touches of "nature." But *Windsor Forest*, or *Coopers Hill*, or Vergil's *Georgics*, for that matter, if passed for poems of "natural description," are passed under false pretenses.

Certain dogmatic assertions regarding Vergil's three chief bodies of poetic work must be made. Most fundamental of these is that *Eclogues*, *Georgics*, and *Aeneid* alike are substantially concerned with politics in the larger sense: they are all *de re publica*, concerned with the common weal. The *Eclogues* depict chiefly rural scenes and rural persons, and the persons are chiefly herdsmen of one kind or another, keepers of flocks though not necessarily shepherds. Withal, the poems are filled with allusions to political topicalities: the expropriatory land grants to Octavian's veterans in the neighborhood of Mantua, the assassination and deification of Julius Caesar, the generosity of Gaius Asinius Pollio. On the whole, the relationship of the pastoral persons to the political events is a passive one; the poems express various moods — hopeful, elegiac, prophetic — in reaction to the deeds

11

of political men, but they make no attempt to intervene in or direct events. The *Aeneid*, on the other hand, is set in courts and on battle-fields, and is designedly doctrinal and exemplary. In Aeneas is presented at once the model of Roman virtue, to be emulated by all citizens, and the model of a great and virtuous ruler who is, the reader is left in little doubt, both type and forerunner as well as ancestor of Augustus. Between the two extremes of pastoral and epic fall the *Georgics*.

Like the *Eclogues*, the *Georgics* deal with rural matters, but with farming rather than herding. The difference between the two kinds of poems is parallel to the difference between the passive and the active forms of husbandry. In the pastoral convention the keeping of herds is a leisurely occupation which allows the herdsman abundance of time in which to compose his songs and airs, to play the syrinx, to fall in love, to cultivate a personality which remains nonetheless somewhat vapid. In the georgic the landscape is not peopled with distinct actors, and narration is conducted through an unidentified poetic voice much resembling the voice of an epic narrator. Such personality as may be attributed to the georgic narrator is a grave and austere one, deeply concerned with affairs both agricultural and political, and full of practical knowledge in the first sphere which he proceeds to transfer to the second. The narrator inhabits a somber and real world — the world of work — rather than any pastoral Arcadia. Vergil's *Georgics*, after all, are concerned with γεωργικός, the working (ἔργον) of the earth (γῆ); their chief classical antecedent was the grim and practical *Works and Days* of Hesiod. Hesiod's poem is concerned equally with practical advice on farming, with the related matter of due times and seasons in agriculture and the prognostication of weather, and with the unhappy age of iron in which it was Hesiod's lot to live. *Mutatis mutandis* each of these elements reappears not only in Vergil's *Georgics* but also in *Coopers Hill* and *Windsor Forest*. Vergil's *Georgics* alter the balance among these elements, for Vergil was not really a farmer in the sense that Hesiod probably was. In Vergil's *Georgics* the rural scene and the practical

12

lore of agriculture are converted into symbols and paradigms of political affairs. Some of the topicalities of the *Eclogues* reappear in the
Georgics; Caesar's assassination, for instance, is touched on at the
climax of *Georgic* I, and *Georgic* IV in optimistic mood concerns
itself in part with the felicitous rule of Augustus. But in contrast with
the *Eclogues*, the *Georgics* respond actively to political events; they
presume to instruct, to warn, to give advice in politics as in farming,
and in truth the farming lore, howsoever effectively deployed, is only
incidental to the real politically hortatory purpose of the poems.

   The relevance of this analysis of the *Georgics* to *Coopers Hill* and
Windsor Forest should be obvious. Though to be sure neither English poem pretends to offer much in the way of agricultural advice,
both offer some. *Coopers Hill*, for instance, comments on the ferti-
lizing benefits conferred on soil flooded by a river, and on practical
and impractical methods of preserving crops from inundation. Both
poems retain vestigial traces of weather prognostication, of concern
with the calendar of due times and seasons. Even the stag hunt of
Coopers Hill and the hunts of *Windsor Forest* (as certainly Howard's
Dewell of the Staggs) owe something to the suggestive duel of the
bulls in *Georgic* III. Most important, however, both *Coopers Hill* and
Windsor Forest treat a rural scene as the paradigm for a hortatory
political discourse.

   If the definition of *Coopers Hill* as a georgic poem is correct, that
is, as a political-didactic poem employing rural nature as the vehicle
of its discourse, then Johnson's classification of its kind as local
poetry is misleading and largely irrelevant. *Coopers Hill* in reality,
like *Windsor Forest*, belongs to a special subspecies of political-
didactic poetry. The larger kind to which it thereby belongs is one that
flourished in the seventeenth century. Its most impressive innovator
was Ben Jonson, particularly in his eulogistic poems on King James.
As Jonson himself is by far and away Denham's most influential
poetical master, so Jonson's *Epigrammes* IV and V — "On King
James" and "On the Union" — may be regarded as at least the tiny
English seeds from which *Coopers Hill* grew. Jonson's royal

13

masques and eulogies preceded the luxuriant flourishing in all the arts of adulation centered on the person of the king which typified the court of Charles I. *Coopers Hill* is but a late and sober manifestation of the same artistic phenomenon. Its immediate precursor was Waller's *Upon His Majesties repairing of Pauls*, which an obtuse critic might consider an early example of a "building poem," a poem that showed Denham how the mere existence of a grand external object could be construed as an exemplary act on its part, and one from which a pertinent lesson in political morality might be drawn. In one light, therefore, *Coopers Hill* and *Upon His Majesties repairing of Pauls* might be seen as both exemplifying the same poetical kind, although Waller's poem can hardly be considered a georgic. A similar difficulty of distinction attends all consideration of the relationship of *Coopers Hill* to other poems of its period with which it is properly comparable.

Royal eulogy is not the distinctive note of the class of political poems to which *Coopers Hill* essentially belongs, for the wider class must be one that subsumes the gravity and seriousness of the georgic. Yet all the poems of the class are concerned with the equipoise of the commonwealth and the person and qualifications of the prince. A list of poems that also exemplify the dignified kind to which *Coopers Hill* belongs would include, besides those mentioned, preeminently such poems as Marvell's *Horatian Ode on Cromwell's Return from Ireland*, his *First Anniversary of the Government under His Highness the Lord Protector*, and his *Poem upon the Death of his late Highness the Lord Protector*. Waller is always more trivial in his effects, but his efforts in the same kind would probably include his Cromwellian eulogy, *Of a War with Spain, and Fight at Sea*. Dryden carries the genre into the Restoration, with *Astraea Redux* and *Annus Mirabilis*, and even with *To my Honor'd Friend Sir Robert Howard*.[11]

---

11. Ruth Nevo (*The Dial of Virtue* [Princeton, 1963], pp. 30–42) recognizes the general affinity of *Coopers Hill* with other mid-seventeenth-century panegyrics of "high seriousness," including some of those here suggested. But her view, if I do not misrepresent it, of *Coopers Hill* as treating contemporary political events with "a due generality" is only a special product

Dryden also approaches the specifically georgic aspect of *Coopers Hill* with *To my Honor'd Friend, Dr. Charlton, On . . . Stonehenge, by him Restor'd to the True Founders.*[12] That poem interprets a feature of the landscape, Stonehenge on Salisbury Plain, as a symbolic statement about the place of restored kingship in the English commonweal, although to be sure that feature is drawn out of Charlton's contentious book rather than directly from the landscape. What distinguishes these poems from the usual run of princely panegyric is not so much their judicious and generalizing air as that each one interprets emblematically one or more particular places, scenes, or events. Each one is a "local poem" insofar as it is grounded firmly either in topography or history, in place or event, in space or time, or in both, rather than in fiction, myth, or mere poetically created symbol. But the direct princely and political application of all these poems separates them even from such profound topographical poems as those written by Marvell on Nun Appleton House and its gardens.

---

of the texts problem. Generalization is far more typical of the "B" text of *Coopers Hill*, that produced in 1653–54 and first published in 1655, than it is of any of the three versions of the "A" text produced between 1640 and 1642. Despite Edmund Gosse's extremely muddled and misinformed attempt to find in the early versions "the very doctrine of the Neuters" (*From Shakespeare to Pope* [Cambridge, 1885], pp. 104–109), the "A" text is both more particular in details and more firmly Royalist and propagandistic in purport than its successor text. In 1642, after all, Denham had a king to support; in 1654 he did not.

12. This poem is also analyzed by Wasserman, *The Subtler Language*, pp. 13–33.

Nature's Emblems

IF DR. JOHNSON'S ASSIGNMENT of *Coopers Hill* to the category of local poetry needs to be rejected as inadequate, and his apparent definition of the kind as "description of a landscape, embellished by retrospection or meditation," needs to be reversed in emphasis, T. H. Banks is equally incorrect in the opposite conclusion, "that the nature description is relatively unimportant . . . serving merely as a peg on which to hang ethical and philosophical reflections." [13] Even more than Johnson's or Pope's formulations, this statement obscures the vital connection that exists in Denham's poem between the landscape he describes and the political formulations he derives from it. If Johnson and Pope misstate the relationship they may do so because they lack an adequate terminology in which to state it accurately. Banks's statement reveals a total failure to apprehend the relationship, a failure that is a product of the wide gap between the sensibility of the seventeenth century and the type of sensibility brought into being by the nineteenth century. Although Pope's statement of the nature of the process taking place in *Coopers Hill* may lack precision, his own performance in *Windsor Forest* shows him to have had a sound intuitive knowledge of the procedures of the earlier poem. But *Coopers Hill* was first written between 1640 and 1642, seventy years before *Windsor Forest*, in an earlier world of the mind which could still discourse intelligibly about the sort of mental act performed by Denham in viewing the Thames Valley from the summit of Cooper's Hill.

The nature of that act may be seen in simplified form by an ex-

---

13. Banks, *Poetical Works*, p. 48.

amination of Jonson's *Epigramme* V, "On the Union." Jonson's poem deals with the union of the crowns of England and Scotland in the person of James I and VI:

When was there contract better driven by *Fate*?
    Or celebrated with more truth of state?
The world the temple was, the priest a king,
    The spoused paire two realmes, the sea the ring.

This comparison of the uniting of the two kingdoms with a marriage contract may seem to the modern mind a mere example of conceited wit, yet Jonson insists on the *truth* of what might be taken for a metaphor. The two kingdoms in sober fact were joined together in 1603 in a union that promised, however mistakenly, to put an end to the perpetual border warfare between England and Scotland, and it was literally true that a single king was the officiant or instrumental agent of the union. Similarly, since the two kingdoms do share between them a single island, the waters surrounding each were now joined in an unbroken circle round the realms of a single monarch — the wedding ring of the two kingdoms. In other words Jonson is not, in intention at least, exercising his wit by yoking together heterogeneous ideas: the sea and a ring, England and Scotland and a bridal couple, King James and a priest. On the contrary, he is discovering meanings actually implicit in king, kingdoms, and sea; he is reading hieroglyphs presented to him by nature and history. To borrow from the "B" text of *Coopers Hill*, the union as Jonson sees it "is to him who rightly things esteems, / No other in effect than what it seems" (lines 29–30).

Among the various versions of *Coopers Hill*, from first to last, occur several references to emblems, and it is in emblem literature and the modes of thought associated with it that an explanation of Denham's use of the landscape in *Coopers Hill* must be sought. Although the vogue for emblem literature in the sixteenth and seventeenth centuries is usually said to have begun with Alciati's collection of 1531, at the very roots of the concept of the emblem is a confusion fostered by the pseudoclassical work, *The Hieroglyphics of Hora-pollo*.[14] That book, purporting to explain and interpret the hiero-glyphic writing of the Egyptians, asserted that hieroglyphs were in fact condensed symbolic pictures, "in little comprehending much."[15] Pictorial emblems were then attempts to create anew something like Egyptian hieroglyphs, enigmatic pictures that would convey pro-found truths to the eyes of the initiate and the learned, and conceal them from the profane view of the lay. The terms *emblem* and *hieroglyphic* came in time to be largely interchangeable, and gave rise to still another species of confusion. Sir Thomas Browne, in *Religio Medici* — first published in 1642, the same year as the first pub-lication of *Coopers Hill* — by an unassailable process of logic arrived at an explanation for some of the obscurity he encountered in the reading of Genesis: "truely for the first chapters of *Genesis*, I must confesse a great deale of obscurity, though Divines have to the power of humane reason endeavoured to make all goe in a literall meaning, yet those allegoricall interpretations are also probable, and perhaps the mysticall method of *Moses* bred up in the Hieroglyphicall Schooles of the Egyptians" (Part One, sect. 34). In other words Moses, the author of Genesis, having received his schooling in Egypt, ob-viously learned to write in hieroglyphs. Since hieroglyphs are alle-gorical or symbolic pictures, Genesis must have originally been writ-ten in symbolic pictures, whence the obscurities in its present text. Therefore a special skill at interpreting allegory, like the skill re-quired to decipher hieroglyph or emblem, is required to decipher the obscure parts of Genesis.

But if, through the instrumentality of Moses, God had written Scripture, he had also written the other book of his Creation. Be-side "the Booke of Gods word" stood "the Booke of Gods workes,"

---

14. See *The Hieroglyphics of Horapollo*, trans. George Boas, Bollingen Series XXIII (New York, 1950).

15. The phrase is taken from the Overburian "What a Character Is" (1622): "Character is also taken for an Ægiptian Hierogliphicke, for an imprese, or shorte Embleme; in little comprehending much."

in Bacon's phrase (*Advancement of Learning* [1605]) expressing a commonplace of the age. And the fact that God had chosen to write his Scripture in hieroglyphics indicated his probable predilection for that form of writing also in his Book of Works. Sir Thomas Browne had likewise revealed that assumption in a prior section of *Religio Medici*:

Thus there are two bookes from whence I collect my Divinity; besides that written one of God, another of his servant Nature, that universall and publik Manuscript, that lies expans'd unto the eyes of all; those that never saw him in the one, have discovered him in the other: This was the Scripture and Theology of the Heathens; the naturall motion of the Sun made them more admire him, than its supernaturall station did the Children of Israel; the ordinary effect of nature wrought more admiration in them, than in the other all his miracles; surely the Heathens knew better how to joyne and read these mysticall letters, than wee Christians, who cast a more carelesse eye on those common Hieroglyphicks, and disdain to suck Divinity from the flowers of nature. (Part One, sec. 16)

Emblems and hieroglyphics were in the air in which *Coopers Hill* was written. Only a few years before Denham's poem Francis Quarles had published his immensely successful *Emblems* (1635) and *Hieroglyphics of the Life of Man* (1638), and Quarles is at one with Browne in considering that God's Book of Works is written in hieroglyphics: "Before the knowledge of letters, God was knowne by Hierogliphicks; And, indeed, what are the Heavens, the Earth, nay every Creature, but Hierogliphicks and Emblemes of His Glory?"

If, then, the heavens, the earth, and every creature in God's Book of Works is a hieroglyph, it must be possible to read the hieroglyphs "expans'd unto the eyes of all." And a patriotic Englishman might well feel that few pages of the Book of Works were more crammed with significant hieroglyphs than the Thames Valley between Windsor and London. In brief, what Denham attempts from the summit of Cooper's Hill is to *read* the landscape "expans'd" before him. His "historical retrospections and incidental meditations" are neither hung upon the peg of the landscape, nor superadded as embellishment to the description of the landscape. They are rather the *meaning* of the landscape, the message written in the landscape in God's hieroglyphics. Everything within that landscape, whether made by God or man — and the distinction is not always either clear or relevant — is a hieroglyph, impresa, or short emblem. The pall of cloud covering London is an accurate hieroglyph of the self-defeating busyness of the Londoners, engendered as it directly is by that very busyness. St. Paul's in the City had already been recognized by Waller as the emblem "of a heart / Large both in magnanimity and art." [16] Windsor Hill and Windsor Castle were their "Masters Embleme." The castle's founder had not *selected* its site, but had *accepted* what had been thrust on him by Nature (or God), had shown in effect his own skill at reading hieroglyphs. The Order of the Garter, seated at Windsor, had in its own emblems and devices either echoed or preadumbrated Nature's emblems: the blue garter around the English arms foreshadowed the united ring of sea around Great Britain celebrated by Ben Jonson, the selection of the Soldier-Saint George of Cappadocia as patron of the order had prefigured the Soldier-Saint Charles I. St. Anne's Hill, denuded of its crowning chapel, served as a lively hieroglyph for the despoliation of the church; the Thames, flowing past Windsor, Cooper's Hill, St. Anne's Hill, and London, vividly represented all that connected those points: the flow of history, the all-encompassing constitution of the commonweal, God's design and providence, the flow of the poet's own verse. The meadow of Runnymede, a low place embraced between stream and rugged hill, was a natural hieroglyph for the great event that took place there: the meeting between King and subjects.

When Denham undertook to read the hieroglyphics on the great public manuscript expansed before him from Cooper's Hill he was not undertaking the decipherment of a language totally alien. Like Champollion, he was equipped with a key to his text. The hiero-

---

16. See App. B, below.

glyphic or emblematic frame of mind had already produced a common language of interpretation, a large part of the vocabulary of which was both older than and independent of either Alciati or Horapollo. When Denham beheld the battlemented towers of Windsor delicately poised above a peaceful and beautiful countryside, he was already predisposed to recognize the conjunction of Mars and Venus. That Windsor Castle was also a dwelling place of King Charles and Queen Henrietta Maria merely reinforced the validity of the hieroglyph, for a common feature of Renaissance portrait iconography was the depiction of king and queen, or duke and duchess, as Mars and Venus.[17] The adulterous liaison between that pair of deities was only one fable concerning their relationship; an independent tale, stemming from Hesiod's *Theogony*, viewed them as legitimately married, parents of a daughter, Harmonia. Mars and Venus together therefore denote at one and the same time harmony and royalty. Consequently Denham can also recognize that the battlements of Windsor constitute a crown — emblem of royalty — and specifically a turreted crown like that worn by Cybele, the Great Idaean Mother of the Gods. In *Coopers Hill* Denham can be seen to have expanded upon each of the ideas compressed into the hieroglyph of Windsor Castle: strength and beauty, warlikeness and peacefulness, Mars and Venus, king and queen, harmony, kingship, maternity, fertility.

The emblematic habit of mind, in a word, encouraged the persistence of topoi, most of ancient, some of more recent, provenance. Even in the earliest draft of *Coopers Hill*, for instance, Denham had touched on one of the most enduring and widespread classical-Renaissance topoi, that of the musical structure of the world with its moral-religious-political implications. Thus he describes (or reads) Windsor Forest:

---

17. See Erwin Panofsky, *Studies in Iconology* (1939; 1962), pp. 160–164 and illustrations. Few seventeenth-century monarchs can have been as devoted to iconological allegory as was Charles I; witness not merely the masques of his reign but the paintings he commissioned from Rubens.

35117

Here nature whether more intent to please
Us, or her selfe with strange varieties
(For things of wonder move no lesse delight
To the wise makers, then beholders sight)
Though these delights from severall Causes move
(For so our Children thus our frends we love)
Wisely shee knew the harmony of things
(Aswell as that of soundes) from discord springs:
Such was the discord which did first disperse
Forme, order, beauty, through the universe,
While moisture, dryness, Coldnes, heate, resists
All that we have, & that we are subsists.

Here Denham only glances at the music topos, but his aside is not
a decorative simile; it is the substance of his statement, the validation
of the hieroglyph of cosmic and political harmony he finds in Nature's composition of Windsor Forest.[18] For the music topos was perhaps the most strongly felt of all those he had available to him.
Waller's poem on *His Majesties repairing of Pauls*, the immediate
poetic antecedent of *Coopers Hill*, is conducted very largely within
the topos of music:

. . . in [Charles's] art of regiment is found
A pow'r, like that of harmony in sound.
Those antique minstrels sure were *Charles*-like Kings,
Cities their lutes, and subjects hearts their strings.[19]

In his essay "Of Empire" Bacon had made exactly the same political
application of the music topos as Waller, placed in the same con-

---

18. Both the all-pervasive acceptance of the music topos among Denham's contemporaries
and the possibilities for misunderstanding which thereby arose are illustrated by the Henry E.
Huntington Library "Draft I" manuscript of *Coopers Hill* (Ellesmere 8899), in which the
word "soundes" is mistranscribed as "Soules," reflecting the belief deriving ultimately from
Pythagoreanism, that the soul is the "harmony" of the body. The same manuscript carries
a shoulder note at this point, reading "Body of Man."

19. See App. B, below. Ruth Nevo (*The Dial of Virtue*) is so impressed by the pervasiveness of the music topos among Denham's poetical contemporaries that she has used Waller's
phrase, "Cities their lutes, and subjects hearts their strings," as the title for the first chapter of
her study.

text of counterstriving contraries as Denham's lines on Windsor Forest: "To speake now of the true Temper of *Empire*: It is a thing rare, and hard to keep: For both Temper and Distemper consist of Contraries. But it is one thing to mingle Contraries, another to enterchange them. The Answer of *Apollonius* to *Vespasian*, is full of Excellent Instruction; *Vespasian* asked him; *What was Neroes overthrow?* He answered; *Nero could touch and tune the Harpe well; But in Government, sometimes he used to winde the pins too high, sometimes to let them downe too low.*" All this may seem like the theorizing of poets and bookish men, even when delivered from the pen of Lord Verulam, so that to a modern ear similar words from the lips of the practical and resourceful Earl of Strafford may sound eerily inappropriate. Yet on April 13, 1641, in a two-hour speech before the High Court of Parliament in defense of his own life, Strafford spoke some sentences that must have influenced the composition of the last part of *Coopers Hill*, whose author was present to hear them, though perhaps they provided no specific verbal formulations for the poem:

The prerogative of the Crown and the propriety of the subject have such mutual relations that this took protection from that, that foundation and nourishment from this; and as on the lute if anything be too high or too low wound up, you have lost the harmony, so here the excess of a prerogative is oppression, of a pretended liberty in the subject disorder and anarchy. The prerogative must be used as God doth his omnipotency, at extraordinary occasions; the laws . . . must have place at all other times, and yet there must be a prerogative if there must be extraordinary occasions.[20]

But prolonged consideration of the ways Denham in *Coopers Hill* treats the Thames landscape as an expansed hieroglyphic or emblem-

---

20. Quoted by C. V. Wedgwood, *The Great Rebellion: The King's Peace 1637–1641* (New York, 1956), pp. 414–415, and *Thomas Wentworth* (London, 1961; 1964), p. 360. Perhaps Gosse would characterize Strafford's language as "the very doctrine of the Neuters." As my life of Denham, *Harmony from Discords* (p. 28), reveals, Denham was present at Strafford's trial as a witness for the defense.

atic manuscript to be read or interpreted can only lead, profitlessly at the moment, into an attempt to read or interpret the poem itself. And every judicious attempt to read the poem must take proper cognizance of the problems presented by the variant texts, and settle on one of the four drafts as the basis for any attempted explication. In like manner, consideration of matters influencing the first composition and subsequent revisions of the poem should be deferred to separate discourse on its composition and publication.

Composition
and Publication

ALL USUAL METHODS of determining the date of initial composition of *Coopers Hill*, through external or internal evidence, in the long run fail. What was in effect a third distinct draft of the poem was printed in August 1642, and initial composition must therefore have preceded that date by a sufficient span of time to allow two distinguishable earlier drafts to have entered separately into manuscript circulation. But there seems no way other than guesswork to judge how much time should be allowed for the manuscript circulation prior to that first printing. The fourth surviving edition of the poem, and first edition of the "B" text, bears on its title page the notice "Written in the yeare 1640." That date seems certainly to allow ample time for circulation of the manuscript drafts, and no objections that can be raised against it are insuperable, yet it fails to be really persuasive.

At the same time the fact must be confessed that no topical allusion within the poem is either so precise or so unmistakable as to require acceptance of a composition date later than 1640. Waller's poem on St. Paul's, which must be accepted as having preceded *Coopers Hill*, may have been composed as early as 1635, more likely was written close to 1639, but certainly was already in existence by 1640. The omens of impending civil war noticed even in Draft I of *Coopers Hill*, although they became publicly clearer with each year, might well have been discerned in 1640 by a shrewd observer. Nonetheless, for several reasons, mid-1641 or slightly earlier seems a likelier time for the inception of composition, although in no sense can the indications for that date marshaled here be claimed to constitute proof.

One traditional approach to the composition of *Coopers Hill* which earlier editors and critics have dabbled with but failed to exploit is that which assumes a change in Denham's political beliefs which is supposed to have come about with the outbreak of civil war. According to this conception Denham remained a neutral constitutionalist, critical of the king, until armed rebellion against the constitutional office of kingship drove him into the ranks of the Royalists. Edmund Gosse, who makes a hash of the evidence, assumes Denham's conversion to have taken place between the 1642 and 1643 editions of *Coopers Hill*, and asserts that the latter edition removes the neutralist doctrine contained in the first. This claim is nonsense, for 1643 is a straight copy of 1642, with the mere difference of an attempt to correct several typographical errors that appear in the earlier edition. If *Coopers Hill* in 1642 was a neutralist poem it remained one in 1643, and the latter edition constitutes a real political anomaly, published as it was in the Royalist capital of Oxford during a severe war-caused shortage of paper, and issued from a press wholly occupied with printing on behalf of the King's cause. *Coopers Hill* in 1642 and 1643 was in fact a poem of distinctly Royalist bearing. T. H. Banks, who appears unable to resist any of Gosse's crazy assertions, even when he has to find a completely different evidential basis for them, is inclined on the whole to place Denham's conversion to royalism sometime between 1641, in which year he places Denham's tragedy *The Sophy*, and 1642, which he perhaps accepts as the date of *Coopers Hill*. Yet, though he knows that *Coopers Hill* in 1643 was substantially identical with *Coopers Hill* in 1642, he quotes with Gosse the final twelve lines of that text as evidence of Denham's retained neutralist sympathies. Only a narrow view or relative ignorance of the kinds of formulaic statements open to Royalist writers in the seventeenth century could construe these lines as neutralist, though to some extent a misprint in 1642 which is perpetuated by Gosse and Banks may have contributed to their misunderstanding of the tone of the passage.[21] In fact, the poetic insistence on balancing of oppo-

---

21. The 1642 edition reads: "their boundlesse power *tell* Princes draw / Within the Channell, and the shores of Law," a very much stronger statement than what Denham actually

sites, on *concors discordia*, which typifies these lines, is a specific mark or trait of Royalist literature throughout the middle of the seventeenth century. The proclaimed Royalist aims in the civil wars, after all, never included the total abolition of parliaments or the establishment of absolute monarchy. The ideal contemplated always included a harmony of all opposed forces, a balance of king and subject. It was the parliamentarian side that wished for root-and-branch reformations and did away ultimately not merely with bishops and kings but also with its own House of Lords. In short, *Coopers Hill* must be recognized as having been from inception — not merely in the Draft III editions of 1642 and 1643 — a committed Royalist poem.

This much granted, a shift in political position detectable between *Coopers Hill* and earlier poems by Denham might serve to demark the time of composition of *Coopers Hill*, particularly if the earlier works can be more firmly dated. Banks has suggested *The Sophy* as a repository of neutralist sentiments, and accepts 1641 as its probable date of composition. But *The Sophy* was actually first printed at precisely the same time as *Coopers Hill* — August 1642 — and the evidence for its performance sometime in the preceding year, despite an assertion on its title page, is extremely tenuous.[22] In any event, interpretation of *The Sophy* as a vehicle of neutralism is a product of the same fallacy as that which seeks to interpret *Coopers Hill* in the same way. *The Sophy* is also a work of deliberate balance, and tendentiously selective excerption, such as has been used to show its antimonarchist sentiments, might equally well be employed to demonstrate its hostility to Puritan zealotry. *The Sophy* is a tragedy with a plot drawn from history, a literary form unsuited by its very nature for the promulgation of particular partisan political views. Any attempt to educe from it Denham's political beliefs at the time he composed it is misguided and bound to be fruitless, particularly

---

wrote: "their boundlesse power *let* Princes draw. . . ." The copy text probably read *lett*, in common with several manuscripts, which the compositor misread. Isaac Walton in his copy of 1642 (now in the Huntington Library) changed "tell" to "lett" (see p. 56, below).

22. See my *Harmony from Discords*, pp. 38–40, for a discussion of the likelihood of a performance of this tragedy.

if one is seeking evidence of so nebulous a political position as neutralism. At the same time, there is absolutely no way to be sure composition of *The Sophy* preceded composition of one or more of the circulated drafts of *Coopers Hill*.

Two other works of possible relevance then only remain. One is "On the Earl of Strafford's Tryal and Death." Denham did not publish this poem until he included it, in revised form, in his collected *Poems and Translations* of 1668, but it seems reasonable to assume that the poem was originally written not long after the events it commemorates, in a version that survives in several manuscripts.[23] About this elegy four points may legitimately be made: (1) it cannot in any case have been written *earlier* than Strafford's execution on May 12, 1641; (2) in neither version (original or revised) can it be construed, nor has anyone attempted to construe it, as anything other than sympathetic to Strafford, and sympathy toward Strafford is definitive of a Royalist attitude; (3) it is a poem organized entirely along a series of resolved antitheses such as equally typify Denham's other balance-of-opposites poems of the same period; (4) the early text of the poem ends with a line — itself embodying a resolved antithesis — directly echoed from Waller's *Upon His Majesties repairing of Pauls*, the sole Waller poem also echoed even in Draft I of *Coopers Hill*, and openly alluded to in all subsequent drafts. The "Strafford" poem then would seem to show Denham as an unequivocal Royalist in, probably, mid-1641 (not that his alleged neutralism at any time can be substantiated). It also shows the same stylistic tendency toward balancing and antithesis which is typical of both *The Sophy* and *Coopers Hill*, and which, at least in the latter poem, can also be incontestably associated with political royalism. And last, it shows in common with *Coopers Hill* the influence of exactly the same single Royalist poem by Waller. This sharing of Waller echoes

---

23. One (British Museum MS Egerton 2421) is printed by Banks, *Poetical Works*; there is another in the Bodleian Library (MS Locke e. 17), and one in the Advocates' Collection (MS 19.3.8) in the National Library of Scotland. Denham's role in Strafford's defense (see n. 20, above) may probably be construed as indicative of his sympathies even so early.

should also go some way toward associating the time of composition of *Coopers Hill* with that of the poem on Strafford.

One other Denham poem of a supposed neutralist cast which belongs to this period needs also to be considered, chiefly by way of destroying the notion that a datable political conversion can be connected in any way with the composition of *Coopers Hill*. Sir George Croke was the most outspoken of the five minority judges who dissented from the ruling of the King's Bench favoring the Crown in John Hampden's ship-money case; Sir John Denham, father of the poet, was another of the dissenters. On Croke's death Denham wrote an "Elegy on the Death of Judge Crooke" which, though he never published it, survives in a number of manuscripts.[24] Banks prints this poem, which he dates to 1641, and assumes it to be a product of Denham's neutralist period, on the grounds, presumably, that a Royalist could not sympathize with a man who had disagreed with the King. But the text of the poem praises, not Croke's opposition to the King, but his constitutional *balance*, which *latterly* has preserved him from the zealous heat of antiroyal Puritanism. And Banks is mistaken in ascribing the poem to 1641. Croke died in February 1641/2, which is, of course, by our reckoning February 1642. Denham's "Elegy" therefore was not written before the poem on Strafford, but perhaps nine months later, certainly nine months after the death of Strafford. February 1642 would have been a very late date for Denham to have attempted a neutralist stance, when the King had already abandoned London. To imagine a conversion to royalism thereafter, in time to allow for composition of three separate drafts of *Coopers Hill*, and entry of two of them into manuscript circulation, all by the end of July, is to strain credibility.

Internal evidence is as ambiguous as external in indicating a precise date for the composition of *Coopers Hill*. Dating by topical allu-

---

24. See my *Harmony from Discords*, p. 48, for discussion of this poem and for identification of a number of manuscript copies. Banks (*Poetical Works*) prints this poem with description of two manuscripts, and includes a slightly erroneous note on Croke.

sions, for instance, necessarily involves a circularity of reasoning. Identification of a formula of words in the poem as an allusion to a contemporary event may seem to limit the date of composition to a time when such an allusion would be lively. But recognition of a formula of words as a topical allusion depends upon a preconception as to the time during which the poem was composed. This may be illustrated by consideration of the verbal formula in *Coopers Hill*, line 5: "Courts make not Kings, but Kings the Court." Professor Earl Wasserman, assuming the poem to be essentially a product of 1642, interprets this line as an allusion to the dispute in the second quarter of that year, as to whether legitimacy of government resided with the High Court of Parliament assembled in Westminster, or with the King and the Parliament he had summoned to his presence at York. But even April 1642 seems impossibly late for at least Draft I of *Coopers Hill* which nonetheless contains that line, and so Wasserman's interpretation must be ruled out. In the circumstances one is then very hesitant to advance the hypothesis that the line is indeed a topical allusion, but an allusion to a dispute of the winter of 1640–41. During that period the Parliament was arrogating to itself in the most strictly legalistic fashion the title of High Court, attacking the Royalist doctrine of the King as fountainhead of law and justice, attacking the majority of judges of the King's Bench who had ruled in the Crown's favor in Hampden's case, and specifically attacking the King's authority to constitute or establish courts of law, the prerogative courts. Most important of all, it was as the ultimate High Court of the kingdom that the Parliament then proceeded to the trial of the Earl of Strafford for treason.

Something of the reverberation in *Coopers Hill* of echoes of Strafford's defense speech of April 13, 1641, has already been indicated, and Professor Wasserman has made out a case that the stag hunt in the second half of the poem is in some sense an allegory of the trial and death of Strafford. Wasserman's argument is somewhat vitiated by his failure to discriminate adequately among the drafts of the poem, but a sifting and realignment of his evidence still leaves his reading a very probable one, if only for the text of the poem (Draft III) published in 1642.[25] One may then with some confidence postulate that *Coopers Hill* was written within the aura of Strafford's trial. But one of the curious details of the Draft III stag hunt, the inexplicably voluntary death of the stag, is not a feature of either Draft I or Draft II. Wasserman has pointed to the parallel between the stag's voluntary and requested death at the hands of Charles, and the letter from Strafford to the same Charles recommending the signing of Strafford's death warrant as a politic means to national reconciliation. The preceding lines of the poem, in which the stag beats off the assaults of the "lesser hounds," Wasserman sees as a parallel to Strafford's skillful legal defense, which forced his enemies at last to an act of attainder as the only sure means to convict him. In Draft III (the 1642 text) the parallel to Strafford, if it is really there, is reinforced by means of a simile in which the beset stag is compared to a hero surrounded by "baser foes." Drafts I and II lack this simile, however, which in Draft III is the vehicle for conveying the voluntariness of the stag's death, and have instead a sinking-ship simile:

As in a Calme the Oare-fynn'd Galleys creepe,
About a winde bound, & unwieldy Shipp;
Which lyes unmov'd, but those that come too neere
Strikes with her thunder, & the rest with feare,
Till through her many leakes the Sea shee drinkes
Nor yealdes at last but still resisting sinks:
So stands the stagg among the lesser hounds . . .

If one is prepared to accept the parallel between the stag hunt and Strafford's end, this earlier culmination only emphasizes the fact that Strafford went down fighting, not that he voluntarily besought death at the King's hand. The stag, to be sure, is killed by Charles, but

---

25. Ruth Nevo (*The Dial of Virtue*, p. 35 n. 16) characterizes Wasserman's interpretation as "conclusively argued," but she herself continues to welter in the muddle of the separate texts. A perhaps endearing characteristic weakness of commentators on *Coopers Hill* is an unwillingness to reject outright any hypothesis proposed by a predecessor.

another end to a royal stag hunt is scarcely conceivable. It is conceivable, though, that this ship simile might have been written when Strafford had been overwhelmed by his foes but not yet executed, or at least before Denham was aware — or poetically aware, which need not be the same thing — that Strafford had requested the King to sign his death warrant.

All other minor clues to dating in the poem are even more evanescent and ambivalent. A few small touches seem unlikely, although not impossible, for 1642, but at any rate external considerations make any time in 1642 seem too late for first inception of *Coopers Hill*. It would be vain to pretend that any of the assumed topical allusions in *Coopers Hill* could withstand rigorous critical skepticism, but their presence may be accepted as at least a working hypothesis. Since all the larger topicalities discernible or imagined in the poem relate to the period from the winter of 1640–41 until the lull following the execution of Strafford in May 1641, a lull that Strafford himself had hoped would be a new period of harmony and goodwill, it seems not unreasonable to date the initial composition of *Coopers Hill* to that period of momentary calm, midyear of 1641.

What in the present edition is called Draft I of *Coopers Hill* presumably entered manuscript circulation when Denham conceived he had created a finished poem. Nonetheless Draft I was followed into manuscript circulation, at a date completely undeterminable, by a revised version, Draft II. Draft II adds for the first time the explicit compliment to Waller's poem on St. Paul's, which had, however, been echoed in one line of Draft I as well as in one line of Denham's original elegy on Strafford. In other details Draft II is much like Draft I, although the verses are slightly more polished. A simile comparing the Thames to a distraught lover is toned down and condensed, and a few lines are added here and there, including one couplet that appears in Draft II only, but was subsequently dropped entirely from the poem.

By the end of July 1642, at the latest, Draft III of *Coopers Hill* must have been completed. This is a draft in every way more polished than either I or II, with many new lines added at various places, including six lines early in the poem on men making and unmaking plots in London, which possibly have no topical reference, or may faintly glance at the Army Plot of the summer of 1641. These lines are unique to Draft III. In many parts of the poem conceptual statements are expanded upon and explained. Drafts I and II, for instance, had stated that, as one result of Magna Charta,

Tyrant, & Slave, those names of hate & feare,
The happier Stile of King, & Subiect beare.

Draft III expands this formulation by showing it to be an exemplification of the cosmic doctrine of harmony through balance of mean opposites rather than of the opposition of extremes:

Happy when both to the same Center move;
When Kings give liberty, and Subjects love.

The ending of the stag hunt also, as remarked above, is given a new direction by the substitution for the sinking-ship simile of the simile of a beset hero.

Since no manuscript copies of Draft III appear to have survived, it is a permissible inference that none entered circulation, and that the draft as Denham finished it was designed for the press. The fact that a bookseller published in August 1642 the highly finished Draft III rather than either of the rougher drafts I and II further suggests that he was not publishing without authority a manuscript that merely found its way, through successive transcriptions, into his hands. Friday, August 5, 1642, appears to have been the day upon which Thomas Walkeley first published *Coopers Hill*. Walkeley also published *The Sophy* under a 1642 imprint, very likely on or about the same day.

The publication of *Coopers Hill* on August 5 fairly requires that Walkeley had his copy text in hand by the end of July at latest. Despite the ill-founded clouding of the authority of Walkeley's edition extrapolated in modern times out of an editor's advertisement prefaced to the 1655 edition of *Coopers Hill*, the most reasonable way to account for Walkeley's possession and publication of *Coopers Hill* and *The Sophy* is that they were provided him by the Mr. John Denham whom his entry in the Stationers' Register recognizes to be their author.[26] In the case of *Coopers Hill* Denham, moreover, provided Walkeley with a new draft which had not yet entered public circulation. Denham in July and August of 1642 was by all indications living at his home in Egham, about twenty miles from London westward on the Thames, and the notion proposed by the 1655 editor that he was at the time "long absen[t] from this Great Town" is preposterous.[27]

The next edition of *Coopers Hill* was essentially a reprint of that of 1642, but one that appeared in wartime Oxford in about April 1643. Denham had meanwhile himself appeared in Oxford, and the coincidence of his appearance in that city with the publication of his poem there is too signal to be overlooked. The Oxford edition contains a small number of corrections of misprints in Walkeley's edition, all of which testify silently to Denham's probable hand in the Oxford reprint as well as in the original London edition.

A third edition of *Coopers Hill* appeared in 1650, by which time Denham was indeed absent from the scene, as a political exile with the court of Charles II. This 1650 London edition was also a reprint of 1642, but one lacking the Oxford corrections of 1643. It was brought out by Humphrey Moseley, who may have issued another edition later in the same year, which has been lost. Moseley retained the printing rights, however, and it was he who brought out also the first edition of the "B" text of the poem, Draft IV, in 1655.

Upon his return from political exile in 1653 Denham had gone for an indeterminable period into a poetic seclusion as the guest of the Earl of Pembroke at Wilton House near Salisbury in Wiltshire. There, we have Aubrey's testimony, he translated Vergil, and a prob-

26. See B. O Hehir, " 'Lost,' 'Authorized,' and 'Pirated' Editions of John Denham's *Coopers Hill*," *PMLA*, LXXIX (1964), 242–53.
27. See J. B.'s note (prefixed to "B" text, below).

able fruit of that translation is *The Destruction of Troy*, a partial translation of *Aeneid* II, which was published by Moseley in 1656. But, though on this point Aubrey is silent, both internal and external evidence indicates that it was during the same period that Denham drastically revised *Coopers Hill*. Scarcely a third of the text of the poem was unaffected by the revision, if any part of it can be said to have been completely unaffected, for even when lines were left verbally unaltered their contexts were changed, and blocks of verses all through the poem were shifted to new relative positions.

The original *Coopers Hill* had been written by a Royalist poet before the outbreak of civil war, as a warning against war and against provoking the dormant strength of the King. The revision of 1653–54 was undertaken by a defeated Royalist whose king had been executed, by an impoverished and homeless returned exile in an England where monarchy had been abolished, but which was now flourishing under the monarchic Protectorate of Cromwell. As the earlier versions of the poem reflected the earlier conditions and mood, the later version reflects the later. The changes effected included such minor but significant ones as the suppression of the name "Charles," which had occurred twice in all three earlier drafts, and such major ones as the expansion of the stag hunt to more than twice its former length. The expansion of the stag hunt without question blurs its apparent relevance to the trial and execution of Strafford, but only a very small part of the additional material consists of "naturalistic detail" as Professor Wasserman would see it. On the contrary, the additions chiefly tend to humanize the stag, attributing to him a wide range of human emotions, including shame at his own previous abandonment of another stag who was formerly hunted to death. The stag is also characterized as the "Prince of the soyl," and his death takes place amidst "the scenes of his past triumphs." If a case can be made for the parallel of the earlier stag hunt to the trial and death of Strafford, a stronger one can be made for the parallel of the revised stag hunt to the end of King Charles I: his dying statement of penitence for his share in Strafford's death; his execution outside the windows of the banqueting hall at Westminster, its ceiling decorated with the allegorical "Triumphs" he had commissioned Rubens to paint. Other new material added to the poem seems to glance at the new prince, the Lord Protector. Finally, the whole direction of the poem was changed by an alteration of its ending. In the earlier drafts constrained royal power had been depicted by the simile of a river that men recklessly confine to a narrow course or seek to divert into a new channel: the calm stream becomes a torrent that overflows all controls. This image had been followed by twelve lines that complete the simile's equation and conclude with an admonition to the subjects: to obey. The new ending postpones the image of the flooding river to the absolutely terminal lines, thus deleting the comparison and altering the image from a simile to an autonomous symbol. The river no longer stands for kingly power, but for the state as a whole, and so the new *Coopers Hill* ends on a picture of mere anarchy:

Stronger, and fiercer by restraint he roars,
And knows no bound, but makes his power his shores.

Although possibly not poetically the most significant change made in the extensive revision of *Coopers Hill*, the change of most moment for literary history was the addition, for the first time, of the celebrated "Thames couplets" imitated, parodied, contemplated, and admired to infinity during the following century:

O could I flow like thee, and make thy stream
My great example, as it is my theme!
Though deep, yet clear, though gentle, yet not dull,
Strong without rage, without ore-flowing full.

These lines, surprisingly, did not at once catch the critical or poetical fancy, despite the fame of *Coopers Hill*. They were first specifically commented on by John Dryden, in his "Dedication of the *Aeneis*" (1697): "I am sure there are few who make verses have observ'd the sweetness of these . . . lines. . . . And there are yet fewer who can find the reason of that sweetness. I have given it to some of my friends in conversation, and they have allow'd the criticism to be just." If few had observed the sweetness of those lines before that date many observed it afterward. At least once prior to 1697 those lines had also been poetically imitated. In 1685 at the death of Charles II, Charles Montague in an elegiac tribute represented the Thames as the "pleasing emblem" of Charles's reign because its channel is "strong and easy, deep and clear."[28] Yet, although *Coopers Hill* itself was widely renowned and imitated before Dryden's comment, one may reasonably suspect that it was Dryden's commendation rather than the intrinsic beauty of these lines which led to their eighteenth-century celebrity.

The study of the Thames lines has also led inevitably to a hunt, for the most part misguided, for their sources. The hunt is misguided because similar or parallel antithetical formulations are without number. It is the particular phrasing that is unique to *Coopers Hill*, but Denham's most truly original feat is the simultaneous application of the river emblem to verse and to life. Of the numerous verbal parallels that have been found only two perhaps deserve notice, and both because of their associations with Ben Jonson, the poet most influential on the work of Denham. One of these parallels has already been instanced by T. H. Banks, from William Cartwright's *In Memory of the most worthy Benjamin Johnson*, first published in *Jonsonus Verbius* (1638):

But thou still putst true passion on; dost write
With the same courage that try'd captaines fight;
Giv'st the right blush and colour unto things;
Low without creeping, high without losse of wings;
Smooth, yet not weake, and by a thorough care,
Bigge without swelling, without painting faire.[29]

A less obvious parallel is presented by Jonson himself, in prose. In *Timber; or, Discoveries* he describes a good style: "There the lan-

---

28. Quoted by Wasserman, *The Subtler Language*, p. 69 n. 30.
29. Banks, *Poetical Works*, p. 53.

guage is plain and pleasing; even without stopping, round without swelling; all well-turned, composed, elegant, and accurate." [30]

Denham did not allow the text of *Coopers Hill* to rest permanently in the state that was printed in 1655. The year before his death he collaborated with Henry Herringman, a rising and ambitious new stationer, in publishing a collection of his works under the title of *Poems and Translations*. The version of *Coopers Hill* he printed in that collection, though substantially the same as that of 1655, differs in a number of not entirely insignificant details. For one thing, four new lines are added to the poem, lines that are in essence a rewriting of the earlier ("A" text) lines that had been replaced by the "Thames couplets," thus extending the poem in length to 358 lines as against the 354 of both the 1642 and 1655 versions. In addition the readings of a few lines are altered, generally by the revival of at least a reminiscence of the readings of the drafts antecedent to 1655. Sometime after publication of the 1668 edition Denham added to the text a further six lines which have only recently come to light. The present is the first edition to incorporate these additional six lines in the poem.

It is the text of *Coopers Hill* first printed in 1668 which has continued to represent Denham's poem to posterity. *Poems and Translations* was reprinted in 1671, and in 1684, 1703, 1709, 1719, 1769, and 1771. A new volume called *The Poetical Works of Sir John Denham* was published in 1780. Denham's works, including *Coopers Hill*, were also republished in various massive collections of British poets: in 1773, twice in 1779 (including Samuel Johnson's collection), in 1795, twice in 1807, in 1810, 1819, 1822, and in 1857. *Coopers Hill* alone was also separately published in 1709 and appeared in innumerable anthologies, as it still continues sporadically to appear today. But not even for scholarly purposes has the only slightly different 1655 version reappeared in print, and the last known edition of the version of 1642, before the present one, is that of 1650. As to the two drafts of the poem which circulated in manuscript before the print-

30. Ben Jonson's *Works*, ed. Francis Cunningham (London, 1807), III, 415.

ing of Draft III in 1642, they have never before been edited or printed in full.

In 1676 at Oxford appeared what can perhaps only be regarded as evidence that *Coopers Hill* had become established as a classic. Moses Pengry, chaplain to the Earl of Devonshire, translated the poem into Latin, and in that year a beautiful large quarto edition of *Coopers Hill Latine Redditum* was issued from the Sheldonian Theatre. Curiously, Pengry employed for his translation the text of *Coopers Hill* published in 1655 despite the availability of the finally revised form in the *Poems and Translations* editions of 1668 and 1671. Even more curiously, perhaps, the Latin translation of *Coopers Hill* achieved some manuscript circulation despite the availability of the Oxford printing.[31]

Although perhaps all that is really germane to the original inspiration of *Coopers Hill*, and to the poetic models that Denham followed in creating his poem, has already been touched on here, one other antecedent poem of peculiar interest may be mentioned. This poem is not brought forward as a probable model or source for *Coopers Hill*; indeed it is a virtual certainty that Denham had never heard of it. Yet the poem in some ways is curiously parallel to *Coopers Hill*. This is a Carolingian Latin poem of 536 hexameters on the subject of *Karolus Magnus et Leo Papa* attributed to Angilbert.[32] Of this poem the first 325 lines (very close to the total length of *Coopers Hill*) bear an intriguing resemblance to the shape of Denham's work. The first twelve lines are an exordium; lines 13–94 a eulogy of the emperor, whose name occurs as *Karolus* and *Carolus* — naturally suggestive of Denham's *Charles* and of his translator's *Carolus* — who is compared with David, a common seventeenth-century topos. Lines 95–136 describe and celebrate the king's architectural activity in his capital "ubi Roma secunda / Flore novo." The next section extends from line 137 to line 325 and begins with the

---

31. See App. A, below.
32. The poem is printed in the *Monumenta Germaniae historica*, in *Poetae latini aevi Carolini*, ed. E. Dümmler, I (1881), 366–379.

description of a rivered plain immediately adjacent to the walls of the city where herds of deer come to graze (cp. *Coopers Hill*, "And thither all the horned hoast resorts"), the phrasing of some of the lines being borrowed from Aeneas' stag shoot in *Aeneid* I.185–193. Here Carolus comes for sport, and the rest of the section is an elaborate description of his hunting, though his ultimate kill is of boars: "Sternit et innumeras porcorum strage catervas." The remainder of the poem is less suggestive of *Coopers Hill*, but not totally alien to its spirit.[33] The last section deals with the relations between Charlemagne and Pope Leo, with the emphasis on the Pope rather than on the emperor, but *Coopers Hill* too deals with ecclesiastical policies and the relationship between church and ruler. One last quality in common between *Coopers Hill* and *Karolus Magnus et Leo Papa* is the indebtedness of both poems to Vergil. The verbal debts to all of Vergil's works are, of course, much more evident in the Latin poem than in the English. No doubt this fact should be discounted, for thousands of poems must be verbally indebted to Vergil, but the odd resemblances between these two poems written so far apart are at least worth considering, if only as a notable curiosity and coincidence.

---

33. *Karolus Magnus et Leo Papa* is cited by Ernst Curtius, *European Literature and the Latin Middle Ages*, trans. W. R. Trask, Harper Torchbooks: The Bollingen Library (New York and Evanston, 1963), p. 158, and very briefly schematized (less fully than here), *ibid.*, n. 40.

The Exemplars
of *Coopers Hill*

THE DISTINGUISHABLE VERSIONS of *Coopers Hill*, as evident from the discussion of the poem's composition and publication, are five in number. But the differences between the text published in 1655 and that published in 1668 are too minimal to require considering those editions as representing separate drafts of the poem. Moreover, though a modern fashion has grown up of referring to the 1655 edition as "the first authorized edition," it is in fact the only edition of *Coopers Hill* about which some suspicion may justly be entertained. If Denham's 1668 cancellations of 1655 readings in favor of readings slightly closer to the text of 1642 are not merely final alterations, they may indeed be rejections of spurious readings. Such being the possibility, there can be little justification for reproducing the 1655 text *in extenso*, or for canonizing its idiosyncrasies.

From prior discussion it is also evident that the massive revision of *Coopers Hill* effected in 1653–54 is the great watershed between drafts of the poem. The three drafts preceding the revision are all sufficiently distinct to require separate identification and editing as drafts I to III, but sufficiently closely related to warrant being grouped together under the loose designation of the "A" text. The two versions printed in Denham's lifetime after the revision are enough alike to be classified together as Draft IV, and more broadly distinguished from the other drafts as constituting together the "B" text. Throughout the present work, it should be clear, the designation of various versions of *Coopers Hill* as drafts I to IV is a very precise distinction, the division into "A" text and "B" text a loose one. The term "A" text, especially, in general means drafts I to III, but Draft III alone is often viewed as the "A" text proper, drafts I and II as mere preliminary forms of the "A" text.

41

All known or available texts of *Coopers Hill* are classifiable on the basis of the gross distinction between the "A" and the "B" texts, and as belonging to one of the four more finely distinguished drafts. These drafts or texts are represented among some five printed editions of the poem issued in Denham's lifetime, one closely posthumous edition, and an indeterminate number of manuscript transcriptions. Of these latter, five have been employed for the present edition, together with another minor manuscript document and Denham's transcription of a few unprinted lines; further manuscript evidence that may come to light is extremely unlikely to affect the conclusions here drawn. Although the first three drafts all represent versions of the "A" text, drafts I and II are represented only in manuscript. Therefore those drafts may be segregated as preliminaries to the "A" text proper, or Draft III. Accordingly the thirteen exemplars employed for the present edition distribute themselves as follows:

One. Preliminary texts. Draft I: (1) MS Ellesmere 8899, (2) MS Harleian 367.71. Draft II: (3) Folger MS V.a.160, (4) Folger MS V.a.322, (5) MS Harleian 837.3, (6) manuscript marginalia in a copy of exemplar 8, below.

Two. "A" Text. Draft III: [London version] (7) Walkeley's 1642 edition, (8) Moseley's 1650 reprint; [Oxford version] (9) Hall's 1643 edition.

Three. "B" Text. Draft IV: (10) J. B.'s 1655 edition, (11) *Poems and Translations* edition, 1668, (12) Denham's holograph additions to *Poems and Translations*, 1668, (13) *Poems and Translations* edition, 1671.

A detailed description of each of these thirteen exemplars follows.

ONE. PRELIMINARY TEXTS

Draft I

1) Manuscript Ellesmere 8899 is a manuscript of *Coopers Hill* which was acquired in 1917, through Sotheby's, by the Henry E. Huntington Library, San Marino, California, as part of the Ellesmere Col-

lection included in the contents of the Bridgewater House Library. The volume in which it is found is a very miscellaneous gathering which appears to have been bound up for the third Earl of Bridgewater (1686–1701), but which includes several pieces in the handwriting of the first Earl (d. 1649). Of the 73 items in the volume (MSS EL 8854–8926), one other — MS EL 8876, "Mr Hampdens Speech against Peace at the Close Committee" (1643) — also belongs to Denham's canon. Little in the way of external evidence serves to date the transcription of the *Coopers Hill* manuscript. A copy of Cleveland's elegy on Strafford (MS EL 8864), in the handwriting of the first Earl of Bridgewater, was probably made not long after the composition of the poem and the execution it commemorates (May 1641). Therefore at least one item in the volume can be dated as early as 1641. In addition, the same unidentified hand that transcribed *Coopers Hill* also copied the verses "Upon Bringing in the Plate" (*Rump Songs*, I, 87), which concerns events of mid-1642 (MS EL 8895). Neither fact, however, reveals the date of the transcription of *Coopers Hill*.

Among a number of other indecisive indications on the manuscript itself that it was transcribed during the lifetime and effectual reign of Charles I, the chief must be reckoned the shoulder note to line 90 (= "A" text, line 112). The line unambiguously alludes to Charles I and Henrietta Maria, so that the note, "K: & Q: Maty nowe," must be contemporary with that royal pair. Moreover, it is hard to imagine this note being so matter-of-factly added to the text after the outbreak of civil war, when the Queen's Majesty was in Paris, and the King in Oxford, or with the Scots, or a captive.

Manuscript EL 8899 consists of twelve folio pages (six leaves) of quite uniform textual length. Nine pages contain exactly 28 lines each, two (pp. 7 and 9) contain 30 each, while only the last (p. 12) contains, understandably, fewer, namely the terminal 14 lines. The total of 326 lines constitutes the shortest full-length version of *Coopers Hill*, but the testimony of MS Harleian 367.71 (exemplar 2, below) suggests that a couplet lacking in MS EL 8899 may have fallen out

43

in transmission, so that this text should properly consist of 328 lines. The pages of MS EL 8899 are unnumbered, but sequence is indicated by catchwords. On the first page, above the body of the text, appears an inscription in the same hand and ink as the rest of the manuscript: "Coopers Hill / (Betweene this & Windsore, whence this Survey)." To the title a subsequent hand has added a comma and the words "by Sr: John Denham." The addition therefore cannot be earlier than Denham's knighthood of April 1661.

This manuscript is in an impure secretary hand showing italic traits, and its orthography is extremely skeletal, being characterized by an obsessive use of manuscript abbreviations and contractions and by a sparsity of capitalization and punctuation. Several transcription errors seem almost certainly the product of misheard dictation (e.g., "like Could Anteus" for "like ould Anteus"). Others appear to indicate previous corruptions already present in the parent copy, which therefore was improbably a Denham holograph. Specific variant readings of this manuscript are detailed in the apparatus to the present editions of Draft I and of the "A" text; a few are discussed below in the critical reading of Draft I, and elsewhere.

Manuscript EL 8899 was unknown to Banks and consequently not made use of in his edition of *Coopers Hill*. Without this full-length copy of the first draft it would have been extremely difficult to recognize the independent existence of the first draft and so to determine the correct number and sequence of the drafts. This manuscript proved by itself to be the key to the real relationship between the two manuscripts known to and used by Banks, and between the manuscripts and the printed texts. The addition of further exemplars to the manuscript corpus has only confirmed conclusions originally drawn from those three manuscripts alone.

2) Manuscript Harleian 367.71 is number 71 among eighty-two separate manuscripts bound up in a volume titled *Historical Tracts* and designated MS Harleian 367 in *A Catalogue of the Harleian Manuscripts in the British Museum*. The *Catalogue* describes the volume

44

as "a Booke in fol. wherein are contained many Papers & Fragments, with various Poems, written by the hands of Mr. John Stow, & others; now bound up together." The *Coopers Hill* manuscript is technically one of the "Fragments," and its scribe is unknown. Like the Bridgewater volume containing MS EL 8899, in fact, MS Harleian 367 is a very miscellaneous collection of unrelated pieces, offering no certain external clues to the date at which the copy of *Coopers Hill* it contains was transcribed. Moreover, unlike MS EL 8899, this manuscript of *Coopers Hill* offers no internal evidence whatsoever as to its date, although it is beyond question of the seventeenth century.

Manuscript Harleian 367.71 as it now stands is manifestly a defective copy of *Coopers Hill*. The opening of the poem is missing; what survives consists of five leaves (ten pages), foliated 169–173 relative to their position in the volume. The foliation, being continuous, shows that the manuscript was already defective when the leaves were numbered, and other evidence discussed below indicates that the manuscript was defective even when first bound into the volume. Catchwords are not employed, but the surviving pages of the poem are paginated, independently of the volume, pages 3–12, thus suggesting that the total loss consists of one leaf or two pages, and therefore that this manuscript, like MS EL 8899, consisted originally of six leaves. At present the text begins with a line ("Not to looke back soe farre to whome this Isle") corresponding to line 81 of the "A" text, but to line 59 of MS EL 8899.

Altogether MS Harleian 367.71 retains 270 lines of *Coopers Hill*, but the lines are distributed over the pages far from uniformly. Leaving out of account the last page (p. 12), which contains only the terminal 4 lines of the poem, page content varies from 26 to 34 lines, averaging about 29 lines per page (although no page contains an odd number of lines — that is, no couplet is broken between pages). Therefore, the missing pages may be conjectured to have contained from a minimum of 52 lines to a maximum of 68, with probability centering on the average, namely 58 lines. This last figure coincides exactly

with the number of lines contained in the directly comparable portion of MS EL 8899.

The surviving 270 lines of MS Harleian 367.71 include a single
couplet (equivalent to "A" text, lines 115–116) which MS EL 8899
lacks; the remaining 268 lines of the two manuscripts are textually
identical. From the coincidence two reasonable conclusions can be
drawn: first, as already suggested in discussion of that manuscript,
the defect of a couplet in MS EL 8899 is accidental and not organic
to the text; second, the lost portion of MS Harleian 367.71 corresponds
closely, probably exactly, to the first 58 lines of MS EL 8899. Both
manuscripts, therefore, are representatives of the same (first) draft of
Coopers Hill, which apparently properly should extend to a total
length of 328 lines.

Manuscript Harleian 367.71, written also in an impure secretary
hand, with more distinct italic traits, contrasts sharply in orthography with the frugality of MS EL 8899. Relatively few contractions
are employed, and those only of the commonest; in the contrary
spirit, redundant *e*'s and redundant doubled consonants abound.
Capitalization is also abundant, but follows no discernible convention. The hand is undistinguished, and the transcription is careless
and untidy, marred by frequent cancellations and corrections, some
pointless, while several manifest transcription errors remain uncor-
rected. Punctuation is sparing but on the whole judicious. Specific
variant readings of this manuscript are detailed in the apparatus to
Draft I and to the "A" text, and a few are discussed separately in the
critical reading of Draft I.

At present on its otherwise almost blank last page MS Harleian
367.71 carries a note that moved Banks, who used this manuscript in
editing *Coopers Hill,* to some unnecessary and profitless speculation.
In full the note reads: "The above is Part of Sir John Denham's
Cooper's Hill — last Edition." The first thing to be observed about
this note is that it is written in a distinctively modern italic, while
considerations completely independent of the script serve to show
that it was not on the manuscript about 1726, nor even possibly by

1808.[34] The intention of the note is clearly to identify the content of the defective manuscript, and therefore it was certainly unknown to Humphrey Wanley, compiler of the first part of the *Catalogue of the Harleian Manuscripts*. Wanley, who died in 1726, catalogued MS Harleian 367, but failed to recognize the *Coopers Hill* transcript, which he describes merely as "A Poem upon the Prayses of Windsor-Castle, and the Places adjacent. Imperf[ect]." Moreover, the volume of the *Catalogue* in which Wanley's work appears was itself not published until 1808, but his failure to recognize the poem as *Coopers Hill* was allowed then to stand unremedied. Whatever its date, therefore, the note appended to the last page of the manuscript shows no more than an astute librarian's recognition of the true identity of the poem and his attempt to rectify the error of the *Catalogue*; and his note was probably written sometime in the nineteenth century later than 1808 (although the capitalization suggests a writer educated in the eighteenth century). Consequently the specification of the text as that of the "last Edition" can carry no special authority. Certainly the annotator cannot have meant the word "last" to be construed as "most recent"; on the contrary, almost certainly he intended to identify the text as that of the *old* edition, the one *prior* to that now current, employing the same idiom as that in "last week," "last year," or *The Tragedies of the Last Age Considered*. In identifying the text as more nearly related to the "A" text than to the "B" the librarian was perfectly correct; so far as he intended to identify the text as explicitly the same as that of the "A" text editions he was incorrect. This subject merits no further discussion.

It is to be regretted that so far no other representative of Draft I of *Coopers Hill* beyond MSS EL 8899 and Harleian 367, both to some extent defective and unsatisfactory, has come to light. The apparent paucity of manuscripts of this draft is, however, explicable in view of the fact that composition and subsequent circulation of this draft very

---

34. My colleague, Professor Thomas G. Barnes of the Department of History, University of California, Berkeley, an experienced paleographer, is more than willing to accept this hand as belonging to the early nineteenth century.

probably could not have preceded printed publication of the third
draft by more than about two years, if that long, and that a second
draft of the poem, presumably preferred by Denham, also entered
into circulation within the interim. It is not surprising therefore if
copies of Draft II appear to be more frequent and full than copies of
Draft I.

Draft II

3) The manuscript of *Coopers Hill* here called Folger MS V.a.160
occurs as the last English poem (numbered 93) in a seventeenth-
century commonplace book now in the Folger Shakespeare Library.
The book appears to have been originally owned by a Matthew Day
of Windsor, who wrote his name on the first leaf, and who may have
been the penman of a few pages in Latin at the beginning and end of
the book, and who may have been either Matthew Day (1574–1661),
five times mayor of Windsor, or his son, the Reverend Matthew
Day, M.A. (1611–1663). A group of English poems, all in the same
hand, quite distinct from the hand of the Latin, occupies 107 numbered pages in the central part of the book, between the Latin pages.
Roughly the first half of this English material consists of poems that
may be associated with the period 1633–34; the last two poems, occupying pages 94–107, are both by Denham: "An Elegie on the
Death of Judge Crooke by Mr. Denham," and *Coopers Hill*. The
transcript of *Coopers Hill* begins on page 95, immediately after the
last fourteen lines of the "Elegie." Beneath a rule occurs the title,
with an added note in the same handwriting as the rest: "Cooper's
Hill. Written by Mr. Denham to Mr. Waller."

Therefore this transcript seems neatly self-bracketed in date. It
could not have been earlier than the composition and circulation of
the "Elegie," which itself could not antedate the death of Judge Croke
in February 1641/2. At the latest, if either of the two Days was the
penman, the transcript could not have been made either after 1661
or 1663. At the same time, the attribution to *Mr.* Denham would
appear unlikely after the poet had become Sir John in April 1661.

Moreover, the handwriting of the English poems appears to undergo a distinct change, which may be interpreted as a maturing, between the first entries and the last, a fact suggesting that the poems were transcribed over a period of some years. Precisely this development of the handwriting has led one modern scholar to argue persuasively that the earlier poems in the volume were transcribed roughly contemporaneously with the events to which they allude, that is to say, in about 1633 or 1634.[35] An implication of that argument is that the two Denham poems were transcribed perhaps about 1642.

Unhappily the authenticity of this manuscript is somewhat open to question. For one thing, the Day commonplace book was at one time the property of J. P. Collier, the notorious forger and manipulator of texts. Any seventeenth-century manuscript that has passed through Collier's hands is *ipso facto* suspect, although Collier normally achieved more sensational results than the two minor poems by Dekker and one doubtful attribution to Shakespeare he might have hoped to serve up out of this volume. And the forgery of 107 pages of minor verse seems like a great deal of effort for the purpose, especially as Collier nowhere else shows any interest in Denham. Moreover, Dr. Giles Dawson and Mr. John Crow, both modern Collier experts, are willing to attest that the handwriting of the book is untypical of Collier's recognized forging styles.[36] But even if Collier himself is cleared of forging this book, the handwriting of the English poems remains slightly disturbing. The ornate, predominantly italic hand to some eyes may more nearly resemble hands typical of the Restoration period than of the 1630's and 1640's suggested both by the content and the progressive changes in the hand.[37] Conse-

---

35. F. David Hoeniger, "Thomas Dekker, the Restoration of St. Paul's and J. P. Collier, the Forger," *Renaissance News*, XVI (1963), 181–200. This article discusses problems raised by the Matthew Day commonplace book, and to that article as well as (through subsequent correspondence) to Professor Hoeniger himself, and equally to Dr. Giles Dawson, curator of books and manuscripts at the Folger Library and authority on Collier's forgeries, I owe much of the substance of the following discussion.

36. *Ibid.*, p. 184.

37. It should be noted that Dr. Dawson, in private correspondence, has stated to me that

quently one hesitates to assert that this manuscript of *Coopers Hill* was unquestionably transcribed in or about 1642, though if its absolute authority could be accepted that date would be strongly supported.

Whatever doubt may be cast on the authenticity of MS Folger V.a.160, none can be cast on the veracity of the text it contains. It is a genuine copy of Draft II of the poem, and so implies the existence of a genuine parent copy. Fortunately the Day commonplace book is not the sole substantiation of Draft II of *Coopers Hill*, and it can be extremely useful when employed with discretion. Moreover, an unexpected warranty of the probable authenticity of this manuscript resides in the fact that by an unusual coincidence this transcript appears very likely to have been the immediate ancestor of another Folger Library copy of *Coopers Hill*, MS V.a.322 (exemplar 4). Its own immediate ancestor was not itself a Denham holograph, but may very well have been an immediate copy of one. The Windsor provenance would make likely, as a purely external consideration, an early receipt of a poem of Egham origin. Therefore MSS V.a.160 and V.a.322 appear to be, of the five manuscripts collated for the present edition, the most directly related to a Denham original. One special characteristic of MS V.a.160 deserves mention, and that is the concern of its scribe for meter. Even his mistranscriptions, or copies of mistranscriptions, are made to be accommodated to the decasyllabic, five-stress line, and in a few instances his attention to meter has been the means of resolving a textual crux among the other exemplars.

The text of *Coopers Hill* in MS V.a.160 extends over thirteen numbered pages (pp. 95–107) of the commonplace book. Below the title on page 95 occur the first 12 lines of the poem, and page 107 contains the final 16 lines. Of the remaining eleven pages, three contain 30 lines apiece, seven contain 28 lines, and one contains only 26. The total of 340 lines coincides exactly with the length and structure of the text

---

he can see nothing in the handwriting of MS Folger V.a.160 (or in that of MS Folger V.a.322) which could not have been written before 1650.

contained in MS V.a.322, and therefore can be considered definitive of Draft II. Although the pages are numbered, catchwords are also used, but only on the even-numbered pages. In a bound book this practice serves only to establish that no leaf has been lost and to correlate the text with the page numbers.

As a whole the text of *Coopers Hill* in MS V.a.160 is carefully transcribed and free of gross idiosyncrasies. It does contain a few false readings, however, which are carried over to MS V.a.322 and there (later) corrected. Individual variant readings of this manuscript are recorded in the apparatus to Draft II and to the "A" text; a number of its more important peculiarities, troublesome or otherwise, are discussed below in the critical reading of Draft II. Banks did not know this manuscript, and consequently made no use of it in his edition of *Coopers Hill*.

4) The manuscript of *Coopers Hill* here called Folger MS V.a.322 occurs toward the end of an anonymous commonplace book of unknown provenance now in the Folger Shakespeare Library. All that is known of the book is that it was once no. 96 in a sale at Sotheby's; the date of that sale is not known, nor even if it was at that time or later that Folger acquired it. The book is in several handwritings, none of which has been identified. The subject matter is roughly chronological, with the earliest part referring to events about 1630, the latest to nothing later than about 1645. Denham's "Elegy on the Death of Judge Crooke" (d. February 1641/2) and *Coopers Hill* occur, as in Folger MS V.a.160, near the end. *Coopers Hill* itself is followed, however, by verses describing an incident purported to have taken place at the Parliament of 1628; the same verses, slightly altered and expanded, and with appropriate changes among the persons named, achieved wider circulation later, ascribing the incident to the Rump.[38] Perhaps then this indicates the entry was made in MS V.a.322 at a time before the piece was altered and brought up to

---

38. *Rump Songs* (1661), I, 61–63.

date. Otherwise there is nothing to date specifically the transcript of *Coopers Hill*.

The text of *Coopers Hill* in MS V.a.322 extends over eleven pages (pp. 216–226) of the commonplace book. Pagination is indicated on the odd-numbered pages (rectos) only. The text begins at the top of page 216, under the title, "Cooper's Hill"; the number of lines per page varies within narrow limits. Of the eleven pages, six contain 32 lines each, two contain 34 lines, one contains 36 lines, the title page contains 30 lines, and the last page contains the terminal 14 lines. After the last line the copyist had apparently first written "Mr Dodderidge," but then struck out that name and wrote "Denham," so that what appears is: Mr ~~Dodderidge~~ Denham. The total of 340 lines of text may be accepted as definitive of Draft II of *Coopers Hill*. The net increase of 12 lines over the length of Draft I includes a specific Draft II couplet (between "A" text lines 218 and 219) shared among the Draft II exemplars exclusively.

As a whole the text of *Coopers Hill* in MS V.a.322 is carefully transcribed and free of gross idiosyncrasies. It is in fact, in point of clarity and accuracy, by far the neatest manuscript exemplar of the poem; its chief deficiency lies in its relative paucity of the traditional or usual shoulder notes. The handwriting is a bastard very strongly governed by secretary; unlike the script in any of the other manuscripts considered, or the practice in the printed editions of *Coopers Hill*, no attempt is made to discriminate *u* from *v*, the form used depending solely on position. Making allowances for this and its few minor flaws, MS V.a.322 may be viewed as containing an almost ideal text of the second draft of *Coopers Hill*. Individual variant readings of this manuscript are recorded in the apparatus to Draft II and to the "A" text; a few of its more important peculiarities are discussed below in the critical reading of Draft II. Banks did not know this manuscript, and so made no use of it in his edition of *Coopers Hill*.

I believe MS V.a.322 to be a direct copy of MS V.a.160 (in the transcript of *Coopers Hill*), but a number of false readings carried

over from the parent copy have been canceled and corrected at a somewhat later date, obviously by someone with access to a superior text.

5) Manuscript Harleian 837.3 is the third of eight manuscripts in
a volume designated MS Harleian 837 and described in the *Catalogue
of the Harleian Manuscripts in the British Museum* as a "Book in
folio consisting of divers Tracts bound up together." Although its
companion pieces in this volume are so few, they are of little service
in determining the date at which the transcript of *Coopers Hill* was
made. Two of the pieces deal with the unpopular first Duke of Buckingham (assassinated 1628), the others are less readily datable as to
content. "Newes from Pernassus," the fourth item in the collection,
is in the same unidentified hand as *Coopers Hill*, but although it is
described as "a Libel on some Member of the House of Commons" I
have been unable either to date or to identify it. Internal evidence in
the manuscript as to the date of its own transcription comes to little
beyond the unique shoulder note, "The Kinge and Queene there,"
affixed to line 41 ["Windsor, the next, (where Mars and Venus
dwells," = "A" text, line 49.] While this might be construed as a
distinct reference to Charles I and Henrietta Maria, it may constitute
no more than a general elucidation of the topos in the line.

This manuscript of *Coopers Hill* occupies eight folio leaves, or sixteen unnumbered pages. The leaves are foliated 63–70, relative to their
position in the volume; the sequence of the pages is marked by sub-
script catchwords. The large number of pages in this manuscript is
offset by an average of fewer lines to the page in comparison with the
other manuscripts. Three of the sixteen pages contain 20 lines apiece,
eight contain 21 lines, and five 22; it is notable, therefore, that this
manuscript does not share the usual inhibition against splitting a
couplet between pages. With its total of only 338 lines, the text of this
manuscript is defective to the extent of a couplet found in all other
exemplars of the poem (between its own lines 228 and 229; the couplet
in Draft II is lines 229–230, in the "A" text, lines 237–238). The text
does, however, include the unique, second-draft couplet, lines 209–210

(between "A" text lines 218 and 219). The first page, which contains 20 lines of verse, is headed by the title "COOPERS: HILL:"; Denham's name occurs nowhere on the manuscript.

The script of this manuscript is an almost pure secretary hand showing, however, with bizarre effect, Exchequer mannerisms, and the orthography is affected and mannered. Colons and commas (really atrophied suspension marks) are used more for ornament than for functional punctuation. A doubled nasal is always represented by a tittle, whereas other consonants are often redundantly doubled, and *f* when beginning a syllable is always doubled (to produce such freaks as "ffruyteffull"). A not surprising consequence of the scribe's concern for visual appearance is that MS Harleian 837.3 contains a significantly higher proportion of demonstrable textual inaccuracies than any of the other manuscripts of *Coopers Hill* examined. Yet, despite its ostentation, this hand is self-consistent, and in the long run unambiguous, although it has achieved one totally irresolvable ambiguity. That occurs in line 68 ("A" text, line 76), where in place of the name "Cibele" the copyist's secretary script may be read equally as "Civile," "Ciuile," or "Cinile."

The chief variant readings of MS Harleian 837.3 are recorded in the apparatus to Draft II and to the "A" text. In a number of readings of individual words, as the apparatus discloses, this manuscript tends to coincide with readings of the printed "A" text editions rather than with the other manuscripts. Whether this fact speaks for an original Denham copy of Draft II already embodying readings later to become canonized in Draft III, and therefore a sort of "late state" of Draft II, or for some kind of contamination by Draft III of the text embodied in MS Harleian 837.3, is not easily decided. This manuscript was one of the two known to and used by Banks in editing *Coopers Hill*. He noticed the uniquely second-draft couplet, but seriously mistranscribed it for his apparatus. On his limited evidence Banks misconstrued the relationship of the manuscripts to the sequence of the printed texts, and imagined they represented a state of *Coopers Hill* intermediate between the "A" and the "B" texts.

6) The document labeled *1650ms* in the apparatus to Draft II and to the "A" text of *Coopers Hill* in the present edition is neither a manuscript of the poem nor a further copy of Draft II. Rather it constitutes vestigial evidence of the onetime existence of another copy of Draft II beyond those here examined. The evidence consists of manuscript marginalia added, perhaps around 1700, to a copy of the 1650 "A" text edition of *Coopers Hill* (exemplar 8, below) now in my possession. The marginalia consist of eight manuscript shoulder notes and an interpolated manuscript couplet. An earliest date for these additions to the volume is furnished by the entry on the blank verso of the title page, in the same hand and ink, of a brief biographical notice of Denham, manifestly abridged from Anthony Wood's account of Denham in *Athenae Oxonienses* (1691–92).

Of the eight shoulder notes added to *1650ms*, three seem to be unique while five correspond closely to shoulder notes in MS EL 8899. Therefore it might be conjectured that the shoulder notes were added to *1650ms* under the inspiration of a manuscript that strongly resembled MS EL 8899, and so must have been a transcript of Draft I. But the shoulder notes still remain appropriate to the Draft III text of 1650, and so might have survived through any number of copies of successive drafts as a separate shoulder-note tradition. The only alteration to the *text* of the poem is entirely in the direction of Draft II. Between lines 218 and 219 of the text (on p. 12 of the edition) a star has been inserted, calling attention to the bottom of the page, wherein written out in full occurs a transcript of the unique Draft II couplet already mentioned in discussion of the Draft II manuscripts. Consequently the lost manuscript consulted by the annotator of *1650ms* must be regarded as having been a representative of Draft II.

All the manuscript marginalia of *1650ms* are recorded in the apparatus to Draft II and to the "A" text. Examination of certain of the unique shoulder notes in this volume has proved surprisingly fruitful in elucidating the progressive evolution of the texts of *Coopers Hill*.

two. THE "A" TEXT
Draft III
LONDON VERSION

7) The first printed edition of *Coopers Hill* was published in London in August 1642 by the bookseller Thomas Walkeley. The text of this edition is the earliest surviving representative of the third distinguishable draft of the poem. Walkeley also published Denham's *The Sophy* and probably received copy for both works at the same time, for he entered both together in the Stationers' Register on Saturday, August 6: "two bookes vizt, A *Tragedy* called, *The Sophy* & a *Poem* called *Coopers Hill*, both of them by Mr John Denham." George Thomason's copy of *Coopers Hill* (1642), now in the British Museum, is dated August 5, which suggests that publication and entry in the Register closely coincided. The volume is a small one, about 7"x5", and collates thus: COOPERS / HILL. / A Poëme. / (rule) / (device) / (rule) / London Printed for *Tho. Walkley*, / and are to be sold at his shop at the Signe / of the Flying Horse between York-house / and Britaines Burse. 1642. 4o. pp. [2 (1, title)] + 19 (1–19, the poem) + [3 (1–3, blank)], signn. A–C⁴. (Wing D993.)

Two copies of this 1642 edition now in the Huntington Library have been collated chiefly for the present edition. They are the Robert Hoe copy (call number 122026) and the Isaac Walton copy (call number 134086-7). Of these the Walton copy, which has passed through the subsequent ownerships of T. Park, Charles N. Bancker, and Beverley Chew, is by far the most interesting, not only for its associational value, but for a significant manuscript emendation of the text in line 351 (p. 19). There the printed word "tell" is crossed out, and the word "lett" substituted, in what may be Walton's handwriting. This correction agrees with the reading of all the manuscripts as well as with the Oxford edition of 1643 (exemplar 9, below). The fact argues that Walton, or whoever made the alteration, had access either to a copy of the 1643 edition or to a manuscript, and that he judged the reading of *1642* to be incorrect. The edition of 1650 reads "till" and the "B" text editions drop the line in question entirely.[39]

Although *Coopers Hill* (1642) is a fairly conscientious example of book production for what must have been an inexpensive issue, it contains a considerable number of compositorial errors, some manifestly the result of misreading the copy text. A few of these errors, though by no means all, are corrected in the Oxford edition of 1643, for which an emended copy of *1642* probably served as copy text.

Draft III, or the "A" text proper, of *Coopers Hill*, first exemplified in *1642*, extends the text to 354 lines, a net increase of 14 lines over Draft II, although the increase is in fact compounded of very many alterations and revisions. Yet, despite the differences that distinguish Draft III from drafts I and II preserved in the manuscripts, the manuscripts are frequently capable of serving as valuable correctives of the printed "A" text. The manuscripts also support and supplement the Oxford corrections of Walkeley's 1642 edition. For instance, *1642* is followed by both *1643* and *1650* in the fairly nonsensical reading, "For things of wonder more, no less delight" (line 225), where the "B" text reads, "For things of wonder give no less delight" (line 199). The manuscripts unanimously reveal that the compositor of *1642* misread "more" for "move," and therefore should have produced "For things of wonder *move* no less delight" — the reading adopted for the present edition of the "A" text.

The "piracy" of which recent bibliographies (following Banks) have assumed all three "A" text editions of *Coopers Hill* to stand convicted is a charge that may colorably be brought only against Walkeley's 1642 edition. It is a charge that arises out of an uncritical acceptance and misconstruction of a prefatory statement by J. B., the otherwise unknown editor of the 1655 first edition of the "B" text (exemplar 10, below). Although a positive exoneration of *1642* cannot be

---

39. A minor puzzle is provided by the fact that Gosse (*From Shakespeare to Pope*, p. 106), purportedly quoting *Coopers Hill*, lines 350–354, from Walkeley's 1642 edition, also gives the manuscript and Oxford reading "let." Perhaps Gosse knew another copy of *1642* in which the emendation had been made, but his extreme confusion about the textual relationship between *1642* and *1643* (he identifies the latter with the "B" text) makes it equally likely that he is inadvertently quoting *1643*.

brought forward, in the form of irrefutable proof that Denham consented to or cooperated in Walkeley's publication of the poem, the substance of J. B.'s allegation can be readily rejected. At the time of publication Denham was not in any significant sense away from London, nor can anyone seriously maintain that the "A" text is not a genuine version of *Coopers Hill* from Denham's pen, as J. B. alone asserts. Moreover, Denham himself never implied any such rejection of *1642*, and *The Sophy*, registered and published by Walkeley at the same time as *Coopers Hill*, has never by anyone been called a piracy. Two further points in favor of the authority of *1642* are the emendations of *1643*, in which Denham almost certainly had a hand, and the apparent total failure of any *manuscript* copies of the "A" text proper to survive. The significance of this last fact resides in the very nature of seventeenth-century "piratical" or unauthorized publication.

For a printer to print a poem, a copy of it must come into his hands. If the copy does not come directly from the author, it must be a copy from someone else, which is to say, a copy in circulation. But no evidence exists to show that the text Walkeley printed was in circulation, whereas ample evidence exists that drafts I and II were in circulation. It seems logical therefore to conclude that the text of *1642* never entered manuscript circulation, and that it failed to do so because that version of *Coopers Hill* passed directly from the poet's hands into the hands of the printer. The Draft III revision indeed was probably carried out with publication in mind, and the subsequent occurrence of at least three printed editions of the new text within a period of eight years must have effectively ended the manuscript circulation of drafts I and II.

Banks used the text of *1642* as the basis for the *apparatus criticus* of his edition of *Coopers Hill*. As has been observed, he adopts the "B" text of *1668* as the received text of the poem, and attempts to treat the entire "A" text as a mere set of variants from the standard. Consequently it simplifies his task to assert that the texts of *1643* and *1650* are identical with that of *1642*, and so to exclude them both from his apparatus.[40] The flaws in the theory behind his procedure are accompanied by independent flaws in the practice: Banks records in his apparatus by no means all the significant variants of even *1642* from the "B" text, still less those of the other "A" text exemplars.

For reasons that seem sound to me, the text of *1642* has not been used in this edition as the basis of the "A" text of *Coopers Hill*. That distinction has been reserved to *1643*. Nevertheless all variants of *1642* from what has been adopted as the standard text are recorded in the apparatus.

8) The second London edition of *Coopers Hill* was brought out very early in 1650 by the bookseller Humphrey Moseley. Although this was chronologically the third published edition of the poem, it was issued in disregard and in probable ignorance of the Oxford edition of 1643, which in any event fell outside the purview of the Stationers' Company. Moseley acquired from Thomas Walkeley the printing rights to *Coopers Hill* in a transaction recorded in the Stationers' Register on November 3, 1649. The approximate date of actual publication is indicated by George Thomason's copy of the poem in the British Museum, on which Thomason has noted "Jan. 21, 1649[/50]." Together with *Coopers Hill*, Moseley printed in the same small volume Denham's "To Mr. Richard Fanshaw Esquire upon his . . . translation of *Pastor-Fido*" (which had already appeared with Fanshaw's *Pastor Fido* issued by Moseley in 1648), and also the "Prologue" and "Epilogue" to *The Sophy*. The latter verses had appeared in the 1642 edition of *The Sophy* by Thomas Walkeley, and so probably belonged to him; perhaps it was an attempt to rectify the transgression that led, on February 4, 1649/50, to a further transfer

---

40. The subjugation of the readings of *1643* to those of *1642* is effected with admirable thoroughness: in his Appendix D Banks quotes at length from Gosse on Denham, including Gosse's quotation of the last lines of the "A" text, noticed in the preceding note. As that note points out, Gosse, though purporting to quote from *1642*, actually gives the *1643* reading "let" for "tell" in line 351. Banks in turn quoting Gosse silently "corrects" the reading, thus expunging even this ghostly reminder of *1643*. Similarly he suppresses the readings of his two manuscripts for this word.

from Walkeley to Moseley of the rights to print *The Sophy*, for apparently Moseley never did publish Denham's tragedy.

The format of *1650* is slightly larger than that of *1642*, the volume measuring roughly 7½" x 6", and collating thus: COOPERS / HILL / A Poeme. / The Second Edition with Additions. / (rule) / *Written by* IOHN DENHAM *Esq*; / (rule) / (device) / (rule) / LONDON / Printed for *HUMPHREY MOSELEY*, / and are to be sold at his Shop, at the Signe / of the Princes Armes in St. *Pauls* / Church-yard. 1650. 4o. pp. [2 (1, title)] + 22 (1–18, Coopers Hill; 19, A Prologue to the Sophy; 20, An Epilogue to the Sophy; 21–22, To Mr. Richard Fanshaw), signn. A-C^4. (Wing D995.)

The "Additions" referred to on the title page are the three additional Denham poems; the text of *Coopers Hill* has in no way been expanded over, or substantially altered from, the text of *1642*. This Moseley edition, in fact, is in every way a reprint of Walkeley's edition, without intervention of any emendations, derived either from manuscript or from the corrections embodied in *1643*. Denham himself was in political exile on the Continent at the time this edition was issued, and so apparently had no hand in it whatsoever. Nevertheless the charge of piracy against this edition is meaningless; Moseley, having derived his title to print the poem directly from Walkeley, and in due course, was obliged by neither law, ethics, nor morality to consult Denham in the matter. Had he done so, however, he might have achieved a somewhat better text. As it is, *1650* can only perpetuate the misreadings or other compositorial errors of *1642* when it does not compound them by further errors of its own, for example, "till" for "tell" in line 351, where the manuscripts and *1643* show the proper reading should be "let" (or "lett"). Consequently, *1650* must be judged the least reliable and least authoritative of the three surviving "A" text editions of *Coopers Hill*. Yet to resolve all doubts, all the variants of *1650* from what has been selected for the present edition as the standard "A" text have been recorded in the apparatus.

The defects of *1650* are the more to be regretted in that copies of that edition are by no means inaccessible: in addition to the British Museum and the Bodleian, Wing lists five American libraries as holders of copies. Besides these, there are copies in the library of the University of California, Berkeley, and in my possession, and probably elsewhere.

Some evidence suggests that Moseley may have followed this "Second Edition" of *Coopers Hill*, of January 1649/50, with a "Third Edition," in perhaps October 1650. Such an edition, corresponding in every other way to the description of *1650*, is listed as published in October 1660 by Bishop White Kennet, *A Register & Chronicle Ecclesiastical & Civil* (1728). I have argued elsewhere that the date 1660 cannot be correct for this edition, if it ever existed, and have suggested that the date may be an error for 1650.[41] In any event, no substantial trace of this possible edition appears to have survived.

OXFORD VERSION

9) The historical second edition of *Coopers Hill* was not Moseley's 1650 "Second Edition," but a reprint of *1642* brought out by Henry Hall, printer to Oxford University, about April 1643. As one of the two licensed printers to the university, Hall enjoyed exemption from the regulations of the London Stationers' Company, and the normal isolation of the Oxford printers from the affairs of the company was exaggerated by the Civil War, which opposed Oxford, as the Royalist capital, to London. A consequence for the publication history of *Coopers Hill* was that generations of Oxonians (John Aubrey, Anthony Wood, even Samuel Johnson) continued to regard *1643* as the *first* edition of the poem, whereas for the Stationers' Company it had no existence at all, and *1642* was counted correctly as the first edition, *1650* incorrectly as the second.

Since a certain intricacy is unavoidable in the subsequent examination of *1643*, it may be well to set forth the collation, as a

---

41. " 'Lost,' 'Authorized,' and 'Pirated' Editions of John Denham's *Coopers Hill*," pp 242–253.

relatively fixed matter, at once. The volume is small, about $7\frac{1}{4}''$ x 5″, and collates thus: COOPERS / HILL. / (rule) / A Poëme. / (rule) / (device) / (rule) / *Printed in the Yeare M.DC.XLIII.* 4o. pp. [2 (1, title)] + 10 (1–10, the poem), signn. A-B². (Madan 1570; Wing D994.) As can be noticed (and as Aubrey notes) the book is printed on one and a half sheets — at least formally. It might be more correct to say that it is printed on a half sheet and a quarter sheet, for the direction of the chain lines, as far as they are discernible, is vertical rather than horizontal as would be true in a quarto made up in the usual fashion.[42] This aberrance, moreover, is only one of several peculiarities observable among the surviving copies of this edition of *Coopers Hill.*

John Aubrey, who owned a copy of *1643* now in the Bodleian Library, is also the author of the first recorded comment on the quality of paper used for its printing, and the first to intimate the circumstances under which publication occurred: "In 1642/3, after Edghill fight," he writes, "[Denham's] poeme called *Cowper's Hill* was printed at Oxford, in a sort of browne paper, for then they could gett no better." Wing's *Short-Title Catalogue* lists six libraries as holders of copies of *1643*; among them these libraries hold a total of eight copies. Additionally, one other copy has come into my possession. Of these nine copies, eight altogether—including Aubrey's own copy—are printed on a very poor quality, unwatermarked, wool-fiber paper which can no doubt be equated with Aubrey's "sort of browne paper." This paper Dr. A. H. Stevenson believes to be a hitherto unnoticed English-made paper upon which the Royalist printers at Oxford were forced to fall back when wartime exigencies cut off the customary supply of French-made papers from Normandy.[43] This "bad" paper appears also in several other products of

---

42. In the practice of cutting, before printing, double-sized sheets of poor quality, unwatermarked paper, Hall anticipated by more than a century a usage of late eighteenth-century printers discussed by Allen T. Hazen, "Eighteenth-Century Quartos with Vertical Chain-Lines," *The Library,* Transactions of the Bibliographical Society, XVI (1935–36), 337–342.
43. The views of Dr. Stevenson, who very kindly examined several samples of papers

the Oxford press of the same period, including many issues of the Royalist newssheet, *Mercurius Aulicus*, also printed by Henry Hall.

The single known exception to the rule that the Oxford *Coopers Hill* was printed on "bad" paper is the copy originally owned by Thomas Barlow, later Bodley's librarian and a bishop. Barlow's copy, which is now also in the Bodleian, is printed on a good Norman pot paper, and typographical evidence shows it to have been the last printed of the nine known copies. A parallel situation exists in the case of another small quarto printed by Hall, Peter Heylyn's *Theeves, Theeves* (Wing H1740; Madan 1328), which, like *Coopers Hill*, was printed on a sheet and a half, and on the same "bad" paper. Of four copies examined of this scarcer pamphlet, three were printed throughout on the "bad" paper; the exception was again Barlow's copy in the Bodleian, of which the full sheet was printed on a good Norman pot and the half sheet on the usual "bad," wool-flecked paper. The interest of this parallel goes beyond whatever sidelights it may shed on Barlow's privileged position as a bookbuyer. As far as a check on the title pages of books produced by Henry Hall during 1643 has revealed, *Coopers Hill* and *Theeves, Theeves* are the only two to share exactly the same imprint (Madan's 209) in exactly the same typesetting and spelling (*Printed in the Yeare M.DC.XLIII.*), and exactly the same ornament or device (between scrolled leafy vines a seminaked savage, with skirt and headdress of feathers or leaves, the whole about 2 x 4 mm). Madan was not able to date *Coopers Hill* more precisely than to the imprint year, but *Theeves, Theeves* was purchased by Thomason in London on May 1, which leads Madan to deduce a printing about April 26. A date close thereto for the printing of *Coopers Hill* therefore seems likely.

The only other indication of a printing date for the Oxford *Coopers Hill* which we have is Aubrey's assertion that it was printed in "1642/3," a dating that at least comes within close range of April.

---

both in the British Museum and in the Bodleian Library at my request, were communicated in private correspondence.

But Aubrey also says that the printing took place "after Edghill fight," an undeniable but not very precise claim, since the battle took place on October 23, 1642. Nevertheless, March or April of 1643 seems very strongly indicated as the period during which Hall printed Denham's poem "in a sort of browne paper."

Now Denham's own movements during these months remains uncertain. He was captured by the Parliamentary forces at Farnham on December 1, 1642, and brought to London. Sometime thereafter he was released, and immediately, all authorities agree, went to Oxford to join the King. When precisely this was, however, nobody knows. Yet the obvious implication, that he arrived in Oxford before the publication of *Coopers Hill*, and that the publication of *Coopers Hill* in some way arose out of Denham's presence in Oxford, fits all the facts of the matter which may be ascertained. For one thing, certain political episodes in London in December and January of 1642–43 led Denham to compose his satirical verses on *Mr. Hampdens Speech Against Peace*, of which George Thomason acquired a printed copy on March 23. The fact suggests, although it does not prove, that Denham was already at liberty at the time, and, if at liberty, in Oxford or on his way there.[44]

Much more indicative of Denham's hand in the Oxford publication of *Coopers Hill*, however, are the corrections the Oxford edition makes to the text of Walkeley's 1642 edition. A glance through the apparatus of the present "A" text, which records the minutest variations among the editions, reveals how singularly close *1643* remains to *1642*. For this closeness only two explanations seem at all possible. By far the less probable is that both editions were set in type from precisely the same manuscript copy text, but that the Oxford compositor, while mostly both reading and misreading the manuscript in exactly the same way as his London predecessor, was sometimes more careless although in a few crucial instances more

---

44. For a sketch of Denham's movements in 1642 and 1643, see my *Harmony from Discords*, pp. 54–66.

careful and accurate in his readings than Walkeley's compositor. This hypothesis would also entail belief that Walkeley, after completing his edition, had turned over the manuscript to someone who then took it to Henry Hall in Oxford. Even in this fairly absurd sequence of events, however, it can be recognized that the only logical intermediary between the two printers would have been Denham himself.

The more reasonable hypothesis is that Hall used a printed copy of *1642* as the basis of his edition. This would readily account both for the identities between the two editions, including the identical misreadings, and for the independent deviations of *1643*, which would be simply the errors of Hall's compositor. Only the corrections in *1643* need then to be accounted for. At least five of these (at lines 187, 194, 211, 296, and 351) are manifestly not the sort to be corrected spontaneously by a compositor, as the fact that the misreadings of *1642* were either allowed to stand unchanged or else further corrupted in Moseley's edition of 1650 clearly demonstrates. An error, or failed correction, in *1643* tends to much the same demonstration. In line 244 the reading of *1642* and *1650* is "Dyana"; in *1643* it is "Dyana'"—with a clearly printed but superfluous apostrophe. But three manuscripts, including the metrically conscious MS Folger V.a.160, agree on the reading "Dian'" which improves the scansion of the line. Presumably then Denham really wrote "Dyan'" for Draft III; this became corrupted to "Dyana" in *1642*, and an attempt to correct it in *1643* succeeded only in adding the apostrophe to the end of the word, but not in deleting the *a*. Someone must have made these corrections in the copy of *1642* used as the Oxford copy text, and no likelier identity for the corrector than John Denham occurs readily to the reason.

Under the circumstances of Oxford publishing in the year 1643 the possibility that the printer Henry Hall initiated the issuance of *Coopers Hill* as a private commercial venture is extremely remote. Setting aside the crux of the corrections, it must be recognized that Hall had the use of only one printing press, and in 1643 his hands were full, past all precedent, by printing work for the royal war effort.[45] As eight of our nine copies of *Coopers Hill* attest, along with dozens of other contemporary products of the Oxford press, paper was extremely scarce, and no frivolous or speculative publications could be issued.[46] *Coopers Hill* in fact appears to have been published precisely because of its estimated value as Royalist propaganda, and that it was already held in some esteem even at the time of printing is indicated by Barlow's good-paper copy.[47] Obviously the one person most likely to have brought a copy of Walkeley's 1642 edition to Oxford, to have corrected the text of that edition to reflect the author's true intentions, and to have arranged publication of the poem as a contribution to the King's cause, was John Denham himself.

The Oxford edition of 1643, then, shows every sign of being an edition that emanated directly from Denham. Its text shows what appear to be his own corrections of errors in the London edition of 1642, and consequently must be regarded as superior to the text of that earlier edition. Consequently it is the Oxford text, subject to necessary minor emendation, which has been adopted as the basis for the "A" text offered herein. For the purpose all nine known copies have been carefully checked, and three — those in the Huntington Library, San Marino; in the Newberry Library, Chicago; and in my private possession — have been minutely collated. All discrepancies

---

45. According to Falconer Madan, the two printers at Oxford, Henry Hall and Leonard Litchfield, had until 1655 no more than a single press each. During the prewar decade the average output of these presses had been only 25½ pieces annually ("The Oxford Press, 1650–75," *The Library*, VI [1925], 113–147). In 1642 there were 191 Oxford imprints, in 1643 there were 238; some of these were either London counterfeits or duplicates, issued clandestinely by Royalist printers to alleviate the strain on Oxford's facilities (*Oxford Books*, II: *Oxford Literature 1450–1640, and 1641–1650* [Oxford, 1912], pp. x–xi).

46. Recourse to the coarse unsuitable paper of *Coopers Hill* and *Theeves, Theeves* was not the sole symptom of the Oxford paper shortage. The scarcity grew so acute that the news-sheet *Mercurius Aulicus* was often obliged to fake sequence numbers and folio signatures to conceal from the enemy the fact that not all scheduled numbers could be issued, for want of paper (see Madan, *Oxford Books*, II, x–xi).

47. Madan's surprised comment on the oddity of such a "pastoral and unwarlike" poem as *Coopers Hill* appearing among the proclamations and polemical tracts that constituted the fruits of printing in Civil War Oxford (*ibid.*, II, 326) not only betrays his innocence of the political nature of the poem, but at the same time discloses something of the qualities prerequisite of any book that hoped to see Oxford publication in 1643, and the improbability of mere piratical ventures on the part of either printer.

among the copies have been recorded in the apparatus to the "A" text, along with all deviations from the text that has been adopted as standard.

THREE. THE "B" TEXT
Draft IV
J. B.'S EDITION

10) The first appearance of the "B" text of *Coopers Hill* took place probably late in the year 1655 in an edition published by Humphrey Moseley and accompanied by a note "To the Reader" signed with the initials J. B. (J. B.'s note in full is prefixed to the "B" text, p. 137, below.) This 1655 edition has given rise, by virtue of both the textual revolution in *Coopers Hill* to which it attests and the ambiguities of J. B.'s note, to much of the confusion that has since clouded all discussion of Denham's poem. The identity of J. B. is only one of the mysteries surrounding this publication, so that the establishment of a few certainties is a vital prerequisite to any further speculation about the edition. The precise date of publication is not ascertainable: no Stationers' Register entry refers to the copy, since Moseley had held the printing rights since 1649. Unfortunately, too, George Thomason perhaps felt no compulsion to add a third edition of *Coopers Hill* to the copies of *1642* and *1650* he already possessed, for no copy of *1655* has survived in his collection.[48] Like the earlier editions of *Coopers Hill*, this edition is a small quarto pamphlet, of dimensions perhaps 8" x 6" untrimmed, and collates in a similar fashion. COOPERS / HILL. / Written in the yeare 1640. / Now Printed from a perfect Copy; And / A Corrected Impression. / (rule) / (device) / (rule) / *LONDON,* / Printed for *Humphrey Moseley,* and are to be / sold at his Shop, at the Signe of the Princes / Armes in St *Pauls* Church-

---

48. Actually the publication of *1655* can doubtless be closely correlated with the publication of Denham's *The Destruction of Troy* (1656), which Moseley brought out around February 1655/6, probably quite shortly after *Coopers Hill* (see my *Harmony from Discords,* p. 110).

yard. 1655. 4o. pp. [4 (1, title, 2, blank, 3–4, To the Reader)] + 18 (1–18, the poem) + [1], signn. A², B-C⁴, D². (Wing D996.)

The gratuitous self-assertiveness of this volume, outside of even J. B.'s note, is quite marked. Unlike any other edition of *Coopers Hill*, this one clamors to provide unsolicited information: the precise year of the poem's original composition, the exact nature of the copy text used in printing. In the face of such eagerness skepticism appears churlish; consequently, though no one has quite believed anything that J. B. actually says, his edition has been invested with an unwarranted aura of authority — an aura only. Not a single scholar accepts without question 1640 as the date of initial composition of the poem, still less the absurd contention that the initial version then composed was verbatim the "B" text that J. B. prints. Nor has anyone shown a disposition to accept J. B.'s explicit assertion that the entire "A" text is nothing but a barbarous mutilation and "false Transcript" of the "B" text. Accordingly, out of politeness, it has become customary to call *1655* the "first authorized edition" of *Coopers Hill*, and to label the "A" text editions that preceded it "piracies." Something by way of a defense of the authority of the "A" text editions has already been attempted above; a few remarks on the disingenuousness of J. B.'s edition are now in order.

J. B. nowhere asserts that he has been deputized by Denham to issue a corrected text of *Coopers Hill*. He takes responsibility and credit entirely to himself, although he claims to have obtained his "perfect Copie" of the poem from "the Author's owne papers." Without knowledge of J. B.'s identity, it is vain to speculate on the true nature of his relationship to Denham. Any number of fictions can be constructed to fit the available facts. A hostile construction could with little difficulty picture J. B. as himself the one pirate in the sequence, or at least as an ignorant busybody. The most charitable construction will accept him as Denham's somewhat ill-informed agent, the purpose of whose note to the reader is, in effect, to *withdraw* the authority of all previous versions of the poem, so that Denham's most recent draft (Draft IV) could supersede in the public consciousness all earlier drafts already in circulation.

Although Moseley's compositor undoubtedly did make use of "A Corrected Impression" (probably a copy of *1650*) together with a manuscript of the new draft of *Coopers Hill*, the gap between the old "A" text and the new "B" text, as the present edition exists to testify, is a wide one. Almost certainly the revisions were made during Denham's stay at Wilton in 1653–54, and they were not trivial ones. Even though the text of J. B.'s edition coincides exactly in length with the 354 lines of the "A" text editions, the coincidence must be regarded as essentially accidental. Denham's own later edition of the poem, published in his *Poems and Translations* of 1668 (exemplar 11, below) contains 358 lines, and the question remains open whether the extra four lines of that version were added by Denham after 1655, or whether their absence from J. B.'s edition betokens a defect in his text (the four lines in question are a rewriting of lines in the "A" text).

J. B.'s edition of *Coopers Hill* is not only carelessly printed (entire words are dropped) but it differs from the unquestionably authorized "B" text of 1668 in several significant readings. Again the question is open whether the differences represent defects in J. B.'s "perfect Copie" or further revision by Denham himself after 1655. All the variant readings of *1655* are recorded in the apparatus to the present "B" text. Here only a number of assertions need be made to counter a mass of false assumptions: (1) everything asserted by J. B. is in some degree false, or at least misleading; (2) J. B.'s edition is not the "first authorized edition"; it was neither authorized nor the first authentic text of the poem; (3) the earlier editions of *Coopers Hill* were neither "piracies" nor "false Transcripts"; (4) this edition was not "expanded"; like the "A" text editions it contains exactly 354 lines of verse. It is the gross distinctions between the "B" text and the "A" text which set apart *1655* from *1642, 1643*, and *1650*, as well as from the manuscript drafts. These distinctions, as earlier remarked, are chiefly the inclusion in the "B" text, for the first time, of the famous "Thames couplets," and of the great expansion of the stag-hunt episode (to which J. B. alludes) *at the expense of the compression* of the other sections of the poem.

Banks was familiar with *1655*, and recorded its variants sporadically in his apparatus. To some extent he accepted J. B.'s claims for his edition, but seems not to have recognized the actual extent or intent of those claims. Banks in fact appears to be the inventor of the notion that J. B.'s edition was "authorized," and to have been the first to apply the label "piracy" to the "A" text editions. Nonetheless he tacitly refuses to accept J. B.'s more extreme claims (e.g., to unique textual authenticity), and accords no greater weight in his critical apparatus to J. B.'s deviations from *1668* than he does to those of *1642* and the two manuscripts he knew.

J. B.'s edition of *Coopers Hill* was apparently little known in its own time; no reference to or quotation from *Coopers Hill* which can be dated earlier than 1668 clearly requires the "B" text as its basis, and several, even later than 1655, clearly depend on the "A" text. It is an oddity, therefore, that Moses Pengry's Latin translation of the poem, *Coopers Hill Latine Redditum*, though published in 1676, follows with extreme fidelity J. B.'s edition rather than Denham's own edition of 1668. At the same time it would probably be incorrect to regard *1655* as a rare book. Wing lists four holders in Great Britain, four in the United States. In addition to the copies thus indicated, at least two other copies have come to my attention, including my own.

POEMS AND TRANSLATIONS EDITION, 1668

11) The only truly authorized edition of *Coopers Hill*, and the last edition to appear in Denham's lifetime, was the version of the "B" text which appeared in Denham's collected *Poems and Translations* issued early in 1668 by Henry Herringman. Herringman acquired the printing rights to *Coopers Hill, The Sophy,* and various others of Denham's published poems by transfer from the widow of Humphrey Moseley, recorded in the Stationers' Register. Denham's own hand in the matter is beyond question, as evidenced by his

own prose statements within the collection as well as by ample exterior testimony.[49] Not a single word in the entire volume, however, so much as alludes to any prior edition of *Coopers Hill*, or makes any assertion about the relative authenticity of texts. The text is fundamentally the same as that of *1655*, but differs in being longer by four lines (lines 193–196), and in a number of significant readings.

   Poems and Translations (1668) is a fairly complicated volume, but the complete collation of it is here unnecessary. Some copies contain an errata sheet, but none of the errata pertain to the text of *Coopers Hill*, which does, however, contain three typographical errors. *Coopers Hill* is the first poem in the volume, followed by *The Destruction of Troy* with a separate title page and imprint date (1667), but continuous pagination and sequence of signatures. *The Sophy* also occurs in the volume, with separate title page dated 1667 and with separate pagination. In all copies examined the title page and preliminary matter of the entire volume begin with signature A. As far as is relevant to *Coopers Hill* the collation is as follows: POEMS / AND / TRANSLATIONS, / WITH THE / SOPHY. / (rule) / Written by the Honourable / Sir *JOHN DENHAM* / Knight of the *Bath*. / (double rule) / *LONDON*. / Printed for *H. Herringman* at the Sign of the / *Blew-Anchor* in the *Lower-Walk* of the / *New-Exchange*. 1668. 8o. pp. [12 (1–2, blank, 3, title page, 4, blank, 5–10, The Epistle Dedicatory To the King, 11–12, table)] + 186 (1–22, *Coopers Hill*) + [6 (1, errata, 2, blank, 3, title page, 4, blank, 5–6, preliminaries)] + 99 (1–44, 43–97) + [1]. Signn. [π] A⁵, B–M⁸, N⁵ [π], Aa-Ff⁸, Gg⁴. (Wing D1005.) In the printing of *Coopers Hill* page 17 is misnumbered or rather misprinted as page 27.

   With the corrections of misprints only, the text of *1668* has been accepted for the present edition as the definitive "B" text of *Coopers Hill*. But, although the text clearly reflects Denham's own careful preparation of the "B" text for the printer, a copy of *1655* must

---

49. The late Sir W. W. Greg had in his possession a presentation copy of *1668*, signed by Denham. Denham's own copy, with copious holograph additions, is now in the possession of Mr. James M. Osborn of Yale (see exemplar 12, below).

nevertheless have served as the basic copy text. This fact is indicated by a curious accident of the printing. In *1655* line 109 of the poem had appeared as "He, who not needs that Embleme which we paint"; for *1668* Denham altered the reading to "Nor doth he need those Emblemes which we paint." By chance, in *1668* this line appears as the first line at the top of a page (p. 8), a fact that would require the word "Nor" to appear as catchword at the bottom of the preceding page (p. 7). In fact the catchword that appears is "He," indicating that the compositor who set the page did so from a copy text in which line 109 appeared in the *1655* form, most probably an actual copy of *1655*. This erroneous catchword persisted through the reprint editions of *Poems and Translations* issued in 1671 and 1684. It was the text of *1668* which Banks adopted as the single basic text of *Coopers Hill*, and which has been reprinted in most anthologies since.

12) Sometime after publication of *1668* Denham transcribed in his own copy and marked for insertion in the text of *Coopers Hill* six new lines of the poem. Denham's copy has recently come to light and has passed into the possession of Mr. James M. Osborn of Yale University. Mr. Osborn has published these lines in the *Times Literary Supplement*, September 1, 1966, and through his kindness they have now for the first time been incorporated into the text of the poem. Since the Denham-Osborn holograph is a unique transcript of these lines they have had to be reproduced verbatim (except for expansion of abbreviations) without opportunity of collation.

13) For the present edition the edition of 1671 has also been collated with *1668*, on the chance that a few variants might constitute authorial corrections not caught in *1668*. Of these variants only one is of much interest: the correction of tense in line 242 of "Give" to "Gave." This correction may be Denham's, and is the reading followed by most reprints of *Coopers Hill* before that of Banks. In the present edition it is recorded in the apparatus.

MINOR EXEMPLARS

As lesser exemplars of *Coopers Hill* must be counted the exemplars of the Latin translation. The translation has no known authorial warranty, the exact date at which it was made is unknown, but its interest resides in the fact that the act of translation forced the translator to *interpret* the poem, and thus to some extent to reveal how one of Denham's contemporaries read the poem. The translator, as Anthony Wood reveals, was Moses Pengry, chaplain to the Earl of Devon (to whose son, William Lord Cavendish, the translation was dedicated), although the published translation bore the name neither of Pengry nor of Denham. The edition, a handsome large quarto, was issued at the Sheldonian Theatre in 1676. According to Madan the issue, which is now scarce, consisted of 1,025 copies.[50] Wood's copy, now in the Bodleian Library, bears the inscription: "Anthony à Wood Oxon, given to me by Moses Pengry. Bac. Div. & Fellow of Brasenose Coll. who translated this poem from Engl. into Latine, June 15. 1676. Chapl. to yᵉ Earl of Devon." [51] The translation, into hexameters, is a close rendition of the text of *1655*, even to the lack of the four lines belonging exclusively to *1668* and thereafter, and occupies exactly the same number of lines—354.

Manuscript copies of *Coopers Hill Latine Redditum* also exist, of which I have seen two, each including some slight variants. One is interleaved in a copy of the 1709 separate edition of *Coopers Hill* now in the Huntington Library; it maintains the line alignment of the English and Latin texts, including a blank in the Latin for the four lines not translated. The other is a manuscript now in the possession of Mr. James Osborn of Yale University, through whose kindness I was enabled to procure a photostatic copy.[52]

---

50. Falconer Madan, *Oxford Books*, III: *Oxford Literature 1651–1680* (Oxford, 1931), p. 332.

51. Madan's transcription of this note contains at least three misprints. The present transcript was kindly provided by D. G. Neill, assistant librarian, Department of Printed Books, Bodleian Library, Oxford, in a letter dated January 16, 1964.

52. For a fuller presentation of *Coopers Hill Latine Redditum*, see App. A, below.

COOPERS HILL: THE TEXTS

Draft I

THE TEXT IS exemplified in two independent manuscripts: MS Elles-mere 8899 (326 lines, lacking lines 93–94) and MS Harleian 367.71 (lacking lines 1–58). Manuscript Ellesmere 8899, as the only fully ex-tensive representative, has been used as the basis. Abbreviations, with the exception of ampersand within a line, have been expanded, and punctuation has been silently supplied, usually on the authority of other exemplars. Unique Ellesmere readings have been rejected, how-ever, whenever the Harleian manuscript and other available exem-plars of *Coopers Hill* agree on a contradictory variant. In all such cases the rejected reading is recorded in the apparatus. In a few in-stances the Ellesmere and the Harleian manuscripts disagree on a reading over which all other available exemplars divide according to exactly the same alternatives. Since such a binary division is ulti-mately irresolvable, and may reflect either an ambivalence in Den-ham's intention or an initial variance or obscurity in the parent copies from which all existing exemplars descend, selection of one reading over another for the edited text has been governed by ulterior con-siderations. Most significant of these has been the desire that each of the binary variants shall be represented at least once among the four texts of *Coopers Hill* presented in this edition. For the text of Draft I the alternate reading has not only been preserved in the ap-paratus, but an effort has been made also to indicate the distribution of the split among the other drafts.

No effort has been made in the apparatus to comprehend such variants as spelling, capitalization, or distribution of punctuation be-tween the Draft I manuscripts and other exemplars. The intention has been to record all variations of line, phrase, or word, without exception. Nonetheless whenever the apparatus records a manuscript variant an exact transcription of the variant has been aimed at. From the apparatus, therefore, the reader should be able to reconstruct the exact verbal text of each manuscript, although he will not have available all the individual vagaries displayed by each.

KEY TO THE CRITICAL APPARATUS

EL.8899   Manuscript Ellesmere 8899 in the Bridgewater Collection at the Henry E. Huntington Library

H.367   Manuscript item 71 in volume MS Harleian 367 of the Harleian Collection in the British Museum

II   Consensus of the exemplars of Draft II

A   The "A" text of *Coopers Hill*

B   The "B" text of *Coopers Hill*

Σ   Consensus of all other drafts of *Coopers Hill* (i.e., all exemplars of *II*, *A*, *B*)

Draft I

COOPERS HILL (*1641?*)

Sure we have Poets that did never dreame
Uppon Pernassus, nor did tast the Streame
Of Hellicon, And therefore I suppose
Those made not Poets, but the Poets those:
And as Courts make not Kings, but Kings the Court,   5
So where the Muses & their Troopes resorte
Pernassus stands; if I can bee to thee
A Poet, thou Pernassus art to me,
Whose topp when I ascend, I seeme more high
More boundlesse in my Fancy then myne Eye: 10
As those who raysed in body or in thought
Above the Earth or the Ayres middle vault,
Behould how Windes & Stormes & Meteors growe
How Clowdes condence to Rayne, congeale to Snowe
And See the Thunder form'd (before it teare   15
The Ayre) Secure from danger & from feare
So from thy lofty topp my Eye lookes downe
On Pauls, as men from thence unto the Towne   Paules & London
My minde uppon the Tumult & the Crowde
And Sees it wrapt in a more dusky Cloud   20
Of busines, then of Smoke, where men like Ants

---

12 Ayres] Earths   13 Meteors] Meterrs   17 topp my] topping
    EL. 8899   *EL. 8899*   *EL. 8899*

    Title] For general annotation of *Coopers Hill* see the "A" and "B" texts (drafts III and
IV).
    18. The absence from the text at this point of the complimentary allusion to Waller's
poem on St. Paul's is one of the major distinguishing features of Draft I of *Coopers Hill.*

Preying on others to supply their wants
Yet all in vaine, increasing with their Store
Their vast desires, but make their wants the more.
Oh happines of Sweete retyr'd content   25
To be at once Secure, and Innocent.
Windsore the next (where Mars with Venus dwells,   Windsore
Beauty with Strength) above the Valley Swells,
Into myne Eye: As the late married Dame
Who proud, yet seemes to make that pride her shame   30
When nature quickens in her pregnant wombe
Her wishes past & now her hopes to come
With such an Easie & unforct ascent
Windsor her gentle Bosome doth present
Where no stupendious Cliffs nor threatning heights   ·35
Accesse deny, nor horrid Steepe affrights
But such a Rise as doth at once invite
A pleasure & a Reverence from the Sight
Thy Masters Embleme in whose face I saw   Kings Matie.
A frendlike sweetnes & a Kinglike Awe   40
Where Majesty & love soe mixt appeare
Both gently kinde, both Royally Severe
So Windsor humble in it selfe seemes proude
To be the Base of that Maiesticke loade
Then which noe Hill a nobler burthen beares   45
But Atlas only, which supports the Spheares
Nature this Mount soe fitly did advaunce
Wee might conclude then nothinge is by Chance
Soe plac't as if shee did on purpose rayse
The Hill to Robbe the builder of his praise   50
(For none commends his iudgement that doth chuse
That which a blind man only could refuse)
Such are the Towers which the holy temples grace

---

27 dwells,] dwells)   28 Strength)] Strength,   48 then] that *II, A*
    EL. 8899   *EL. 8899*   53 holy] hoary *II, A*

Of Cibele, when all her heavenly Race
Doe homage to her, yet shee cannot boast   55
(Amongst that numerous & Celestiall hoast)
More Heroes then can Windsor, nor doth Fame's
Immortall Booke record more noble names
Not to looke backe soe farre to whom this Isle
Must owe the glory of soe brave a Pile   60
Whether to Caesar, Albanact, or Brute   Not knowne who
The Brittish Arthur, or the Danish Knute   built Windsore
This amongst us no lesse contest did move
Then when for Homers birth seaven Citties strove
Like him in birth thou shouldst be like in Fame   65
As thine his fate, if myne had beene his Flame
But whosoere it was, Nature design'd
First a brave place, & then as brave a mynde
Nor to recount those severall Kings to whome
It gave a Cradle or to whome a Tombe   70
But thee (greate Edward) & thy greater Sonne   E: 3
(Hee that the Lillies wore, & he that wonne)   Blacke Prince
And thy Bellona who deserves her share   Queene
In all thy Glories; Of that Royall payre
Which wayted on thy Tryumph; she brought one   Kings of   75
Thy Sonne the other brought, and shee that Sonne Fraunce
                                                 & Scotland
Nor of lesse hopes could her greate ofspring prove
A Royall Eagle cannot breede a dove.
Then didst thou founde that order, Whether Love Order of the
                                                 Garter
Or victory thy Royall thoughts did move   80

---

54 Cibele] Cecilie   amonge *H. 367*   75 *Shoulder*] The Kings
    EL. 8899   did] doth *EL. 8899*   of ffra: and Scotland
61 *Shoulder*] *not in* 70 or] & *EL. 8899*   *H. 367*
    H. 367   71 *Shoulder*] *not in* 78 breede] bred *H. 367*
63 This amongst] Those   *H. 367*   79 *Shoulder*] The Garter
                         73 *Shoulder*] *not in*   *H. 367*
                             H. 367

59. The surviving text of MS H.367.71 begins at this line.

Each was a noble cause nor was it lesse
I'th'institution then the greate Successe
Whilst every part conspires to give it grace
The King the Cause the Patron, and the place   St. George
Which forraine kings & Emperors esteeme   85
The second honor to their diadem
Had thy greate destiny but given thee skill
To know aswell as power to Act her will
That from those Kings who then thy Captives were
In after tymes should springe a Royall paire   90
Who should possesse all that thy mighty power   K: & Q: Maty.
Or thy desires more mighty did devoure   nowe
To whome thire better Fate reserves what Ere
The victor hopes for, or the vanquisht feare,
That blood which thou & thy greate Grandsire shead   95
And all that since these Sister nations bledd
Had beene unspilt had happie Edward knowne
That all the blood he spilt had beene his owne
Thou hadst extended through the Conquered East
Thyne & the Christian name & made them blest   100
To serve thee, while that losse, this gaine would bring
Christ for their God, & Edward for their Kinge.
When thou that Saint thy patron didst designe
In whome the Martyre & the Souldier ioyne
And when thou didst within the Azure Rounde,   105
(Who Evill thinkes may Evill him confound)   the Garter
The English Armes incircle, thou didst seeme
But to foretell, & prophesie of him   K: James
Who has within that Azure Round confin'd,

---

82 I'th'] In th' *EL. 8899*   91 Who] wch *EL. 8899*   106 *Shoulder] not in*
84 *Shoulder] not in*   *Shoulder] not in*   *H. 367*
     H. 367   *H. 367*   108 *Shoulder] not in*
90 tymes] Ages *EL. 8899*   93–94 *not in EL. 8899*   *H. 367*
                        93 better] bitter *H. 367*

Those Realmes which nature for their bounds design'd: 110
That bounde which to the World's extreamest Ends,   Sea
Endles her selfe her liquid Armes extends.
In whose Heroicke face I see the Saint
Better exprest then in the livelyest paint
That fortitude which made him famous heere,   115
That heavenly Piety which Saints him there:
Whoe when this Order he forsakes, may hee
Companion of that Sacred Order bee;
Here could I fix my wonder, but our Eyes
(Nice as our tasts) affect varieties;   120
And though one please him most, the hungry Ghuest
Tasts every dish, & Runns through all the feast
So havinge tasted Windsor, casting rounde
My wandring Eye, an emulous hill doth bound   St. Anns hill
My more contracted sight, whose topp of late   125
A Chappell crown'd till in the common Fate
The neighbouring Abby fell, may no such storme   Chertsey Abbey
Fall on our tymes, where Ruyne must reforme.
Tell my (my muse) what monstrous dire offence
What crime, could any Christian King incense   K: Hen: 8   130
To such a Rage? was't Luxury or Lust
Was he so temperate? so chast, so iust?
Were these their Crimes? they were his owne much more,
But they alas were rich & he was poore,
And having spent the treasures of his Crowne   135
Condemnes their Luxury to feede his owne:

---

111 *Shoulder] not in*
   H. 367
113 the] a *EL. 8899*
115 which] that *H. 367*
116 which] that *H. 367*
117 Whoe when] when
   EL. 8899

120 affect] affects
   EL. 8899
124 *Shoulder]* St. Amis
   Hill *H. 367*
127 *Shoulder]* Chersey
   Abby *H. 367*
128 tymes] time
   EL. 8899

130 *Shoulder] not in*
   H. 367
132 chast] wise *EL. 8899*
133 Were] Was *EL. 8899*
135 treasures] treasure
   H. 367

And yett this act (to varnish ore the shame
Of Sacriledge) must beare devotions name;
And he might thinke it iust, the cause & time
Considered well; for none comitts a Crime 140
Appearing Such, but as tis understood
A Reall, or (at least) a seeming good.
While for the Church his Learned pen disputes,
His much more Learned Sword his pen confutes:
Thus to the Ages past he makes amends, 145
Their charity destroyes their faith defends.
Then did Religion in a Lazie Cell,
In Empty Ayrie contemplation dwell,
And like the blocke unmoved lay; but ours
As much too Active, like the Storke devours: 150
Is there no temperate Region can be knowne,
Betweene their frigid & our torrid Zone;
Could wee not wake from that Lethargicke dreame,
But to be restles in a worse extreame;
And for that Lethargie was there no Cure, 155
But to be cast into a Calenture;
Can knowledge have no bounde but must advance,
So farre to make us wish for ignorance:
And rather in the darke to grope our waye
Then (ledd by a false guide) to Erre by day? 160
Partinge from thence twixt Anger Shame & fearre
Those for what's past, & this for what's too neere,
My Eye descending from the Hill surveyes:
Where Thames amongst the wanton valleys strayes. Thames
Sweete Thames, the eldest & the noblest Sonne 165
Of ould Oceanus; doth swiftly Runne,

143 While] Whilst   152 Betweene] Betwixt Σ   157 must] to EL. 8899
EL. 8899   153 Lethargicke] Le-   164 amongst] among
148 contemplation] con-   thurgick H. 367   H. 367
templations Σ

84

Hasting to pay his tribute to the Sea
Like mortall life to meete eternitye;
And though his cleerer sand, no golden veines
(Like Tagus & Pactolus streames) conteynes   170
His genuine & lesse guilty wealth t'explore
Search not his bottome, but behould his shore,
Ore which, he kindly spreads his spatious winge
And hatches plenty for the ensuinge Springe,
Nor with an Angrey & unruly wave,   175
(Like Profuse Kings) resumes the Wealth he gave:
Noe unexpected inundations spoyle
The Mowers hopes nor mocke the Plowmans toyle
And as a parting lover bids farewell
To his Soules ioy, seeing her Eyelidds swell   180
He turnes againe to save her falling teares,
And with a parting kisse secures her feares:
Soe Thames unwilling yet to be devorc't
From his lov'd channell, willingly is forc't
Backward against his proper course to swell,   185
To take his second, though not last farewell.
As a wise king first settles fruitefull peace
In his owne Realmes & with their rich increase
Seekes warre abroade & then in triumph brings
The Spoyles of Kingdomes, & the Crownes of Kings,   190
So Thames, to London doth at first present
Those tributes, which the neighbouring Countreys sent:

---

167 tribute] Tributes *H. 367*
168 meete] seeke *EL. 8899*
170 streames] streame *H. 367*

171 t'explore] explore *EL. 8899*
173 winge] wings *EL. 8899*
174 Springe] Springs *EL. 8899*
179 *Shoulder*] Simile *EL. 8899*

185 Backward] Backwards *H. 367*
187 *Shoulder*] Simile *EL. 8899*
188 rich] owne *EL. 8899*
189 warre] (*sic A*) warres *H. 367, II*

179–186. This extended simile is unique to Draft I of *Coopers Hill*, and so constitutes another of its major distinctive features.

But at his second visite, from the East
Spices he brings & treasures from the West:
Findes wealth where tis, & gives it where it wants,   195
Citties in deserts, woods in Citties plants:
So that to us no thing, no place is strange,
While his faire Bosome is the Worlds exchange:
O could my lines fully & smoothly flow,
As thy pure flood: heaven should noe longer knowe   200
Her ould Eridanus, thy purer Streame,
Should bathe the God's & be the Poets Theame
Here Nature whether more intent to please   Windsor forrest
Us, or her selfe with strange varieties
(For things of wonder move no lesse delight   205
To the wise makers, then beholders sight)
Though these delights from severall Causes move
(For so our Children thus our frends we love)
Wisely shee knew the harmony of things
(Aswell as that of soundes) from discord springs: 210
Such was the discord which did first disperse
Forme, order, beauty, through the universe,
While moisture, dryness, Coldnes, heate, resists
All that we have, & that we are subsists,   Body of Man
While the steepe horrid roughnes of the wood,   215
Strives with the gentle Calmenes of the flood:
Such huge extreames, when nature doth unite
Wonder from thence results, from thence delight:
The Streame is so transparent pure & Cleare
That had the selfe enamoured youth gaz'd here,   Narcissus   220

---

200 noe] not *EL. 8899*
203 *Shoulder*] The Ffor-
     rest *H. 367*
207 these] those *EL. 8899*
210 soundes] Soules
     EL. 8899

     discord] (*sic II*) dis-
     cords *H. 367, A, B*
211 Such] And *H. 367*
213 While] Whilst
     EL. 8899
214 *Shoulder*] *not in*
     H. 367

217 unite] invite
     EL. 8899
219 The] Thy *H. 367*
220 *Shoulder*] *not in*
     H. 367

So fatally deceav'd, he had not beene,
While he the bottome, not his face had seene.
And such the roughnes of the hill, on which
Dian' her toyles, & Mars his tents might pitch
And as our angry supercilious Lords,   225
Big in theire frownes, & haughty in their Words
Looke downe on those whose humble fruitefull paine
Their proud & barren greatenes must Sustayne,
So lookes the hill upon the streame, Betweene
There lyes a spacious and a firtile greene   Egham   230
Where from the woods the Dryades oft meete   meade
The Nayades, & with their nimble feete
Soft dances leade; although their Ayry Shape
All but a quicke poeticke sight escape:
There Faunus & Silvanus keepe their Courts,   235
And thither all the horned host resorts
(When like the Elixar with his Evening beames
The Sunne hath turn'd to Gould the Silver Streames)
To graze the Ranker mead, that noble heard,
On whose sublime & shady fronts is rear'd   240
Natures greate Masterpeece to shew how soone
Greate things are made, but sooner farre undone:
Here have I seene our Charles (when greate affaires   Kinge
Give leave to slacken & unbend his Cares)
Chasing the Royall Stagge, the gallant beast   245
Rous'd with the noyse twixt hope & feare distrest,
Resolves tis better to avoyde, then meete
His danger, trusting to his winged feete

---

224 Dian'] Diana *H.367*   233 leade] leads *EL. 8899*   239 that] the *EL. 8899*
225 *Shoulder*] Simile   236 horned] honored   242 farre] much *H.367*
    EL. 8899   *EL. 8899*   243 *Shoulder*] *not in*
226 haughty] haught   237 like . . . with] with   *H. 367*
    EL. 8899   . . . of *EL. 8899*   244 Give] geves *EL. 8899*
227 paine] paines   238 hath] has *H. 367*   unbend] unbinde
    EL. 8899   *H. 367*

But when he sees the doggs now by the view,   250
Now by the Sent, his speede with speede pursue:
He tryes his frends amongst the lesser heard,
Where he but lately was obey'd & fear'd:
Safety he seekes, the heard unkindly wise:
Or chases him from thence, or from him flyes;   255
(Like a declying Statesman left forlorne
To his frinds pitty & pursuers scorne)
Wearied, forsaken & pursu'd, At last
All Safety in dispaire of safety plact.
Courrage he then assumes, resolv'd to beare   260
All their assaults, when tis in vayne to feare:
But when he sees the eager chace renew'd
Himselfe by doggs, the doggs by men pursu'd;
When neither speede nor Art, nor frends nor force
Could helpe him, towards the Streame he bends his course: 265
Hoping those lesser beasts would not assay,
An Element more merciles then they:
But feareles they pursue, nor can the flood
Quench their dire thirst, (Alas) they thirst for blood.
As in a Calme the Oare-fynn'd Galleys creepe,   270
About a winde bound, & unweildy Shipp;
Which lyes unmov'd, but those that come too neere
Strikes with her thunder, & the rest with feare,
Till through her many leakes the Sea shee drinkes
Nor yealds at last but still resisting sinks: 275
So stands the stagg among the lesser hounds,
Repells their force & wounds returnes for wounds,
Till Charles from his unerring hand letts fly,
A mortall shaft, then glad & proud to die

---

251 amongst] (*sic II, A*)   268 dire thirst] dire   272 Strikes] Strike
     amonge *H. 367, B*   thirsts *H. 367*   *EL. 8899*   Strickes
255 left] lost *EL. 8899*   269 *Shoulder*] Simile   *H. 367*
                                    EL. 8899

By such a wound, he falls. The Cristall flood
Dying he dyes, & purples with his blood.   280
This a more Innocent & happie chase,
Then when of ould (but in the selfe same place)   Runney Meade
                                                    where the greate
Faire Liberty pursu'd & meant a prey   Charter was first
To Tyrany, here turn'd & stood at Bay,   Sealed
When in that remedy all hope was plast,   285
(Which was or should at least have beene the last)
For Armed Subiects can have no pretence,
Against their Princes, but their iust defence:
And whether then or no I leave to them
To iustifie, who els themselves condemne;   290
Yett might the fact be iust if we may guesse
The iustnes of an Action from successe.
There was that Charter Seal'd, where in the Crowne   Magna Charta
All marks of Arbitrary power layes downe:
Tyrant, & Slave, those names of hate & feare,   295
The happier Stile of King, & Subiect beare:
And yet not long in force this charter stood,
The Counterparte was often Seald in blood:
The Subiects Arm'd, the more theire princes gave,
But this advantage tooke the more to crave: 300
And as by giving the Kings power growes les,
So by receiving, their demands increase;
To limitt Regall greatnes all Conspire,
While each forgetts to lymitt his desire,
Till kings (like ould Anteus) by their fall   305
Reinforc't, their courrage from dispaire recall;
When a Calme River rais'd with suddaine Raines,

---

282 *Shoulder*: Runney]   296 Stile] still *H. 367*   305 ould] Could
     Rumney *H. 367*   Subiect] Subects   *EL. 8899*
285 that] the *EL. 8899*   *EL. 8899*   307 *Shoulder*] Simile
293 *Shoulder*] *not in*   299 theire] the *EL. 8899*   *EL. 8899*
     EL. 8899

Or Snowes dissolv'd, oreflowes the adioyninge plaines;
The husbandmen with high rais'd banks secure
Their greedy hopes, & this hee can endure: 310
But if with Bays, & Dams they strive to force
His current to a new or narrow Course,
No longer then within his banks he dwells,
First to a torrent then a deluge swells:
Stronger & fercer by restraint he Roares, 315
And knowes no bound, but makes his power his shores;
Thus kings by grasping more then they could hould,
First made their subjects by oppression bould,
And popular sway by forcing Kings to give,
More then was fitt for subiects to receave 320
Ranne to the same extreame, & one excesse,
Made both by striving to be greater, lesse:
Nor any way but seeking to have more,
Makes either loose, what they possest before.
Therefore their boundles power lett princes draw 325
Within the Chanell & the shoares of Lawe:
And may that Law which teaches Kings to sway
Their Septers, teach their subjects to obey.

---

316 bound] boundes   318 oppression] oppres-
     H. 367   sions H. 367

Draft II

SUMMARY NOTE ON THE TEXT

THE TEXT is exemplified in three manuscripts: Folger Shakespeare Library MSS V.a.160 and V.a.322 (each 340 lines long), and MS Harleian 837.3 (338 lines, lacking lines 229–230); also some manuscript marginalia in one copy of the 1650 London printing, as far as they are pertinent.

Folger MS V.a.160 has been used as the basis. Abbreviations, with the exception of ampersand, have been expanded, and all variant readings have been compelled to justify themselves in the face of not only the other Draft II exemplars, but those of the other drafts as well. All rejected readings are recorded in the apparatus. In instances of binary division on a reading among the Draft II exemplars which also reflects a binary division among all available exemplars of *Coopers Hill*, the principle followed is that set forth in the Summary Note on Draft I: a reading is selected which will ensure that each of the binary variants is represented at least once among the four drafts presented in this edition, and an attempt has been made to indicate in the apparatus the distribution of the split among the other drafts.

The Draft II apparatus, like that of Draft I, attempts to comprehend only variants of line, phrase, or word, and not those of spelling, capitalization, or punctuation. Nonetheless the intention has been to allow no significant variable to pass unnoticed, and to reproduce all recorded variants literatim. From the apparatus, therefore, the reader should be able to reconstruct the exact wording of each of the three Draft II exemplars, although he will not have available an exact record of each jot and tittle of each.

KEY TO THE CRITICAL APPARATUS

V.a.160   Transcript of *Coopers Hill* in commonplace book, MS V.a. 160 in the Folger Shakespeare Library

V.a.322   Transcript of *Coopers Hill* in commonplace book, MS V.a.322 in the Folger Shakespeare Library

H.837   Manuscript item 3 in volume MS Harleian 837 of the Harleian Collection in the British Museum

1650ms   Manuscript marginalia in a copy of *Coopers Hill*, London, 1650, in my possession

I   Consensus of the exemplars of Draft I

EL.8899   (Draft I) Manuscript Ellesmere 8899.

H.367   (Draft I) Manuscript Harleian 367, item 71

A   The "A" text of *Coopers Hill*

B   The "B" text of *Coopers Hill*

Draft II

COOPERS HILL (*early 1642?*)

Sure we have Poetts that did never dreame
Vpon Parnassus; nor did tast the streame
Of Helicon, & therefore I suppose
Those made not Poetts but the poets those.
And as Courts make not kings but kings the Court   5
Soe where the Muses & theyr troopes resort
Parnassus stands; if I can be to thee
A Poett, thou Parnassus art to me,
Whose top when I ascend I seeme more high,
More boundlesse in my fancy then my eye: 10
As those whoe rais'd in body or in thought
Above the earth or the Aires' middle vault,
Behold how windes & stormes & Meteors grow,
How cloudes condense to raine, congeale to snow
And see the thunder form'd before it teare   15
The Aire, secure from danger & from feare;
Soe to this height exalted I looke downe
On Pauls, as men from thence upon the towne.   Paules
Pauls' the late theame of such a Muse whose flight   Mr. Waller's
                Poem.
Hath bravely reacht & soar'd above thy height,   20
Now shalt thou stand, though time or sword or fire

---

10 my eye] myne eye   18 *Shoulder*] *not in*   19 *Shoulder*] *not in*
 H. 837, EL. 8899   *V. a. 160, V. a. 322*   *V. a. 322, H. 837*

 Title] For general annotation of *Coopers Hill* see the "A" and "B" text (drafts III and IV).
19–24. This allusion to Waller's poem *Upon His Majesties repairing of Pauls* first enters
the genesis of *Coopers Hill* at this point. It had not been present in Draft I.

93

Or zeale more feirce then they thy fall conspire,
Secure, while thee the best of Poetts sings
Preserv'd from ruine by the best of Kings.
Then London where my eye, the place, the crowd   London   25
My minde surveyes wrapt in a thicker cloud
Of businesse then of smoake; where men like Ants
Toyle to prevent imaginary wants,
Yet all in vaine, increasing with theyr store
Theyr vast desires, but make theyr wants the more.   30
As food to unsound bodies, though it please
The appetite, feedes only the disease.
Where with like hast, though sev'rall wayes they run,
Some to undoe, & some to be undon.
Where Luxury & wealth like warre & peace   35
Are each the others ruine & increase:
As rivers lost in Seas, some secret vaine
Thence reconveyes, there to be lost againe.
Oh happinesse of sweete retir'd content
To be at once secure & Innocent.   40
Windsor, the next (where Mars & Venus dwells   The Kinge and
Beauty with strength, above the valley swells   Queene there
Into mine eye, as the late married Dame
Whoe proud, yet seemes to make that pride her shame
When Nature quickens in her pregnant wombe   45
Her wishes past & now her hopes to come;
With such an easie & unforc't ascent
Windsor her gentle bosome doth present;
Where noe stupendious cliffs, noe threatning heights
Accesse deny, noe horrid steepe affrights,   50

---

25 *Shoulder*] *not in*   41 *Shoulder*] *not in*   47 ascent] assent
   V. a. 160, V. a. 322   *V. a. 160, V. a. 322*   *V. a. 322*
33 though] through   49 cliffs] Clyffe *H. 837*
   H. 837

   31–38. First added in this draft.

But such a Rise as doth at once invite
A pleasure & a reverence from the sight.
Thy masters Embleme: in whose face I saw
A freindlike sweetnesse & a kinglike awe,
Where maiestie & love soe mixt appeare,   55
Both gently kinde, both royally severe;
Soe Windsor humble in it selfe, seemes proude
To be the base of that maiestick loade,
Then which noe hill a nobler burthen beares
But Atlas only that supports the Spheares.   60
Nature this mount soe fitly did advance
We might conclude that nothing is by chance;
Soe plac'd as if she did on purpose raise
The hill, to robb the builder of his praise.
For none commends his iudgement that doth chuse   65
That which a blindeman onely could refuse;
Such are the Towers which th'hoary Temples grace
Of Cybele when all her heavenly race
Doe homage to her, yet she cannot boast
Amongst that numerous, & caelestiall hoast   70
More Heroes then can Windsor, nor doth Fame's
Immortal booke record more noble names.
Not to looke backe soe farre (to whome this Isle
Must owe the glorie of soe brave a pile)
Whether to Caesar, Albanact, or Brute   75
The Brittish Arthur or the Danish Knute:
Though this of old noe lesse contest did move
Then when for Homer's birth seaven Citties strove,

---

54 kinglike] Kinglye
    H. 837
59 burthen] Burden
    H. 837
61 this mount soe fitly
    did] soe fitly did this
    mount *V. a. 322*

62 We might] She might
    V. a. 160, V. a. 322
    Wee may *H. 837*
63 she] he *V. a. 322*
67 th'hoary] hoarye
    H. 837
    the hoary *V. a. 322*

68 Cybele] Ciuile *H. 837*
75 Whether . . . Alba-
    nact] Whither . . .
    Abbanact *V. a. 160*

95

Like him in birth, thou shouldst be like in fame
As thine his fate, if mine had bin his flame.   80
But whosoere it was, Nature design'd
First a brave place, & then as brave a minde;
Nor to recount those sev'rall kings to whome
It gave a Cradle, or to whome a Tombe;
But thee great Edward & thy greater sonne   85
He that the Lillies wore & he that wonne:
And thye Bellona whoe deserves her share   The kings of
In all thy glories of that royall paire   France &
                                                  Scotland.
Which waited on thy Triumph, she brought one
Thy sonne the other brought & she that sonne: 90
Nor of lesse hopes could the great ofspring prove
A Royall Eagle cannot breed a Dove.
Then didst thou found that order (whether Love   The Garter.
Or Victorie thy royall thoughts did move)
Each was a noble cause; nor was it lesse   95
In th'institution, then the great successe,
Whilst every part conspires to give it grace
The king, the cause, the Patron & the place;
Which forraine kings & emperors esteeme
The second honor to theyr Diademe.   100
Had thy great destiny but given thee skill
To know, as well as power, to act her Will,
That from those kings whoe then thy captives were
In after times should spring a royall paire
Whoe should possesse all that thy mighty power   105

---

80 fate] face *V. a. 160*,   91 of lesse] lesse of   96 th'institution] the In-
    V. a. 322   *V. a. 322*   stitucon *H. 837*
81 whosoere] whosoe'res   the] that *H. 837*   97 conspires] doth stryve
    H. 837   92 breed] prove *H. 837*   *H. 837*
83 Nor] Nott *H. 837*   93 whether] whither   102 well as power, to act]
87 thye] great *V. a. 160*,   *V. a. 160*   power to Actuate
    V. a. 322   *Shoulder*] *not in*   *H. 837*
                                   V. a. 322   her] thy *V. a. 322*
                               94 move] prove *H. 837*

Or thy desires more mighty, did devoure,
To whome theyr better fate reserves what ere
The Victor hopes for, or the Vanquisht feare,
That blood which thou & thy great grandsire shed,
And all that since these sister nations bled   110
Had bin unspilt had happie Edward knowne
That all the bloud he spilt had bin his owne:
Thou hadst extended through the conquer'd East
Thine & the Christian name & made them blest
To serve thee, while that losse this gaine would bring   115
Christ for theyr God & Edward for theyr king.
When thou that saint thy patron didst designe
In whome the martyr & the souldier ioyne;
And when thou didst within the Azure round
(Whoe evill thinks may evill him confound)   120
The English Armes encircle, thou didst seeme
But to fortell & prophesie of him,
Whoe hath within that Azure round confin'd
These Realmes which Nature for theyr bounds design'd:
That bound which to the worlds extreamest ends   125
Endlesse her selfe her liquid Armes extends.
In whose heroique face I see the saint
Better exprest, then in the liveliest paint.
That Fortitude which made him famous heere,
That heavenly Piety which Saints him there;   130
Whoe when this order he forsakes, may he
Companion of that sacred order be.
Heere could I fix my wonder, but our eyes
(Nice as our tasts) affect varieties.
And though one please him most, the hungry guest   135
Tasts every dish & runnes through all the feast

---

109   grandsire] Grand-   123   hath] has *H. 837*   *V. a. 160, V. a. 322*
       sires *V. a. 322*   129   which] that *H. 837*   which] that *H. 837*
119   didst] plac't *H. 837*   130   Piety] Diety
                                133   Heere] There *H. 837*

97

Soe having tasted Windsor, casting round
My wandring eye, an Emulous hill doth bound   St. Anne's Hill
My more contracted sight, whose top of late
A Chappell crown'd, till in the common fate   140
The neighb'ring Abby fell; may noe such storme   Chersy Abby.
Fall on our times where ruine must reforme.
Tell me my Muse what monstrous dire offence,
What crime could any Christian king incense
To such a rage? was't Luxurie or Lust?   145
Was he soe temperat, soe chast, soe iust?
Were these theyr crimes? they were his owne much more,
But they (alas) were rich & he was poore;
And having spent the treasures of his crowne
Condemns theyr Luxury to feede his owne: 150
And yet this Act to varnish ore the shame
Of sacriledge, must beare devotions name.
And he might thinke it iust, the cause, & time
Consider'd well, for none committs a crime
Appearing such, but as 'tis understood   155
A reall or at least a seeming good.
While for the Church his learned pen disputes
His much more learned sword his pen confutes.
Thus to the Ages past he makes amends,
Theyr charity destroyes, theyr fayth defends.   160
Then did Religion in a Lazy Cell
In empty ayrie contemplations dwell,
And like the block unmoved lay, but ours
As much too active, like the storke devours.
Is there noe temp'rat Region can be knowne   165
Betwixt theyr frigid & our torrid zone?
Could we not wake from that Lethargique dreame
But to be restlesse in a worse extreame?

---

138 *Shoulder*] *not in*   142 on] *in H. 837*   153 &] the *V. a. 160,*
   V. a. 160, V. a. 322   151 Act] Art *V. a. 322*   *V. a. 322*

And for that Lethargie was there noe cure
But to be cast into a Calenture?   170
Can knowledge have noe bound? but must advance
Soe farre, to make us wish for ignorance?
And rather in the darke to grope our way
Then ledd by a false guide to erre by day?
Parting from thence, 'twixt Anger, shame & feare   175
Those for what's past & this for what's too neare,
My eye descending from the hill survayes
Where Thames amongst the wanton valleyes strayes.   Thames:
Sweet Thames the eldest & the noblest sonne
Of old Oceanus, doth swiftly runne,   180
Hasting to pay his tribute to the Sea
Like mortall Life to meete Eternitie:
And though his cleerer sand noe golden vaynes
(Like Tagus & Pactolus streames contaynes)
His genuine & lesse guilty wealth t'explore   185
Search not his bottome but behold his shore.
Ore which he kindly spreads his spacious wing
And hatches plenty for th'ensuing spring;
Nor with an angry & unruly wave
(Like profuse kings) resumes the wealth he gave.   190
Noe unexpected inundations spoile
The mowers hopes, nor mocke the plowmans toyle.
Then like a Lover he forsakes his shores,
Whose stay with iealous eyes his spouse implores,
Till with a parting kisse he saves hir teares,   195
And promising returne secures her feares.
As a wise king, first settles fruitfull peace

---

178 amongst] among   192 mocke] make   195 hir] his *V. a. 160,*
     H. 837   *H. 837* worke   *V. a. 322*
     strayes] playes/   *V. a. 160; (corrected*   196 secures] secure
     strayes *V. a. 322*   *later) V. a. 322*   *V. a. 322*

193–196. This four-line simile replaces the grotesque eight-line simile occupying the corresponding place in Draft I (lines 179–186).

In his owne Realmes & with theyr rich increase
Seeks warrs abroad & then in triumph brings
The spoyles of kingdomes & the Crownes of kings.   200
Soe Thames to London doth at first present
Those Tributes which the neighb'ring Countries sent,
But at his second visit from the East
Spices he brings & treasures from the West,
Finds wealth where 't is & gives it where it wants,   205
Cities in desarts, woods in Cities plants;
Soe that to us noe thing noe place is strange
While thy faire bosome is the worlds exchange,
And on thy streames as many nations floate
As when mankinde all soiourn'd in one boate.   210
O could my lines fully & smoothly flow
As thy pure floud, heaven should noe longer know
Her old Eridanus, thy purer streame
Should bathe the Gods & be the Poetts theame.
Heere Nature, whether more intent to please   The forrest.   215
Vs or her selfe with strange varieties,
For things of wonder move noe lesse delight
To the wise makers then beholders sight:
Though these delights from sev'rall causes move,
For soe our children, thus our freinds we love;   220
Wisely she knew the harmony of things
As well as that of sounds from discord springs:
Such was the discord which did first disperse
Forme, order, Beauty through the universe.
While Moisture, drinesse, coldnesse heat resists,   225

---

207 noe thing] nothing *V. a. 322*	210 one] a *H. 837, 1650ms*	219 these] those *V. a. 322, EL. 8899*
208 While] (*sic I, B*) Whilst *H. 837, A*	215 whether] whither *V. a. 160*	224 order, Beauty] Beauty, order *V. a. 160, V. a. 322*

209–210. This couplet (mistranscribed in Banks) is unique to Draft II, but is represented in four exemplars.

All that we have and that we are subsists.
While the steepe horrid roughnesse of the wood
Strives with the gentle calmnesse of the flood,
Such huge extreames when Nature doth unite
Wonder from thence results, from thence delight.   230
The streame is soe transparent pure & cleere,
That had the selfe inamor'd youth gaz'd heere,
Soe fatally deceiv'd he had not bin
While he the bottome not his face had seene;
And such the roughnesse of the hill on which   235
Dian' her toyles & Mars his tents might pitch:
And as our angry supercilious Lords
Bigg in theyr frownes & haughty in theyr words
Looke downe on those, whose humble fruitfull paine
Theyr proud & barren greatnesse must sustaine   240
Soe lookes the hill upon the streame. Betweene
There lies a spacious & a fertile greene   Egham Meade.
Where from the woods the Dryades oft meete
The Nayades, & with theyr nimble feete
Soft dances leade, allthough theyr ayrie shape   245
All but a quicke Poeticke sight escape.
There Faunus & Silvanus keepe theyr courts
And thither all the horned hoast resorts
(When like th'Elixar with his evening beames
The Sun hath turn'd to gold the silver streames)   250
To graze the ranker Meade: That noble Heard

---

226 and] or *V. a. 160,*   239 paine] raine   245 ayrie] **angry**
     V. a. 322   *V. a. 160; (corrected*   *V. a. 160; (corrected*
229–230 *not in H. 837*   *later) V. a. 322*   *later) V. a. 322*
229 Such . . . unite] And   veyne *H. 837*   247 There] Thus
     . . . invite *V. a. 160,*   240 sustaine] maintaine   *V. a. 160, V. a. 322*
     V. a. 322   *V. a. 160*   248 thither] hither
234 seene] beene   243 Dryades] Druides   *V. a. 160*
     V. a. 322   *H. 837*   horned hoast] hornid
236 Dian' . . . tents] Di-   Beasts *H. 837*
     ana . . . Tent *H. 837*   250 hath] has *H. 837*

On whose sublime & shady fronts is rear'd
Nature's great Masterpeece, to shew how soone
Great things are made but sooner farre undone.
Heere have I seene our Charles when great affaires   255
Give leave to slacken & unbend his cares,
Chasing the royall stagg: The gallant beast
Rows'd with the noyse, 'twixt hope & feare distrest
Resolves 't is better to avoyde then meete
His danger, trusting to his winged feete: 260
But when he sees the Dogs now by the veiw
Now by the sent, his speede with speede pursue,
He tryes his freindes amongst the lesser herd
Where he but lately was obeyed & fear'd
Safety he seekes. The herd unkindly wise   265
Or chases him from thence or from him flyes,
Like a declining statesman left forlorne
To his freindes pittie & pursuers scorne.
Wearied, forsaken, & pursude at last
All safety in despaire of safety plac'd   270
Courage he thence assumes, resolv'd to beare
All theyr assaults when 't is in vaine to feare,
But when he sees the Eager chase renew'd
Himselfe by doggs, the doggs by men pursude,
When neyther speede nor art, nor freinds nor force   275
Could helpe him, tow'rds the streame he bends his course
Hoping those lesser beasts would not assay
An element more mercilesse than they,
But fearelesse they pursue, nor can the floud
Quench theyr dire thirst, alas they thirst for bloud,   280

---

252 fronts] front   257 Chasing] Choosinge   259 then] and V. a. 322
     V. a. 322   H. 837   265 Safety] Lastly H. 837
254 farre] (sic EL. 8899) 258 Rows'd with the]   268 &] or V. a. 160,
     much H. 837, H. 367,   Rowsed with   V. a. 322
     A   are B   V. a. 160   Rows'd
                                 with V. a. 322

102

As in a Calme the Oare-finn'd Galleyes creepe
Aboute a windebound & unweldy Shipp
Which lyes unmov'd, but those that come too neare
Strikes with her thunder & the rest with feare,
Till through her many leakes the Sea she drinks,   285
Nor yeildes at last but still resisting sinkes;
Soe stands the stagg among the lesser hounds,
Repells theyr force & wounds returnes for wounds
Till Charles from his unerring hand lets fly
A mortall shaft, then glad & proud to dye   290
By such a wound, he falls, the Christall floud
Dying he dyes & purples with his bloud.
This is a more innocent & happie chase
Then when of old but in the selfe same place   Runnye Meade,
Faire Libertie pursude, & meant a pray   where the   295
To Tyranny heere turn'd & stood at Bay.   Charter was
                                                                    first seal'd.
When in that remedy all hope was plac't
Which was, or should at least have bin the last;
For armed subiects can have noe pretence
Against theyr princes, but theyr iust defence,   300
And whether then or noe I leave to them
To iustifie, whoe else themselves condemne;
Yet might the fact be iust, if we may guesse
The iustnesse of an action from successe.
Heere was that Charter seal'd wherein the crowne   Magna   305
All markes of Arbitrary power layes downe.   Charta.
Tyrant & slave, those names of hate & feare
The happier stile of king & subiect beare.
And yet not long in force this Charter stood

---

287   among] amongst   the Charter] ye gt.   (sic I) have been att
      H. 837   Charter V. a. 160   least H. 837, A, B
294   *Shoulder*: Runnye]   297   plac't] plac'd   301   whether] whither
      Rumney V. a. 160,   V. a. 160   V. a. 160
      V. a. 322   298   at least have bin]   303   might] may H. 837
                                                         304   from] by V. a. 322

103

The Counterpart was often seald in bloud.   310
The subiects arm'd, the more the Princes gave,
But this advantage tooke the more to crave;
And as by giving the kings power growes lesse,
Soe by receiving theyr demands increase:
To limitt regall greatnesse all conspire,   315
While each forgetts to limitt his desire;
Till kings, like old Antaeus by theyr fall
Reenforc't, theyr courage from despaire recall.
When a Calme river rais'd with suddaine raines
Or snowes dissolv'd oreflowes th'adioyning plaines,   320
The husbandmen with high rais'd banks secure
Theyr greedye hopes, & this he can endure;
But if with bayes & damms they strive to force
His channell to a new or narrow course,
Noe longer then within his banks he dwells,   325
First to a torrent, then a Deluge swells;
Stronger & feircer by restraint he roares
And knowes noe bounds, but makes his power his shores.
Thus kings by grasping more then they could hold
First made theyr subiects by oppression bold;   330
And popular sway (by forcing kings to give
More then was fitt for subiects to receive)
Ran to the same extreame, & one excesse
Made both by striving to be greater, lesse:
Nor any way but seeking to have more,   335

---

311 the Princes] (*sic*
    EL. 8899) their
    Princes *H. 837, A, B*
321 husbandmen] Hus-
    bandman *H. 837*
322 Theyr greedye
    hopes] Theyr hopes
    V. a. 160, V. a. 322

324 or] and *H. 837*
325 banks] bounds
    V. a. 160
326 then a] then to a
    V. a. 322
328 bounds] bound
    H. 837, EL. 8899, A
329 could] (*sic I, B*) can
    H. 837, A

330 made theyr subiects
    by oppression] by op-
    pression made theyr
    subiects *V. a. 160*
    oppression] (*sic*
    EL. 8899, B) oppres-
    sions *H. 837, H. 367,*
    A
335 Nor] Nott *H. 837*

Makes eyther loose what they possest before.
Therefore theyr boundlesse power let princes draw
Within the Channell & the shores of Law,
And may that law which teaches kings to sway
Theyr Scepters, teach theyr subiects to obay.   340

---

338 Channell] Channells   339 which] that *H. 837*
     V. a. 160, V. a. 322

The "A" Text, Draft III

(1642)

SUMMARY NOTE ON THE TEXT

THE "A" TEXT of *Coopers Hill*, broadly defined, includes all the closely affiliated versions of the poem (i.e., drafts I–III) which entered circulation prior to the drastic revision Denham effected shortly before 1655. More narrowly, the "A" text may be equated with Draft III, that is, with the text of the poem exemplified exclusively in the *printed* editions published prior to the first appearance of the "B" text in 1655. Both concepts of the "A" text have influenced the presentation of that text here printed.

The text used here to exemplify the "A" text is fundamentally the version of *Coopers Hill* contained in the early printed editions, but it has been collated with, and sometimes corrected by, the two prior drafts (I and II) exemplified only in manuscript. The initial appearance of this (Draft III) text occurred in the first edition of *Coopers Hill*, published at London during the first week of August 1642. A corrected reprint was next issued at Oxford, dated 1643, and published probably in April. The third edition was that which appeared at London in 1650. That edition, describing itself as the "second," is a somewhat careless reprint of the 1642 edition, and shows no trace of the corrections contained in the Oxford edition. No further printed edition of the "A" text survives, although at least one other may have been issued before the first appearance of the "B" text in 1655.

For basic copy the Oxford edition of 1643 has been used here as the only "A" text edition to show unmistakable marks of the poet's own attention. Specifically, the text has been derived from collation of the copies of that edition in the Henry E. Huntington Library, San Marino; the Newberry Library, Chicago; and in my own possession. Critical readings have also been checked against all of the other copies discoverable through the Wing *Short-Title Catalogue*. A few manifest errors in the Oxford edition have been corrected, but without exception the correction has been noted and the actual reading recorded in the apparatus. Otherwise the only departure from the Oxford text, in spelling, punctuation, capitalization, and typeface, has been in the consistent replacement of long *s*. Variants from the Oxford readings have been derived from selected copies of the London editions of 1642 and 1650, particularly those in the Huntington Library and the William Andrews Clark Memorial Library, Los Angeles, and a copy of the 1650 edition in my possession. The five manuscripts (of the earlier drafts) known to me have all also been employed in the collation. The apparatus follows separate principles, however, with regard respectively to the printed editions and to the manuscripts. For the printed editions all variants are recorded, not merely of phrase or word, but also of spelling, capitalization, hyphenization, punctuation, and use of typefaces. It should be possible therefore for the interested reader to reconstruct with absolute fidelity the precise text of any of the three "A" text editions of *Coopers Hill*: 1642, 1643, 1650.

As to the manuscripts, variants are recorded of line, phrase, or word, without exception, but not of spelling or punctuation. Whenever a variant belonging to a single manuscript has been recorded in the apparatus an exact transcription has been aimed at, but whenever a manuscript variant represents the testimony of two or more manuscripts the spelling and punctuation have been compromised, to free the apparatus from a meaningless clutter of scribal idiosyncrasies. Wherever no manuscript variant is recorded, it may be safely assumed that all five manuscripts agree with the text here printed, although quite probably they vary widely literatim and in punctuation. The apparatus always lists manuscript variants *after* printed variants in the same line of the poem. From the apparatus the reader should be able to reconstruct the exact ideal text of each manuscript, although he will not have available all the individual

vagaries displayed by each. Such reconstruction can be more economically effected, however, through the separate presentations of
the texts of drafts I and II on previous pages.

KEY TO THE CRITICAL APPARATUS

1642 First edition, London 1642, small quarto. Wing D993.

1643 [Second] edition, Oxford 1643, small quarto. Wing D994.

1650 "Second" [third] edition, London 1650, small quarto. Wing
D995.

1650ms Manuscript marginalia added in the eighteenth century to
a copy of *1650* now in my possession, and apparently derived from an otherwise unknown manuscript.

a, b (After a date, e.g., *1643a, 1650b*): Presumed earlier or later
state of the impression. Implies that the correlative state is
also instanced among collated copies.[1]

EL.8899 Manuscript Ellesmere 8899 in the Bridgewater House Collection at the Henry E. Huntington Library.

H.367 Manuscript 71 in volume MS Harleian 367 of the Harleian
Collection in the British Museum.

Draft I Consensus of *EL.8899* and *H.367*.

H.837 Manuscript 3 in volume MS Harleian 837 of the Harleian
Collection in the British Museum.

V.a.160 Transcript of *Coopers Hill* in commonplace book catalogued as MS V.a.160 in the Folger Shakespeare Library.

V.a.322 Transcript of *Coopers Hill* in commonplace book catalogued as MS V.a.322 in the Folger Shakespeare Library.

Draft II Consensus of *H.837*, *V.a.160*, and *V.a.322*.

MSS Consensus of all five manuscripts, or *Draft I* and *Draft II*.

B The "B" text of *Coopers Hill*.

* (At end of line as well as in apparatus): correction or
emendation of the Oxford edition (*1643*).

---

1. As to *1643*, *a* or *b* represents an absolute and consistent division among the copies. Three
copies are represented by *1643a*: that in the Huntington, that in Harvard University Library,
and my copy. Six copies are represented by *1643b*: three in the Bodleian Library, one each at the
Newberry Library, at Yale, and at the Dyce Collection (Victoria and Albert Museum).

Draft III

Sure we have Poëts, that did never dreame
Upon *Pernassus*, nor did taste the streame
Of *Helicon*, and therefore I suppose
Those made not Poëts, but the Poëts those.
And as Courts make not Kings, but Kings the Court;   5
So where the Muses, and their Troopes resort,
Pernassus stands; if I can be to thee

---

1 Poëts] Poets *1642, 1650*
2 *Pernassus*] Parnassus
   1642, 1650
3 *Helicon*] Helicon *1642,*
   1650
4 Poëts . . . Poëts those.]
   Poets . . . Poets those.

1642   Poets . . . Po-
ets those *1650*
5 Court;] Court, *1642,*
   1650
6 where . . . Muses, and
   . . . Troopes] where
   . . . Muses and . . .

Troopes *1642*
Where . . . Muses and
. . . Troops *1650*
7 *Pernassus* stands; if
   . . . thee] Parnassus
stands, if . . . thee, *1642,*
1650

Title] Cooper's Hill, Egham, Surrey; see topographical note, p. xxiii.
1–4. Cp. Persius, *Satire* I, Prologue, 1–3:

> Nec fonte labra prolui caballino
> Nec in bicipiti somniasse Parnaso
> Memini, ut repenta sic poeta prodirem.

In Dryden's translation:

> I never did on cleft Parnassus dream,
> Nor taste the sacred Heliconian stream;
> Nor can remember when my brain, inspir'd,
> Was by the Muses into madness fir'd.

5. Courts] Perhaps a topical allusion, as E. R. Wasserman has suggested (*The Subtler Language* [Baltimore, 1959], p. 49) to the "High Court of Parliament." But Draft III was finished at least by the end of July 1642, so that Draft I (which already contains this line) is unlikely to have been so late as May or June, the time of the King's attempted summons of Parliament to York. Perhaps Denham was thinking of the royal prerogative courts, which Charles was compelled to give up in mid-1641. But cp. Heylyn's *Historie of . . . St. George*: "[many places in Britain are] famous for King *Arthurs* table; the *Court* removing with the *Prince*" (2d ed., p. 317).

A Poët, thou *Pernassus* art to mee.
Nor wonder, if (advantag'd in my flight,
By taking wing from thy auspicious height)   10
Through untrac't waies, and airie paths I flie,
More boundlesse in my fancie, then my eie.
Exalted to this height, I first looke downe
On *Pauls*, as men from thence upon the towne.   *Pauls.*
Pauls, the late Theme of such a Muse, whose flight   Mr. *Waller.*   15
Hath bravely reacht and soar'd above thy height:
Now shalt thou stand, though Time, or Sword, or Fire,
Or Zeale (more fierce then they) thy fall conspire,
Secure, while thee the best of Poets sings,
Preserv'd from ruine by the best of Kings.   20

---

8 Poët . . . *Pernassus*]
Poet . . . Parnassus
1642, 1650
9–28 *Draft I*
Whose topp when I as-
cend, I seeme more high
More boundlesse in my
Fancy then myne Eye:
As those who raysed in
body or in thought

Above the Earth or the
Ayres [Earths *EL. 8899*]
middle vault,
Behould how Windes &
Stormes & Meteors
growe
How Clowdes condence to
Rayne, congeale to
Snowe
And See the Thunder
form'd (before it teare

The Ayre) Secure from
danger & from feare
So from thy lofty topp my
[topping *EL. 8899*] Eye
lookes downe
On Pauls, as men from
thence unto the Towne
My minde uppon the Tu-
mult & the Crowde
And Sees it wrapt in a
more dusky Cloud

10. auspicious] Suitable for augury.
10–11. Cp. Denham's translation of *Aeneid* VI.15 (Lucy Hutchinson transcript, VI.16–17):

Boldly presuming with auspicious wings
Through vntraced ayrie ways to take his flight.

13. I first looke downe] About 1840 it was asserted that from Cooper's Hill "the hour and minute hands of St. Paul's Clock, have, by the aid of a telescope been distinctly seen" (communication from the late A. E. Villars, clerk of the Urban District Council of Egham).

14. *Pauls*] The old cathedral, destroyed by the Great Fire of 1666. Its spire was for long the tallest in Europe and remained well into Elizabeth's reign a notable attraction for travelers.

15–20. Allusion to Waller's poem *Upon His Majesties repairing of Pauls* (see App. B, below). This allusion is not contained in *EL.8899*, and probably was added in Draft II.

18. Zeale] Of the antiprelatical Puritans. In 1640 Lord Brooke hoped to live "to see no one Stone left upon another" of the renovated cathedral.

19–20. Cp. Jonson, *Epigramme* IV, "To King James," lines 1–2.

How, best of Kings, do'st thou a scepter beare!
How, best of *Poets*, do'st thou laurell weare!

19. best of Poets] Edmund Waller.   20. best of Kings] Charles I.

As those who rais'd in body, or in thought
Above the Earth, or the Aires middle Vault,
Behold how winds, and stormes, and Meteors grow,
How clouds condense to raine, congeale to snow,
And see the Thunder form'd, before it teare   25
The aire, secure from danger and from feare;
So rais'd above the tumult and the crowd
I see the City in a thicker cloud   *London.*
Of businesse, then of smoake; where men like Ants

Draft II
Whose top when I ascend
I seeme more high,
More boundlesse in my
fancy then my [myne
H. 837] eye:
As those whoe rais'd in
body or in thought
Above the earth or the
Aires' middle vault,
Behold how windes &
stormes & Meteors
grow,
How cloudes condense to
raine, congeale to snow
And see the thunder
form'd before it teare
The Aire, secure from
danger & from feare;
Soe to this height exalted
I looke downe
On Pauls, as men from
thence upon the towne.
Pauls' the late theame of
such a Muse whose
flight
Hath bravely reacht &
soar'd above thy height,

Now shalt thou stand,
though time or sword or
fire
Or zeale more feirce then
they thy fall conspire,
Secure, while thee the
best of Poetts sings
Preserv'd from ruine by
the best of Kings.
Then London where my
eye, the place, the crowd
My minde surveyes wrapt
in a thicker cloud
11 waies, and airie . . .
flie] wayes and ayry
. . . flye *1642* waies
and ayrie . . . flye *1650*
12 fancie, then my eie.]
fancy then my eye,
1642 Fancy then
my eye, *1650*
14 towne] Towne *1650*
Shoulder] *Paules.*
1642 Paules 1650
Paules & London *EL.*
8899 London *1650ms*
not in V. a. 160,
V. a. 322

15 *Pauls,* the] *Pauls* the
1642, 1650
Shoulder] *Master*
Waller. 1642, 1650
Mr. Waller's Poem.
V. a. 160
16 soar'd] soard *1642,*
1650
17 Time . . . Sword . . .
Fire,] time . . . sword
. . . fire *1650*
20 ruine] Ruine *1650*
22 Aires] Ayres *1642*
ayres *1650*
23 stormes, and Meteors]
stormes and meteors
1650
25 Thunder] thunder
1650
26 aire . . . feare;] ayre
. . . feare, *1642, 1650*
28 *Shoulder*] *not in EL.*
8899, V. a. 160, V. a.
322
29 smoake;] smoake,
1642, 1650

21–26. Some attention to meteorology or weather forecasting is customary to all georgic poetry. That Denham conceived of *Coopers Hill* as a georgic may in part account for this passage.

23. Meteors] Any phenomena of the atmosphere, such as rain, hail, lightning.

111

Toyle to prevent imaginarie wants; 30
Yet all in vaine, increasing with their store,
Their vast desires, but make their wants the more.
As food to unsound bodies, though it please
The Appetite, feeds onely the disease;
Where with like haste, though severall waies they runne: 35
Some to undoe, and some to be undone:
While Luxurie, and wealth, like Warre and Peace,
Are each the others ruine, and increase,
As Rivers lost in Seas some secret veine
Thence reconveies, there to be lost againe. 40
Some study plots, and some those plots t'undoe,
Others to make 'em, and undoe 'em too,
False to their hopes, affraid to be secure,

30] *Draft I*: Preying on others to supply their wants
30 imaginarie] imaginary *1650*
33–46] not in *Draft I*
34 Appetite ... disease;] Appetite ... disease, *1642* appetite ... disease, *1650*

35 haste ... waies ... runne:] haste ... wayes ... runne *1642* hast ... waies ... runn *1650* though] through *H. 837*
37 Luxurie ... Warre ... Peace] luxury ... war ... peace

1650
While] Where *Draft II*
39 Seas some] Seas, some *1650*
40 reconveies] reconveighs *1642, 1650*
41–46] not in *Draft II*
43 affraid] afraid *1642, 1650*

33–34. Cp. Sir Robert Howard, *The Duel of the Stags*, lines 147–148:
Sick Minds, like Bodies in a Fever spent,
Turn Food to the Disease, not nourishment.

37–38. In *The Arte of English Poesie* George [or Richard] Puttenham attributes to *"Ihean de Mehune* the French Poet" these lines (ed. E. Arber [London, 1869], p. 217):
Peace makes plentie, plentie makes pride,
Pride breeds quarrell, and quarrell brings warre:
Warre brings spoile, and spoile pouertie,
Pouertie pacience, and pacience peace:
So peace brings warre, and warre brings peace.

The formulation, proverbial in English since the fifteenth century, takes many forms (see A. C. Guthkelch and D. Nichol Smith, eds., Swift's *Tale of a Tub* [Oxford, 1920], pp. 217–218n).

39–40. The current popular theory as to the sources of rivers, based partly on the "fountains of the great deep" mentioned in Genesis (7:11, 8:2) (cp. Vergil, *Georgic* IV.362 ff.).

41–46. These lines occur only in this draft. They were in print a year before "Waller's Plot" of 1643, and their excision ten years later can have had no connection with that plot.

Those mischiefes onely which they make, endure,
Blinded with light, and sicke of being well,   45
In tumults seeke their peace, their heaven in hell.
Oh happinesse of sweete retir'd content!
To be at once secure, and innocent.
Windsor the next (where *Mars* with *Venus* dwels,   *Windsor.**
Beauty with strength) above the valley swels   50
Into my eie, as the late married Dame,
(Who proud, yet seemes to make that pride her shame)
When Nature quickens in her pregnant wombe
Her wishes past, and now her hopes to come:
With such an easie, and unforc'd Ascent,   55
Windsor her gentle bosome doth present:
Where no stupendious Cliffe, no threatning heights
Accesse deny, no horrid steepe affrights,
But such a Rise, as doth at once invite
A pleasure, and a reverence from the sight.   60
Thy Masters Embleme, in whose face I saw

---

44 mischiefes] mischeifes *1650*
45 sicke] sick *1650*
46 heaven ... hell] Heaven ... Hell *1650*
47 content!] content *1650*
49 dwels] dwells *1650* with] and *Draft II* Shoulder] **not in 1643, V.a.160, V.a.322*

The Kinge and Queene there *H. 837*
50 swels] swells *1650*
51 eie] eye *1642, 1650* my] mine *MSS*
52 seemes] seems *1642, 1650*
55 easie ... Ascent] easy ... ascent *1650* Ascent] assent *V. a. 322*

56 present:] present; *1642, 1650*
57 Cliffe, no] cliffs, noe *V. a.160, V. a.322* Cliffs nor *EL. 8899*
58 steepe] steep *1650* no] nor *EL. 8899*
61 face] Face *1650* Shoulder] Kings Matie *EL. 8899* King *1650ms*

49. *Windsor*] Windsor Castle stands out boldly in the prospect westward from Cooper's Hill across the wooded intervening terrain of Windsor Great Park.

49–50. *Mars* with *Venus*; Beauty with strength] Partly the fortified castle in its setting of natural beauty, chiefly Charles I and Queen Henrietta Maria. Mars and Venus together were a favorite Renaissance emblem of harmony; according to Hesiod (*Theogony*, 937, 975), Harmonia was their daughter. It was also commonplace in Renaissance painting to portray princes and their consorts as Mars and Venus.

58. horrid] Bristling or shaggy with rough overgrowth.

61. Thy Masters Embleme] The master is Charles I; the hill and castle of Windsor his emblem. The notion of natural emblems — in Quarles's words, "What are the Heavens, the

113

A friend-like sweetnesse, and a King-like aw;
Where Majestie and love so mixt appeare,
Both gently kind, both royally severe.
So *Windsor*, humble in it selfe, seemes proud*   65
To be the Base of that Majesticke load.
Than which no hill a nobler burthen beares,
But Atlas onely, that supports the spheres.
Nature this mount so fitly did advance,*
We might conclude, that nothing is by chance,   70
So plac't, as if she did on purpose raise
The Hill, to rob the builder of his praise;
For none commends his judgement, that doth chuse
That which a blind man onely could refuse;
Such are the Towers which th'hoary Temples grace*   75
Of *Cibele*, when all her heavenly race   *The Mother of*
Doe homage to her, yet she cannot boast   *the gods.*

---

62 aw;] aw, *1642, 1650*
King-like] Kinglye
H. 837
63 Majestie . . . appeare]
Majesty . . . appeere
1650
64 kind . . . royally]
kinde . . royally *1642*
kind . . . Royally *1650*
65 *Windsor*, humble]
**Windsor*. humble
1643b (humblə
1643a)
proud] proud, *1642,
1650*
66 load.] load, *1642,
1650*

67 hill] Hill *1650*
burthen] Burden
H. 837
68 onely . . . spheres]
only . . . Spheres *1650*
that] w^ch *EL. 8899*
69 mount] *mouut *1643*
Mount *1650*
this mount so fitly
did] soe fitly did this
mount *V. a. 322*
70 chance,] chance *1642,
1650*
We might] We may
H. 837   She might
V. a. 160, V. a. 322
that] then *EL. 8899*

71 she] he *V. a. 322*
72 praise;] praise. *1642,
1650*
73 none] non *1650*
74 onely] only *1650*
75 grace] (*sic MSS*)
*grac'd *1642, 1643,
1650*
th'hoary] hoarye
H. 837   ye holy
EL. 8899
76 *Cibele*] Ciuile *H. 837*
Cecilie *EL. 8899*
Shoulder] wearing a
Crowne of Towers
1650ms   not in
MSS

Earth, may every Creature, but Hierogliphicks and Emblemes?" — is fundamental to
Coopers Hill.
  62–64. Charles I combines in his own person the harmoniously tempered contrarieties of
Mars and Venus: awe, majesty, severity; sweetness, love, kindness.
  76. *Cibele*] This goddess (Cybele) gave difficulty to the scribes of two of the surviving
manuscripts, betokening an unfamiliarity with her name which may account for the shoulder
gloss added first to the present draft. The "B" text drops the name entirely and absorbs the
gloss into the text.

Amongst that Numerous, and Celestiall hoast
More *Heroës*, then can *Windsore*, nor doth Fames
Immortall booke record more noble Names.   80
Not to looke backe so farre, to whom this Ile
Must owe the glory of so brave a Pile;
Whether to *Caesar*, *Albanact*, or *Brute*,
The Brittish *Arthur*, or the Danish *Knute*,
(Though this of old no lesse contest did move,   85
Then when for *Homers* birth seaven Cities strove)
(Like him in birth, thou shouldst be like in Fame,
As thine his fate, if mine had beene his Flame.)
But whoso'ere it was, Nature design'd
First a brave place, and then as brave a minde;   90
Nor to recount those severall Kings, to whom
It gave a Cradle, or to whom a Tombe;
But thee (great *Edward*) and thy greater sonne,   Edward *the third,*
                                                         and the black

---

79 *Heroës,* then . . .   85] Those amonge us   soere . . . design'd
   Windsore] *Heroës,*   noe lesse contest did   *1650*   whosoe'res
   than . . . *Windsor*   move *H. 367*   This   . . . design'd *H. 837*
   1642   Heroes than   amongst us no lesse   90 First . . . minde;]
   . . . *Windsor 1650*   contest doth move   First . . . minde. *1642*
80 Names] names *1650*   *EL. 8899*   Frst . . . minde. *1650*
81 backe . . . farre] back   87 shouldst] should'st   91 Nor] Not *1650*
   . . . far *1650*   *1650*   Nott *H. 837*
82 Pile;] Pile, *1642*   88 beene . . . Flame.]   92 Tombe;] Tombe,
   pile, *1650*   beene . . . Flame *1642*   *1642, 1650*
83 *Shoulder*] Not   been . . . Flame *1650*   or] & *EL. 8899*
   knowne wh[o] built   fate] face *V. a. 160*   93 *Shoulder*] E:3 Blacke
   Windsore *EL. 8899,*   89 whoso'ere . . . de-   Prince *EL. 8899*
   1650ms   sign'd] whosoere . . .   *not in H. 367, Draft II*
                                 designd *1642*   who-

81–82. Cp. *Upon His Majesties repairing of Pauls*, lines 5–6.
         When the first Monarch of this happy Isle
         Mov'd with the ruine of so brave a pile . . .

83–84. Windsor Castle was actually founded by William the Conquerer on the site of an
Anglo-Saxon fortified manor, but Heylyn insists (*Historie of . . . St. George*) that this,
"the fairest and most stately of our English Palaces," was "first built by *Arthur* . . . to bee
the seate of his Round Table" [2d ed., 1633], p. 328).
   87–88. Cp. Pope, *Windsor Forest*, lines 9–10:
               These, were my Breast inspir'd with equal Flame,
               Like them in Beauty, should be like in Fame.

He that the Lillies wore, and he that wonne,

And thy *Bellona*, who deserves her share

In all thy glories; Of that royall paire

Which waited on thy triumph, she brought one,

Thy sonne the other brought, and she that sonne;

Nor of lesse hopes could her great off spring prove,

A Royall Eagle cannot breed a Dove.

Then didst thou found that Order: whether love

Or victory thy Royall thoughts did move,

Each was a Noble cause, nor was it lesse

I'th institution, then the great successe,

Whilst every part conspires to give it grace,

Prince.

Queene Philip. 95

The Kings of France & Scotland.

100

The Garter.

105

---

94 Lillies] Lyllies *1642, 1650*
95 *Bellona,* who] *Bellona* who *1642, 1650*
    thy] great *V. a. 160, V. a. 322*
    Shoulder] Queene *EL. 8899   not in H. 367, Draft II*
96 glories; Of] glories, Of *1642, 1650*
97 one,] one. *1650*
98 sonne;] sonne *1642, 1650*
99 off spring] off-spring *1642, 1650*
    of lesse hopes] lesse of hopes *V. a. 322*
    her] that *H. 837*
    the *V. a. 160, V. a. 322*
100 breed] bred *H. 367* prove *H. 837*
102 move] prove *H. 837*
    Shoulder] Order of yᵉ Garter *EL. 8899*
104 I'th] In th' *EL. 8899, V. a. 160, V. a. 322* In the *H. 837*

94. Lillies wore]   Edward III, who claimed the French crown through his mother Isabella, sister of the childless Charles IV, quartered the fleurs-de-lis ("France Ancient") with his own leopards.
he that wonne]   the Black Prince, in a brilliant victory at Poitiers in 1356, captured King John of France (Jean le Bon), his father's rival.
95. *Bellona*]   goddess of war; "Queene Philip." is Philippa of Hainault, consort of Edward III.
96. that royall paire]   King John of France, captured in 1356, died in London in 1364; King David II of Scotland, captured at Neville's Cross in 1346, was released for ransom in 1357. From 1356 to 1357, then, both kings at the same time were prisoners of Edward III.
97. she brought one]   David II was defeated and captured while Edward III and the Black Prince were both in France, so that England was left in the hands of Queen Philippa.
101 ff. The whole body of legend and history regarding the founding of the Order of the Garter had recently been canvassed by Heylyn in *Historie of . . . St. George,* published in 1631 and "corrected and enlarged" in a second edition of 1633.
103. Each was a Noble cause]   Heylyn accepts both possibilities of "love" or "victory" but flatly rejects the story of the Countess of Salisbury's garter. For "love" as a cause he suggests that the knights "were ioyned together as in a fast tye of amitie and concord: so by their Garter, as a bond of love and unitie." For "victory" as a cause he notes (from Camden) that Edward III called upon SS. Edward and George at the battle of "Callice" in 1349, and in gratitude dedicated his new order to St. George, whom he also made patron of England.

116

The King, the Cause, the Patron, and the place,
Which forraigne Kings, and Emperors esteeme
The second honour to their Diademe.
Had thy great destiny but given thee skill,
To know as well, as power to act her will,   110
That from those Kings, who then thy captives were,
In after-times should spring a Royall paire,
Who should possesse all that thy mighty power,
Or thy desires more mighty did devoure;
To whom their better fate reserves what ere   115
The Victor hopes for, or the vanquisht feare;
That bloud, which thou, and thy great Grandsire shed,

---

105 grace] Grace *1650*
     conspires] doth
     stryve *H. 837*
106 place] Place *1642,*
     1650
     Shoulder] St George
     EL. 8899
108 honour] Honour
     1650
109 skill,] skill *1642*
     thee] the *H. 837*
110 power] Power *1642*
     well, as power to act]
     power to Actuate

H. 837
     her] thy *V. a. 322*
112 after-times] after
     Ages *EL. 8899*
     Shoulder] K: & Q:
     Ma^ty nowe *EL. 8899*
     King & Queen
     1650ms
113 possesse] posesse
     1650
     Who] w^ch *EL. 8899*
114 mighty did] mighty,
     did *1650*

115 fate] Fate *1650*
     better] bitter *H. 367*
116 vanquisht feare;]
     vanquisht feare, *1642*
     Vanquisht feare,
     1650
     Shoulder] Edwd. i
     1650ms
117 bloud . . . thou, and]
     blood . . . thou, and
     1642   blood . . .
     thou and *1650*
     Grandsire] Grand-
     sires *V. a. 322*

106. the Patron] St. George of Cappadocia.
     the place] Windsor Castle, birthplace of Edward III and supposed seat of the Arthurian Round Table.
     107–108. Heylyn reports (*Historie of . . . St. George*, 2d ed., p. 322) that "*Polydore* hath truely noted; that the most mighty Kings of Christendome have reckoned it a speciall honour to be chosen of it" and states further (p. 338), "Nor was there ever any King, or for-raigne Prince, that hath refused it, but *Philip*, D. of *Burgundie* . . . But other Princes, as by our Kings it is conferred upon them for an honour; so by them is accepted also as a favour: the greatest pledge of amitie and faire correspondence betweene friendly Princes."
     112. a Royall paire] Charles I, of the Scottish royal house of Stuart, and Henrietta Maria, daughter of Henri IV of France. They were in fact respectively collateral rather than direct descendants of David II of Scotland and John of France.
     117. thy great Grandsire] Presumably Edward III's grandfather, Edward I, who was at war with France from 1294 to 1303, defeated the Scots at Dunbar in 1296, at Falkirk in 1298, and invaded Scotland in 1303, rather than his great-grandfather, the ineffective Henry III, to whom the phrase might be misinterpreted as applying.

And all that since these sister Nations bled,
Had beene unspilt, had happy Edward knowne
That all the bloud he spilt, had beene his owne;   120
Thou hadst extended through the conquer'd East,
Thine and the Christian name, and made them blest
To serve thee, while that losse this gaine would bring,
Christ for their God, and *Edward* for their King;
When thou that Saint thy Patron didst designe,   St. *George.*   125
In whom the Martyr, and the Souldier ioyne;
And when thou didst within the Azure round,
(Who evill thinks may evill him confound)
The English Armes encircle, thou didst seeme
But to foretell, and Prophecie of him,   130

---

119 beene . . . happy]   125 *Shoulder*] St. Georg   128 Who] who *1650*
     bin . . . hapy *1650*   *1650*   not *in MSS*   129 Armes] armes *1650*
120 bloud . . . beene . . .   126 ioyne] joyne *1642,*   130 Prophecie] Prophecy
     owne;] blood . . .   *1650*   *1650*
     been . . . owne, *1642,* 127 didst] plac't *H. 837*   *Shoulder*] K: James
     1650   *Shoulder*] the Garter   *EL. 8899*
122 Thine and] Thine,   *EL. 8899*
     and *1650*

125–126. The first part of Heylyn's book on St. George and the Garter is entitled *The
Historie of That most famous Saint and Souldier of Christ Iesus; St. George of Cappadocia,*
and bears the epigraph from Psalm 116: "Right precious in the sight of the Lord, is the death
of his Saints."
127–129. A description of the badge of the Garter — the shield of St. George, bearing the
red cross that is also the emblem of England, surrounded by the blue garter bearing the words
honi soit quy mal y pense.
128. "Which combination of mindes, and association of affections, lest possibly it might
be thought to have some other end in it, then what was iust and honourable . . . [Edward
III] caused that French Motto or Impresse to be wrought in with it, which is still observed;
that *viz.* of *Honi soit, qui mal y pense,* Shame bee to him that evill thinketh" (Heylyn, *Historie of . . . St. George,* 2d ed., pp. 323–324).
130–134. Although Denham certainly intends this as a reference to Charles I, the scribe
of *EL.8899* is quite correct in recognizing that the conceit is properly applicable only to
James I. Cp. Jonson, *Epigramme* V, "On the Union":

When was there contract better driven by *Fate?*
Or celebrated with more truth of state?
The world the temple was, the priest a king,
The spoused paire two realmes, the sea the ring.

Denham's logic here is as fuzzy as his history: England and Scotland were as much "confin'd" within the encircling seas before as after the union of the crowns. The "B" text at-

Who has within that Azure round confin'd
These Realmes, which Nature for their bound design'd.
That bound which to the worlds extreamest ends,
Endlesse her selfe, her liquid armes extends;
In whose Heroicke face I see the Saint   135
Better exprest, then in the liveliest paint;
That fortitude which made him famous here,
That heavenly piety, which Saint's him there,
Who when this Order he forsakes, may he
Companion of that sacred Order be.   140
Here could I fix my wonder, but our eies,
Nice as our tastes, affect varieties;
And though one please him most, the hungry guest
Tasts every dish, and runs through all the feast;
So having tasted *Windsor*, casting round   145

---

132 Realmes . . . Nature
. . . design'd.]
realmes . . . nature
design'd, *1650*
These . . . bound]
These . . . boundes
Draft II Those
. . . bounds *Draft I*
Shoulder] Sea *EL.
8899*
135 the] a *EL. 8899*

136 exprest, then . . .
paint;] exprest then
. . . paint, *1642, 1650*
137 which] that *H. 367,
H. 837*
138 Saint's] Saints *1642*
saints *1650*
piety] diety *V. a. 322*
Diety *V. a. 160*
which] that *H. 367,
H. 837*

139 Who when] when
EL. 8899
141 eies] eyes *1642,
1650*
Here] There *H. 837*
142 affect] affects
EL. 8899
144 Tasts . . . runs . . .
feast] Tastes . . .
runs . . . Feast *1650*

tempts to clarify the muddle. An allusion may also be intended to John Selden's *Mare Clausum*, republished on the King's order to assert British maritime claims.

135–136. Rubens actually painted Charles I in the guise of St. George. The picture (see frontispiece), which is now in Buckingham Palace, shows the King rescuing Queen Henrietta Maria from a dragon in a landscape clearly recognizable as the Thames Valley.

137–140. A remarkable unconscious prophecy of Charles I's future roles as soldier and as royal martyr.

139–140. The association of Charles I and St. George through the Order of the Garter was already well established. Charles himself took a special interest in the Garter, ordering, for instance, in the first year of his reign, that all "Knights and companions of the order" should wear "at all times when they shall not weare their Robes . . . an escocheon of the Armes of Saint *George*." The first edition of Heylyn's book on the Garter was illuminated with a frontispiece showing portraits of Edward III and Charles I, with the respective inscriptions "Instituit EDWARDUS" and "Adornavit CAROLUS," together with representations of "GEORGIUS militans" and "St GEORGE Triumphans."

119

My wandring eye, an emulous Hill doth bound   St. *Annes Hill.*
My more contracted sight, whose top of late
A Chappell crown'd, till in the common fate
The neighbouring Abbey fell, (may no such storme   *Chertsey Abbey.*
Fall on our times, where ruine must reforme.)   150
Tell me (my Muse) what monstrous dire offence,
What crime could any Christian King incense
To such a rage? was't Luxurie, or Lust?
Was he so temperate, so chast, so just?
Were these their crimes? they were his own, much more.   155
But they (alas) were rich, and he was poore;
And having spent the treasures of his Crowne,
Condemnes their Luxurie, to feed his owne;
And yet this act, to varnish o're the shame
Of sacriledge, must beare devotions name;   160
And he might thinke it just, the cause, and time

---

146   wandring] wander-
     ing *1650*
     Shoulder] St Amis
     Hill *H. 367   not*
     in V. a. 160, V. a. 322
148   fate] fate, *1642, 1650*
149   neighbouring] nei-
     bouring *1650a*
     Shoulder] Chersey
     Abby *H. 367, Draft II*
150   reforme.] reforme
     1642, 1650
     on] in *H. 837*
     times] time *EL. 8899*
151   offence,] offence?
     1642, 1650

152   *Shoulder*] K:Hen:8
     EL. 8899   H;8
     1650ms
153   was't] wast *1642*
154   chast] wise *EL. 8899*
155   crimes? they . . . own
     . . . more.] crimes;
     they . . . owne . . .
     more *1642*
     crimes; they . . . own
     . . . more *1650*
     Were] Was *EL. 8899*
157   treasures] Treasures
     1650   treasure
     H. 367

159   act] Art *V. a. 322*
160   sacriledge . . . beare
     devotions name;]
     sacriledge . . . beare
     devotions name, *1642*
     Sacriledge . . . bear
     Devotions name,
     1650
161   thinke . . . just, the
     cause, and] thinke
     . . . just the cause,
     and *1642*   think
     . . . just, the cause
     and *1650*
     and time] the time
     V. a. 160, V. a. 322

146–147. St. Anne's Hill is a low elevation southeastward of Cooper's Hill, near the Thames in the present Chertsey Urban District, Surrey, immediately adjacent on the south and east to the present Egham Urban District.

149. The neighbouring Abbey] Chertsey Abbey, a Benedictine monastery founded in the seventh century.

152. Christian King] Henry VIII is meant, but "Most Christian King" was a traditional style of the kings of France. Henry coveted the title, and represented to Pope Julius II that it had been forfeited by Louis XII through making war on the Papacy.

Considered well; for none commits a crime,
Appearing such, but as 'tis understood,
A reall, or at least a seeming good.
While for the Church his learned Pen disputes,   165
His much more learned sword his Pen confutes;
Thus to the Ages past he makes amends,
Their charity destroyes, their faith defends.
Then did Religion in a lazy Cell,
In emptie, ayrie contemplations dwell;   170
And like the blocke unmoved lay, but ours
As much too active like the Storke devours.
Is there no temperate Region can be knowne,
Betwixt their frigid, and our Torrid Zone?
Could we not wake from that Lethargicke dreame,   175
But to be restlesse in a worse extreame?
And for that Lethargy was there no cure,

---

162 well; for . . . crime,]
well, for . . . crime
1642, 1650
165 disputes,] disputes
1642, 1650
While] Whilst
EL. 8899
166 confutes;] confutes,
1642, 1650b con-
fures, *1650a*

167 Ages] ages *1650*
168 charity . . . faith]
Charity . . . Faith
1650
Shoulder] Defender
of the Faith *1650ms*
169 lazy] lazie *1642, 1650*
170 contemplations] con-
templacon *Draft I*

171 blocke] block *1650*
173 knowne,] knowne;
1642
174 frigid] Frigid *1650*
Betwixt] Betweene
Draft I
175 dreame] Dreame
1650
Lethargicke] Le-
thurgick *H. 367*

165. his learned Pen] A reference to Henry VIII's *Assertio Septem Sacramentorum adversus Martinum Lutherum* (1521).

166. learned sword] Renaissance princes were ideally supposed to *reconcile* pen and sword (see R. J. Clements, "Pen and Sword in Renaissance Emblem Literature," *MLQ*, V [1944], 131–141, and "Princes and Literature," *MLQ*, XVI [1955], 114–123).

168. faith defends] Allusion to Henry's title, borne by all his successors, *Fidei Defensor*, a title conferred by Pope Leo X partly in response to Henry's *Assertio Septem Sacramentorum* and partly to compromise Henry's allegation that Julius II had promised to transfer to him the French king's style of "Most Christian King."

171–172. blocke . . . Storke] It is signal that Denham illustrates the contrasting religious moods by means of Aesop's fable of contrasting *kings*.

173. temperate] Well-tempered; essentially a technical term from the humors physiology and four-elements cosmology, indicating a harmonious balance of contraries.

But to be cast into a Calenture?
Can knowledge have no bound, but must advance
So farre, to make us wish for ignorance?   180
And rather in the darke to grope our way,
Then led by a false guide to erre by day?
Parting from thence 'twixt anger, shame, and feare
Thos for what's past, and this for what's too neare:
My eye descending from the Hill survaies   185
Where Thames amongst the wanton valleyes strayes;   *Thames.**
Thames the most lov'd of all the Oceans sonnes,
By his old sire to his imbraces runnes,
Hasting to pay his tribute to the Sea,
Like mortall life to meet Eternity: 190
And though his clearer sand no golden veynes,

---

179   must] to *EL. 8899*
185   descending . . . Hill
      survaies] discending
      . . . Hill, survayes
      1642 descending
      . . . Hill, survaies
      1650
186   Thames . . . valleyes
      strayes;] Thames
      . . . valleyes strayes,
      1642 Thames
      . . . vallies strayes,
      1650

amongst] among
H. 367, H. 837
strayes] strayes/
playes *V. a. 322*
*Shoulder]*not in*
1643, V. a. 160,
V. a. 322
187   Thames . . . lov'd]
      Thames . . . loud
      1642 Thames . . .
      loud *1650*
187–188 *MSS*
Sweet Thames the eldest
& the noblest sonne

Of old Oceanus, doth
  swiftly runne,
189   tribute] Tributes
      H. 367
190   Eternity:] Eternity,
      1642, 1650
      meet] seeke *EL. 8899*
191   sand no . . . veynes,]
      sand no . . . veynes
      1642
      sand, no . . . veynes,
      1650

177–178. Lethargy . . . Calenture] Medical terms for extreme conditions in disease —
"chills and fever."
    179–180. Cp. Denham's "Of Prudence" (1667), lines 103–104:

> Tis strange to know the way, and not t'advance
> That Knowledge is far worse then Ignorance.

    184. thos] Anger and shame (for Henry's religious depredations).
      this] Fear (of the Puritans' threatened depredations).
    189. Cp. Denham's translation of *Aeneid* V.807–808 (Lucy Hutchinson transcript
V.827–829).

                                              their way
> The rivers could not find, nor Xanthus pay
> His tribute to the sea . . .

Like *Tagus* and *Pactolus* streames containes,
His genuine, and lesse guilty wealth t'explore,
Search not his bottome, but behold his shore;
O're which he kindly spreads his spacious wing,   195
And hatches plenty for th'ensuing Spring,
Nor with a furious, and unruly wave,
Like profuse Kings, resumes the wealth he gave:
No unexpected Inundations spoile
The Mowers hopes, nor mocke the Plough-mans toyle: 200
Then like a Lover he forsakes his shores,

---

192 *Tagus* and . . .
     streames containes,]
     Tagus, and . . .
     streames containes
     1642 *Taus,* and
     . . . streams, contains
     1650
     streames] streame
     H. 367
193 t'explore] explore
     EL. 8899
194 Search] Searcht
     1642, 1650
195 O're] Ore *1650*
     wing,] wings *EL.*
     8899
196 Spring,] Spring.
     1642   Springs
     EL. 8899

197 a furious] an Angry
     MSS
198 gave:] gave, *1642,*
     1650
199 spoile] spoyle, *1642,*
     1650
200 mocke . . . toyle:]
     mocke . . . toyle;
     1642   mock . . .
     toyle; *1650*   make
     . . . toyle, *H. 837*
     worke . . . toyle
     V. a. 160, (corrected
     later) V. a. 322
201 Lover] lover *1650*
201–204] *Draft I*
     And as a parting lover bids
       farewell

To his Soules ioy, seeing
  her Eyelidds swell
He turnes againe to save
  her falling teares,
And with a parting kisse
  secures her feares:
Soe Thames unwilling yet
  to be devorc't
From his lov'd channell,
  willingly is forc't
Backward [Backwards
  H. 367] against his proper course to swell,
To take his second, though
  not last farewell.
201 *Shoulder*] Simile
     EL. 8899

192. *Tagus* and *Pactolus*] The Tagus, in Lusitania, and Pactolus, in Lydia, were both rivers celebrated in classical antiquity for their golden sands. Mentioned separately in several authors, they both occur in Ovid's *Metamorphoses* (II.251; XI.142) from whence they became commonplaces for Renaissance schoolboys.

193. guilty wealth] That gold in itself is specifically guilty or evil was a Renaissance commonplace traceable to Ovid (*Metamorphoses* I.137–140). Cp. *Faerie Queene* II.vii; *Comus,* lines 719 ff.; Pope, *Epistle to Bathurst,* lines 9–10.

199–200. Vergilian lines; cp. *Georgics* I.325–326, *Aeneid* II.305–307, and Denham's translation of the latter:

> [the] Torrents raging course
> Bears down th'opposing Oaks, the fields destroys
> And mocks the Plough-mans toil . . .
> (*Destruction of Troy,* lines 293–295).

Whose stay with jealous eies his spouse implores,
Till with a parting kisse he saves her teares,
And promising returne, secures her feares;
As a wise King first settles fruitfull peace
In his owne Realmes, and with their rich increase
Seekes warre abroad, and then in triumph brings
The spoyles of Kingdomes, and the Crownes of Kings:
So Thames to *London* doth at first present
Those tributes, which the neighbouring countries sent; *
But at his second visit from the East,
Spices he brings, and treasures from the West;
Findes wealth where 'tis, and gives it where it wants,
Cities in Desarts, woods in Cities plants,
Rounds the whole Globe, and with his flying towers
Brings home to us, and makes both Indies ours:
So that to us no thing, no place is strange
Whilst thy faire bosome is the worlds Exchange:

205

210

215

---

202 eies . . . implores,]
eyes . . . implores;
1642, 1650
203 her] his *V. a. 160,
V. a. 322*
204 secures] secure
V. a. 322
205 peace] Peace *1650*
Shoulder] Simile
EL. 8899
206 increase] increase,
1642, 1650
rich] owne *EL. 8899*
207 warre] warres
H. 367, Draft II
208 Crownes . . . Kings:]
Crownes . . . Kings.
1642 Crowns . . .
Kings. *1650*

209 Thames . . . *London*]
Thames . . . London
*1642 Thames . . .
London 1650*
210 tributes . . . coun-
tries] *tributes . . .
countriss 1643b
tribntes . . . coun-
triss 1643a
sent;] sent, 1642
sent 1650*
211 at] (*sic MSS*) as
1642, 1650
212 treasures . . . West;]
treasures . . . West.
1642 Treasures
. . . West. *1650*
213 Findes . . . wants,]
Findes . . . wants

1642 Finds . . .
wants, *1650*
215–216] *not in MSS*
216 ours:] ours; *1650*
217 strange] strange,
1642
218 faire] fair *1650*
Whilst thy] While
thy *V. a. 160,
V. a. 322* while
his *Draft I
Between 218 and 219]
Draft II*
And on thy streames as
many nations floate
As when mankinde all so-
iourn'd in one [a *H. 837,
1650ms*] boate.

211–212. Read: "But at his second visit, from the East Spices he brings, and treasures from the West." An allusion to the two Indies "of spice and mine."
218. thy] An alternation between "his" and "thy" in the reading of this line is a minor distinguishing characteristic of the successive drafts.

O could my verse freely and smoothly flow,
As thy pure flood, heav'n should no longer know   220
Her old *Eridanus,* thy purer streame
Should bathe the gods, and be the Poëts Theame.
Here Nature, whether more intent to please   *The Forrest.*
Us or her selfe with strange varieties,
(For things of wonder move no lesse delight *   225
To the wise makers, then beholders sight.
Though these delights from severall causes move,
For so our Children, thus our freinds we love.)
Wisely she knew the harmony of things,
Aswell as that of sounds, from discords springs;   230
Such was the discord, which did first disperse

---

219   verse freely] lines
  fully *MSS*
220   flood, heav'n] flood,
  heaven *1642*
  Flood, Heaven *1650*
  no] not *EL. 8899*
221   *Eridanus,* thy . . .
  streame] *Eridanus*
  thy . . . streame,
  1642, 1650
222   gods, and . . . Poëts]
  gods, and . . . Poets
  1642   Gods and
  . . . Poets *1650*

223   Nature, whether]
  Nature whether *1642*
  Shoulder] Windsor
  forest *EL. 8899*
225   move no] (*sic MSS*)
  *more, no 1642,
  1643, 1650*
  lesse] less *1642*
226   makers] Maker's
  1650
227   these] those
  EL. 8899, V. a. 322
228   Children, thus . . .
  freinds . . . love.]
  children thus . . .

229

230

231

friends . . . love
  1642, 1650
things,] things *1642,
  1650*
Aswell as . . . sounds,
  from . . . springs;]
  Aswell, as . . . sounds
  from . . . springs,
  1642, 1650
  sounds . . . discords]
  Soundes . . . discord
  Draft II   Soules
  . . . discord *EL. 8899*
Such] And *H. 367*

219–222. These lines are precursors of the famous "Thames couplets" that appear only with the "B" text.
221. *Eridanus*] A classical mythical and poetic name for the river Po, but the heavenly Eridanus is the Milky Way. Cp. Pope, *Windsor Forest,* lines 227–230:

  Nor *Po* so swells the fabling Poet's Lays,
  While led along the Skies his Current strays,
  As thine, which visits *Windsor's* fam'd Abodes,
  To grace the Mansion of our earthly Gods.

223–238. Cp. Pope, *Windsor Forest,* lines 11–16:

  Here Hills and Vales, the Woodland and the Plain,
  Here Earth and Water seem to strive again,
  Not *Chaos*-like together crush'd and bruis'd,
  But as the World, harmoniously confus'd:
  Where Order in Variety we see,
  And where, tho' all things differ, all agree.

Forme, order, beauty through the universe;
While drynesse moisture, coldnesse heat resists,
All that we have, and that we are subsists:
While the steepe horrid roughnesse of the wood   235
Strives with the gentle calmnesse of the flood.
Such huge extremes when Nature doth unite,
Wonder from thence results, from thence delight;
The streame is so transparent, pure, and cleare,
That had the selfe-enamour'd youth gaz'd here,   *Narcissus.*   240
So fatally deceiv'd he had not beene,
While he the bottome, not his face had seene.
And such the roughnesse of the Hill, on which
Dyan' her toyles, and *Mars* his tents might pitch.*
And as our surly supercilious Lords,   245
Bigge in their frownes, and haughty in their words,

---

232 order, beauty] Beau-
ty, order *V. a. 160,*
V. a. 322
233 drynesse · moisture,
coldnesse . . . resists,]
drinesse, moysture;
coldnesse . . . resists;
1642, 1650
While] Whilst
EL. 8899
drynesse moisture]
moysture, drynesse
MSS
Shoulder] Body of
Man *EL. 8899*
234 and] or *V. a. 160,*
V. a. 322

237–238] *not in H. 837*
237 extremes when . . .
unite,] extremes,
when . . . unite *1642*
extreames, when . . .
unite *1650*
Such . . . unite] such
. . . invite *EL. 8899*
And . . . invite
V. a. 160, V. a. 322
239 The] Thy *H. 367*
240 selfe-enamour'd]
selfe-enamourd *1642,*
1650
Shoulder] *not in*
H. 367, V. a. 322

242 seene] beene
V. a. 322
244 *Dyan'*] **Dyana' 1643*
Dyana 1642, 1650
Diana *H. 367, H. 837*
Dian' *EL. 8899,*
V. a. 160, V. a. 322
toyles] **royles 1643*
pitch.] pitch *1650*
tents] Tent *H. 837*
245 surly] angry *MSS*
Shoulder] Simile
EL. 8899
246 haughty] haught
EL. 8899

233. drynesse moisture, coldnesse heat] The four "roots" or *rhizomata* of all things, according to Empedocles. The four elements are formed of linked pairs of these qualities: e.g., heat + dryness = fire; coldness + moisture = water.

235–249. Note that Denham's emblematic concept of the Thames does not limit the definition of the river to the stream of water alone: the concept includes both stream and wooded hill, combined into a harmonious landscape. This concept failed Denham in the "B" text, which as a result has a jarring shift of focus at the equivalent point.

244. *Dyan'* . . . *Mars*] Implies an interchangeability between hunting and warfare to be exploited in the stag-hunt episode and thereafter (lines 263 ff.).

Looke downe on those, whose humble fruitfull paine
Their proud, and barren greatnesse must susteine:
So lookes the Hill upon the streame, betweene
There lies a spatious, and a fertile Greene;   *Egham*   250
                                                      Meade.
Where from the woods, the *Dryades* oft meet
The *Nayades*, and with their nimble feet
Soft dances lead, although their airie shap
All but a quicke Poëticke sight escape;
There *Faunus* and *Sylvanus* keepe their Courts,   255
And thither all the horrid hoast resorts,
(When like the Elixar, with his evening beames,
The Sunne has turn'd to gold the silver streames)

---

247 paine] paines *EL. 8899* raine *V. a. 160*; (*corrected later*) *V. a. 322* veyne *H. 837*

248 susteine] maintaine *V. a. 160*

250 spatious . . . Greene;] spatious . . . Greene, *1642* spacious . . . Greene, *1650*

251 *Dryades*] Druides *H. 837*

252 feet] feet, *1642, 1650*

253 shap] shape *1642, 1650* lead] leads *EL. 8899* airie] angry *V. a. 160, V. a. 322*

254 Poëticke . . . escape;] Poeticke . . . escape, *1642, 1650*

255 There] Their *1650* Thus *V. a. 160, V. a. 322*

256 resorts,] resorts. *1642, 1650* thither] hither *V. a. 160*

horrid hoast] horned hoast *H. 367, V. a. 160, V. a. 322* honored host *EL. 8899* hornid Beasts *H. 837*

257 like the Elixar, with] like the *Elixar*, with *1650* like th'Elixar with *Draft II* with ye Elixar of *EL. 8899*

258 has] hath *EL. 8899, V. a. 160, V. a. 322*

250. (*Shoulder*) Egham Mead is an inclusive name for the broad, grassy, and unin-closed floodland "comprising the Meads, called Runney Mead and Long Mead" lying between the village of Egham and the Thames. Cooper's Hill rises directly from the meads.

249–254. The Green, between wooded hillside and stream, is a function of their conjunc-tive opposition, and therefore a natural emblem of harmony. This harmony is perceived by the "quicke Poëticke sight" as a dance of the wood nymphs and the water nymphs, the dryads and the naiads.

253. Cp. Denham's translation of *Aeneid* VI.644 (Lucy Hutchinson transcript VI.660): "Others soft dances lead, & verse recite. . . ."

255. *Faunus*] God of animals.
    Sylvanus] God of woods and groves.

256. horrid] shaggy; but probably a misprint in all "A" text editions, for "hornid" or "horned."

257. Elixar] Elixir, a substance in alchemy for transmuting base metals into gold.

To graze the ranker Meade, that noble Herd,
On whose sublime, and shady fronts is rear'd   260
Natures great Master-peice, to shew how soone
Great things are made, but sooner much undone.
Here have I seene our *Charles*, when great affaires
Give leave to slacken, and unbend his cares,
Chasing the royall Stagge; the gallant beast,   265
Rowz'd with the noyse, 'twixt hope and feare distrest,
Resolv's 'tis better to avoyd, then meet
His danger, trusting to his winged feet:
But when he sees the dogs, now by the view
Now by the scent his speed with speed pursue,   270
He tries his freinds, amongst the lesser Herd,
Where he but lately was obey'd, and feard,*
Safety he seekes; the herd unkindly wise,

---

259 that . . . Herd] that
. . . heard *1642*,
1650 yᵉ . . . heard
EL. 8899

260 fronts] front
V. a. 322

261 Master-peice] Mas-
ter-piece *1642*

262 much] farre
EL. 8899, V. a. 160,
V. a. 322

263 seene] seen *1650*
Shoulder] Kinge
EL. 8899

264 Give] geves *EL. 8899*
unbend] unbinde
H. 367

265 Chasing . . . royall
Stagge; the] Chac-
ing . . . royall Stagge,
the *1642* Chace-
ing . . . Royall Stagg,
the *1650*
Chasing] Choosinge
H. 837

266 noyse, 'twixt] noyse
'twixt *1642*
Rowz'd with the]
Roused with
V. a. 160 rows'd
with *V. a. 322*

267 Resolv's . . . avoyd
. . . meet] Resolves
. . . avoid . . . 'meet

1650
then] and *V. a. 322*

269 dogs . . . view] doggs
. . . view, *1650*

270 scent his] scent, his
1650

271 freinds . . . Herd]
friends . . . Heard
1642, 1650
amongst] amonge
H. 367

272 but] *bur *1643*
obey'd, and feard]
obeyd and fear'd
1650

273 seekes; the herd un-
kindly wise] seekes,

265. the royall Stagge] J. B., the editor of the 1655 first edition of the "B" text, remarks on "that excellent Allegory of the *Royall Stag*," although the actual phrase "the royall
Stagge" has dropped out of the "B" text. J. B. does not indicate what he takes to be the
tenor of the allegory. Wasserman has recently argued (*The Subtler Language*, pp. 72–76) that
the stag hunt is a covert account of the fall and execution of the Earl of Strafford. This
interpretation is very probable, but only for the "A" text.

273. unkindly wise] Wise beyond what is natural to their kind; or perhaps "unkindly-
wise" (as in *1650*): in a manner alien to their (gregarious) nature.

Or chases him from thence, or from him flies;
Like a declining Statesman, left forlorne   275
To his freinds pitty, and pursuers scorne;
Wearied, forsaken, and pursued, at last *
All safety in despaire of safety plac't; *
Courage he thence assumes, resolv'd to beare
All their assaultes, since 'tis in vaine to feare;   280
But when he sees the eager chase renu'd,
Himselfe by dogs, the dogs by men pursu'd;
When neither speed, nor art, nor freinds, nor force
Could helpe him, towards the streame he bends his course;
Hoping those lesser beasts would not assay   285
An Element more mercilesse then they:
But fearlesse they pursue, nor can the floud
Quench their dire thirst, (alas) they thirst for bloud.

---

the heard unkindly
wise *1642* seekes,
the Heard unkindly-
wise *1650*
Safety] Lastlye
H. 837
274 flies;] flies. *1642*
flies, *1650*
275 declining Statesman]
delcining Statesman
1642 declining
States-man *1650*
left] lost *EL. 8899*
276 freinds . . . scorne]
friends . . . scorne.
1642, 1650
and] or *V. a. 160,*
V. a. 322

277 forsaken] *foraken
1643
pursued, at] pursude
at *1642, 1650*
278 safety] *safery *1643*
plac't;] plac't. *1642*
plac't *1650*
279 thence] then *Draft I*
280 assaultes . . . feare;]
assaults . . . feare,
1642, 1650
since] when *MSS*
281 renu'd,] renu'd *1642,*
1650
282 pursu'd;] pursu'd.
1642 pursu'd,
1650
283 freinds] friends *1642,*
1650

284 helpe him, towards
. . . course;] helpe
him towards . . .
course. *1642* help
him towards . . .
course *1650*
286 Element more . . .
they:] Element,
more . . . they. *1642,*
1650
287 fearlesse . . . floud]
fearelesse . . . flood
1642, 1650
288 thirst, (alas) . . .
bloud] thirst (alas)
. . . blood *1642, 1650*
thirsts (alas) . . .
blood *H. 367*

274. The rejection by the herd of a deer distressed in the chase was often mentioned in discourses on hunting, and furnished matter for Shakespeare's Jaques to moralize on (*As You Like It*, II, i, 29–66).

275. Like a declining Statesman] The comparison, perhaps adventitiously, reinforces the parallel with Strafford.

As some brave *Hero*, whom his baser foes
In troops surround, now these assaile, now those,   290
Though prodigall of life, disdaines to die
By vulgar hands, but if he can descry
Some Nobler foe's approach, to him he cals
And begs his fate, and then contented fals:
So the tall Stagge, amids the lesser hounds   295
Repels their force, and wounds returnes for wounds,
Till *Charles* from his unerring hand lets flie
A mortall shaft, then glad and proud to dye
By such a wound, he fals, the Christall floud
Dying he dies, and purples with his bloud: 300

289–295]   *MSS*
As in a Calme the Oare-
finn'd Galleyes creepe
Aboute a windebound &
unwieldy Shipp
Which lyes unmov'd, but
those that come too
neare
Strikes with her thunder
& the rest with feare,
Till through her many
leakes the Sea she
drinks,

Nor yeilds at last but still
resisting sinkes;
Soe stands the stagg
among [amongst
H. 837] the lesser
hounds,
289 *Shoulder*] Simile
EL. 8899
290 those,] those *1642*
thofe *1650*
291 disdaines] disdains
1642, 1650
293 foe's] foes *1642, 1650*

294 fals] falls *1650*
296 returnes] returne
1642, 1650
297 *Charles*] Charls *1650*
298 glad and] glad, and
1642, 1650
299 wound, he . . .
Christall floud]
wound he . . . Chrys-
tall flood *1642, 1650*
300 dies . . . bloud] dyes
. . . blood *1642, 1650*

289–294. The "brave *Hero*" who beats off his baser foes, but begs death at the hand of
a nobler opponent and dies contented, is a total replacement, appearing first in this draft,
not only of the "unwieldy Ship" simile, but of its tone. The resultant greater personalization of the stag and the new qualification of his death as voluntary may indicate a clearer
intention on Denham's part to present an allegory of Strafford's end.

294–300. The stag's improbable gladness at accepting death from the hand of King Charles,
as established by the hero simile, corresponds quite closely, as Wasserman shows, to the facts
of Strafford's last days. Dramatically conducting his own defense before Parliament, he
fought off his accusers until they were forced to convict him by a bill of attainder, upon
which he urged the King to sign the bill for the sake of national peace. Strafford in thus
advising his own execution sought to ease the King's conscience by the statement, "To a
willing man there is no injury done."

299–300. Cp. Sidney Godolphin, *The Passion of Dido for Aeneas* (1658), lines 73–74:

Presses the Queene and mingled with her bloud
Spreads secret poyson through the purple floud . . .

300. A punning twist to a commonplace conceit; cp. also Thomas Sprat, "To the Happy
Memory of Oliver Cromwel," (1658) stanza 5: "Thy purple . . . / Took the deepest Princely
Dye at last."

This a more Innocent, and happy chase
Then when of old, but in the selfe-same place,
Faire Liberty pursude, and meant a Prey
To tyranny, here turn'd, and stood at bay.
When in that remedy all hope was plac't,
Which was, or should have beene at least, the last.
For armed subjects can have no pretence
Against their Princes, but their just defence;
And whether then, or no, I leave to them
To justifie, who else themselves condemne.
Yet might the fact be just, if we may guesse
The justnesse of an action from successe,
Here was that Charter seal'd, wherein the Crowne
All markes of Arbitrary power layes downe:
Tyrant and Slave, those names of hate and feare,
The happier stile of King and Subject beare:
Happy when both to the same Center move;
When Kings give liberty, and Subjects love.

*Runny Meade
where the great
Charter was first
sealed.*

305

310

Magna Charta.

315

---

301 chase] chase, *1642,
1650*
302 *Shoulder*] Runnye
Mead . . . the Char-
ter *H. 837* Rum-
ney meade . . . the
Charter *H. 367, V. a.
322* Rumney
Meade . . . ye gt.
Charter *V. a. 160*
303 Liberty] liberty *1642,
1650*
304 tyranny] Tyranny
1650
305 plac't,] plac't *1642,*

1650
that] ye *EL. 8899*
306 have beene at least,
the last] have been
at least the last *1642*
have been at least the
last *1650* at least
have beene the last
*Draft 1, V. a. 160,
V. a. 322*
308 defence;] defence,
1642, 1650
310 condemne.] con-
demne: *1642, 1650*
311 might] may *H. 837*

312 successe,] successe
1642 successe.
1650
from] by *V. a. 322*
313 Here] There *Draft 1*
314 *Shoulder*] not in
EL. 8899
316 happier stile] hap-
pier style *1642*
happyer style *1650*
happier still *H. 367*
Subject] Subects
EL. 8899
317 move;] move, *1642,
1650*
317–318] *not in MSS*

307–312. This reluctant half-approbation of the barons who wrested Magna Charta from
King John was significantly dropped from the "B" text, where it might have seemed partly
to condone the accomplishment of the "armed subjects" who cut off King Charles's head.
   315–318. A political application of the cosmic law of harmonious balance of opposites:
the harsh extremes of tyrant and slave are moderated to the temperate means of king and
subject.

Therefore not long in force this Charter stood
Wanting that seale, it must be seal'd in blood.   320
The Subjects arm'd, the more their Princes gave,
But this advantage tooke, the more to crave:
Till Kings by giving, give themselves away,
And even that power, that should deny, betray.
"Who gives constrain'd, but his owne feare reviles,   325
"Not thank't, but scorn'd, nor are they gifts, but spoyles,
And they, whom no denyall can withstand,
Seeme but to aske, while they indeed command.
Thus all to limit Royalty conspire,
While each forgets to limit his desire.   330
Till Kings like old *Antaeus* by their fall,

319–320] *MSS*
And yet not long in force
  this Charter stood
The Counterpart was of-
  ten seald in bloud
321 their] the *EL. 8899,*
  V. a. 160, V. a. 322
323–329] *MSS*
And as by giving the kings
  power growes lesse,

Soe by receiving theyr demands increase:
To limitt regall greatnesse
  all conspire,
324 betray.] betray,
  1642, 1650
325 reviles,] reviles *1642,*
  1650

326 but scorn'd . . .
  spoyles,] but scorn'd
  . . . spoyles. *1642*
  bnt scorn'd . . .
  spoyles. *1650*
330 desire.] desire *1650*
  While] Whilst
  H. 367
331 old] Could *EL. 8899*

320. that seale] Love — alluding to the legal validation of documents by affixing a seal.

325–326. If this is an actual quotation it has not been identified. It does represent accurately, however, Charles I's own view of the various political and religious demands made upon him, his rejection of which led to the Civil War. It also anticipates his fatal guiding principle throughout the negotiations for a settlement of one kind or another, both during and after the wars, up until the moment of his death.

331 ff. The ending of the "A" text implies a dialectical view of English history, or at least a vision of that history as a succession of reciprocal alternations between harsh extremes. Denham deplores the interchange of extremes and propounds the possibility and desirability of achieving a harmonious stasis. Schematized, that view of history sees the period from the Conquerer to King John as one of monarchical aggrandizement to the point of tyranny, the predictable reaction to which was the barons' revolt against John and the extortion from him of Magna Charta. Stability might then have been achieved, but baronial dominance degenerated into anarchy which concluded only with the rise of the Tudors. Resurgent monarchy culminated in the tyranny of Henry VIII, who largely extirpated the old nobility while also ravaging the Church. More recently, in reaction to Tudor monarchy, Calvinists and Parliamentarians have been harassing the Stuarts for popular control of both religion and government — the extreme antithesis of the situation under Henry.

At one past time, however, during the reign of Edward III, stability had been achieved, and now, in the person of Charles I, England has another potential Edward, a king willing

Being forc't, their courage from despaire recall,
When a calme River rais'd with sudden raines,
Or Snowes dissolv'd o'reflowes th'adjoyning Plaines,
The Husbandmen with high rais'd bankes secure   335
Their greedy hopes, and this he can endure.
But if with Bays, and Dammes they strive to force,*
His channell to a new, or narrow course,
No longer then within his bankes he dwels,

---

332 recall,] recall. *1642*
1650
Being forc't] Reen-
forc't *MSS*
333 *Shoulder*] Simile
EL. 8899
334 Snowes . . . o're-
flowes th'adjoyning
Plaines,] Snowes
o'reflowes th'adjoyn-
ing Plaines *1642*

Snows . . . o're flowes
the adjoyning
Plaines *1650*
335 bankes] banks *1650*
Husbandmen] Hus-
bandman *H. 837*
336 endure.] endure,
1642, 1650
Their greedy hopes]
Theyr hopes
V. a. 160, V.a. 322

337 Bays] (*sic MSS, B*)
*Bogs *1642, 1643,*
1650
338 course,] course.
1642, 1650
channell] current
Draft I
or] and *H. 837*
339 bankes] banks *1650*
bounds *V. a. 160*

to adopt a temperate stance if his subjects will meet him halfway. But, the "A" text of *Coopers Hill* makes clear in this conclusion, if the subjects persist in pressing for extreme concessions they may in fact provoke the King to a severe reaction, which would reestablish forceful monarchy. Therefore, the poem concludes, let the subjects moderate their demands and learn to obey.

By the time the "B" text came into existence events had nullified the "A" text's implicit prediction of a devastating royal reaction, and so the conclusion of the poem had to be drastically revised. The Antaeus couplet (lines 331–332) was dropped completely and the end of the poem became a depiction of inundating political chaos, replacing the merely admonitory ending of the present text.

333–342. Although this description of a river flood owes much to literary sources (*Georgic* I, Renaissance pastorals, and so on), it is quite appropriate to a view from Cooper's Hill. The Long Meadow and Runnymede at Egham are still susceptible to overflowings of the Thames, and the monks of Chertsey Abbey built in the Middle Ages a causeway across the meads to serve both as road and protection from floods. The causeway still exists in Egham as a thoroughfare leading to the Staines Bridge across the Thames.

337. Bays] embankments or levees alongside a river to prevent inundations. Cp. George Tuberville's translation of Mantuan's "Second Egloge," lines 13–16:

> A bay to beat the waters back
> and cause them to recoil,
> For fear lest Padus would have drown'd
> and overflown our soil.

"Bogs" as in all the printed "A" text editions is likely a compositor's misreading originated in *1642* and mechanically perpetuated.

First to a Torrent, then a Deluge swels;   340
Stronger, and fiercer by restraint, he roares,
And knowes no bound, but makes his powers his shores:
Thus Kings by grasping more then they can hold,
First made their Subjects by oppressions bold,
And popular sway by forcing Kings to give   345
More, then was fit for Subjects to receive,
Ranne to the same extreame; and one excesse
Made both, by stirring to be greater, lesse;
Nor any way, but seeking to have more,
Makes either loose, what each possest before.   350
Therefore their boundlesse power let Princes draw
Within the Channell, and the shores of Law,
And may that Law, which teaches Kings to sway
Their Scepters, teach their Subjects to obey.

---

340 swels;] swels *1642,*   343 can] could *Draft 1,*   both by . . . lesse.
     1650   *V. a. 160, V. a. 322,*   *1642, 1650*
     then a] then to a   *B*   stirring] striving
     V. a. 322   344 made their Subjects   *MSS, B*
341 fiercer . . . restraint,   by oppressions] by   349 more,] more *1642,*
     he] fiercer . . . re-   oppression made   *1650*
     straint he *1642*   theyr subiects   Nor] Nott *H. 837*
     fircer . . . restraint he   *V. a. 160*   350 loose, what] loose
     1650   oppressions] oppres-   what *1650*
342 knowes . . . shores:]   sion *EL. 8899,*   each] they *MSS*
     knows . . . shores   *V. a. 322*   351 let] (*sic MSS*) tell
     1650   347 extreame;] extreame,   *1642*   till *1650*
     bound] boundes   *1642, 1650*   ex-   352 Channell] Channells
     H. 367, V. a. 160,   treams, *EL. 8899*   *V. a. 160, V. a. 322*
     V. a. 322   348 both, by . . . lesse;]   353 which] that *H. 837*

348. stirring]   very likely a compositor's misreading of "striving" — a reading shared
by *MSS* and *B*.

134

The "B" Text, Draft IV

(1655; 1668)

SUMMARY NOTE ON THE TEXT

THIS, the final revised version of *Coopers Hill* and that best known to subsequent generations of readers, appeared first in its fullest form in the collected *Poems and Translations* of Denham published early in 1668. A previous edition of substantially this version of *Coopers Hill*, though lacking four lines (193–196) and containing a number of idiosyncratic readings, had already been published separately in 1655 by an editor who signed himself "J. B." The *Poems and Translations* of 1668 went through five editions: a second in 1671, a third in 1684, a fourth in 1703, and a fifth in 1709. Additionally, *Coopers Hill* appeared again alone in a separate edition of 1709.

The text here printed is that of the 1668 *Poems and Translations*, derived chiefly from a copy in the Henry E. Huntington Library, San Marino, and compared with copies in the William Andrews Clark Memorial Library, Los Angeles, and the Rare Books Department of the University of California Library, Berkeley. That edition was a careful one, carried out with the cooperation of Denham himself, and contains only three typographical errors and no blunders in the text of the poem. The typographical errors have been corrected in the present text, but they are recorded nonetheless in the apparatus. Otherwise the text printed here follows the spelling, punctuation, and typography (except for the elimination of long *s*) of the *Poems and Translations* text of 1668.

Six lines added in holograph to Denham's own copy of *1668* and marked by him for insertion in *Coopers Hill*, although never hitherto incorporated in the text, have here been added in the indicated place, within square brackets. Because, however, these lines have had no representation in the three-hundred-year-old tradition of the received 358-line text, they are not included in the marginal line numeration.

Although the present text has been collated with the texts of the posthumous editions of the poem—1671, 1684, 1703, and both editions of 1709—the apparatus records the variant readings only of 1655 and 1671. The later editions are all reprints of *1668*—1671 and 1684 in fact are reprinted page for page—and they reveal no new readings except such as may be entirely accounted for by the vagaries of printing. As for the editions of 1655 and 1671, and that of 1668 when the present text corrects it, the apparatus follows the principle of recording all variants, not merely of phrase or word, but also of spelling, punctuation, and typography.

KEY TO THE CRITICAL APPARATUS

1655   *Coopers Hill*, J. B.'s edition, London, 1655. Small quarto. Wing D996.

1668   Text of *Coopers Hill* in *Poems and Translations, with The Sophy*, London, 1668. Octavo. Wing D1005.

1671   Text of *Coopers Hill* in *Poems and Translations*, 2d ed., London, 1671. Octavo. Wing D1006.

Lat.   *Coopers Hill Latine Redditum*, Oxford, 1676. Quarto. Wing D997.

  #   (At end of line of poetry as well as in apparatus): correction of *1668*.

Draft IV

COOPERS HILL, "B" Text

TO THE READER

YOU have seen this Poem often, and yet never:
for, though there have been Five Impressions,
this now in your hand is the onely true Copie.
Those former were all but meer Repetitions
of the same false Transcript, *which stole into Print*
by the Author's *long absence from this* Great Town.
I had not patience (having read the Originall)
to see so Noble a Peece so Savagely handled:
Therefore I obtained from the Author's *owne papers*
this perfect Edition. You *may know this by that*
excellent Allegory of the Royall Stag *(which among others*
was lop't off by the Transcriber) *skilfully maintain'd*
without dragging or haling in Words and Metaphors,
as the fashion now is with some that cannot write,
and cannot but write.
Farewell,
J. B.

[Note prefaced to
the first edition of the "B" text
of *Coopers Hill* (1655).]

TO THE READER]   The general tenor of this preface, that the "A" text editions are in effect frauds, is preposterous. J. B. is either deceived or disingenuous, but the purpose of his statement is clear enough: it is to discredit the previous editions of *Coopers Hill* in order to foster dissemination of the present text, whether for commercial or poetic ends, or both. A number of J. B.'s assertions are analyzed in detail in my " 'Lost,' 'Authorized,' and 'Pirated' Editions of John Denham's *Coopers Hill*," *PMLA*, LXXIX (1964), 242–253.

Five Impressions . . . *this now* . . . *Those former*]   Probably implies that "this now" is the fifth edition, not the sixth, as has frequently been supposed, and so requires the supposition of only four of "Those former." Three "A" text editions survive; a fourth may have been issued in October 1650.

the onely true Copie]   The 1668 edition adds four lines to J. B.'s text — four lines that are revised from an "A" text passage he drops — and it reverts to "A" text readings in several minor details, so tacitly refuting this contention.

meer Repetitions]   Undoubtedly the three surviving "A" text editions are "Repetitions," in that *1642* served as copy text for *1643* and *1650*. But *1643* shows some corrections of *1642* almost certainly attributable to Denham himself.

false Transcript]   The idea that the "A" text is a "false Transcript" of J. B.'s "B" text is a staggering improbability. It would mean, among other things, that the fame already accruing to "Mr. Denham's Prospective Poem" was largely misfounded, for the "Transcriber" would be the *sole author* of no fewer than 110 lines of the "A" text which do not appear in J. B.'s text. J. B. apparently was unaware of the existence of drafts I and II in manuscript circulation, which still further confound his thesis.

Print by the Author's *long absence*]   In fact, the London edition of 1642 came out when Denham was in and about London, the Oxford edition of 1643 shortly after Denham's arrival at Oxford. The coincidences strongly suggest Denham's complicity in both publications. See my life of Denham, *Harmony from Discords*, pp. 50–62, for details.

the Originall]   The pretense that the "B" text edition of 1655 represents the "original" *Coopers Hill* is an untenable absurdity.

so Savagely handled]   The differences between "A" and "B" texts are indeed great, but the "A" text is a perfectly viable text, in many ways more self-consistent than the "B."

from the Author's *owne papers*]   A puzzling locution: Why not from the author himself?

this perfect Edition]   Denham's emendations for the text of *Coopers Hill* whose publication he supervised in 1668 testify to his low estimate of the perfection of *1655*.

that excellent Allegory]   The first open suggestion that the stag hunt of *Coopers Hill* is allegorical.

the Royall Stag]   Interestingly, a verbal echo of the "A" text (line 265); in the "B" text the stag is never called "royal." This slip, if it is one, on J. B.'s part suggests he may have viewed the stag hunt as an allegory of the death of Charles I.

which among others was lop't off]   The grounds for claiming that the "Transcriber" lopped off [part of] the stag hunt are that the "A" text stag hunt is only about half as long as that in the "B" text; the explanation of the discrepancy is, of course, that the "B" text hunt has been expanded from the "A" text version, not that the "A" text has curtailed the "B." What J. B. means by "among others" is, however, hard to conjecture. The "A" text and J. B.'s "B" text total 354 lines each; the expansion of the stag hunt in "B" therefore is necessarily at the expense of other sequences in the poem. In all except the hunt passage the general rule is that the "B" text either "lops off" or condenses "A" text material.

without dragging . . . in Words and Metaphors]   Presumably J. B. means only excessive "Words and Metaphors," for certainly the "B" text stag hunt contains a great many more of each than does the "A" text.

as the fashion now is with some]   The objects of this attack are not apparent. Perhaps the real function of these words is to defend by aggression the greatly increased bulk of "Words and Metaphors" with which Denham has in fact loaded his revised stag hunt.

J. B.]   Absolutely no tangible clue serves to identify this person, nor even to suggest his exact position between Denham and Humphrey Moseley, the publisher of the 1655 edition. J. B. shares his initials with at least two of Denham's friends — Sir John Berkeley and Sir John Birkenhead — and with Denham's cousin John Bereblock, as well as with hundreds of contemporaries.

Title]   Cooper's Hill, Egham, Surrey; see topographical note, pp. xxiii–xxvii.

Sure there are Poets which did never dream
Upon *Parnassus*, nor did tast the stream
Of *Helicon*, we therefore may suppose
Those made not Poets, but the Poets those,
And as Courts make not Kings, but Kings the Court, 5
So where the Muses & their train resort,
Parnassus stands; if I can be to thee
A Poet, thou *Parnassus* art to me.
Nor wonder, if (advantag'd in my flight,
By taking wing from thy auspicious height) 10
Through untrac't ways, and aery paths I fly,
More boundless in my Fancy than my eie:
My eye, which swift as thought contracts the space
That lies between, and first salutes the place
Crown'd with that sacred pile, so vast, so high, 15
That whether 'tis a part of Earth, or sky,
Uncertain seems, and may be thought a proud

---

1 Sure there are Poets which . . . dream] If there be Poets, which . . . dreame *1655*	. . . justly . . . suppose, *1655*	fly] ways, and aery . . . flye *1671* waies and ayrie . . . flye *1655*
2 *Parnassus* . . . tast . . . stream] Parnassus . . . tast . . . streame *1655* *Parnassus* . . . taste . . . stream *1671*	4 those,] those. *1655*, *1671*	12 boundless . . . eie] boundless . . . eye *1671* boundlesse . . . eye *1655*
3 *Helicon* . . . therefore . . . suppose] Helicon	6 & . . . train] and . . . traine *1655*	14 lies] lyes *1655*
	7 *Parnassus*] Parnassus *1655*	15 vast, so] vast so *1671*
	8 *Parnassus*] Parnassus *1655*	16 sky] Sky *1671*
	11 ways, and aery . . .	17 Uncertain seems] Uncertaine seemes *1655*

1–4. Cp. Persius, *Satire* I, prologue, 1–3, and Dryden's translation (see note to "A" text, lines 1–4).
1. Sure there are] Cp. "A" text, "Sure we have," in contrast with *1655*, "If there be."
3. we therefore may suppose] Cp. "A" text: "and therefore I suppose" in contrast with *1655*: "we justly may suppose."
5. Courts] See note to "A" text, line 5.
10–11. See note to "A" text, lines 10–11.
10. auspicious] favorable for augury.
13. contracts the space] See note to "A" text, line 13.
15. Crown'd] A "B" text innovation; only in the "B" text are the three loci of the poet's meditation (London, Windsor, St. Anne's Hill) clearly distinguished as bearing crowns.

Aspiring mountain, or descending cloud,
Pauls, the late theme of such a Muse whose flight   M. *W*.
Has bravely reach't and soar'd above thy height: 20
Now shalt thou stand though sword, or time, or fire,
Or zeal more fierce than they, thy fall conspire,
Secure, whilst thee the best of Poets sings,
Preserv'd from ruine by the best of Kings.
Under his proud survey the City lies,   25
And like a mist beneath a hill doth rise;
Whose state and wealth the business and the crowd,
Seems at this distance but a darker cloud:
And is to him who rightly things esteems,
No other in effect than what it seems: 30
Where, with like hast, though several ways, they run

---

18 descending] a falling *1655*

19 *Pauls*] Pauls *1655* Paul's *1671*
    Shoulder] M. *W. 1671* Master *Waller 1655*

21 stand though] stand, though *1655*

22 zeal . . . than] zeal then *1671*   zeale . . . then *1655*

23 *Shoulder*] Edm. Waller Armig. *Lat.*

24 *Shoulder*] Carolus I *Lat.*

25 Under . . . survey . . . City lies] Vnder . . . survay . . . Citty lyes *1655*

27 and wealth the business] and wealth, the busines *1655*

    & wealth the business *1671*

29 him who] him, who *1655*

30 than] then *1655*

31 Where, with . . . hast . . . ways . . . run] Where with . . . hast . . . waies . . . run, *1655*   Where, with . . . haste . . . ways . . . run *1671*

18. The *1668* substitution of "descending" for *1655*'s "a falling" is a manifest improvement; the two possible visual interpretations of the cathedral are now not contradictory but complementary: earth aspires to Heaven, Heaven condescends to earth.

19. *Pauls*] See note to "A" text, line 14. By 1668 Denham, as surveyor general, was himself engaged in planning the new St. Paul's which was built by his successor, Christopher Wren. Denham by his will left a bequest for the "noble and pious worke" of rebuilding.

19–24. Allusion to Waller's *Upon His Majesties repairing of Pauls* (see App. B, below).

22. zeal] of the Puritans (cf. line 153, below, and note thereto; see also note to "A" text, line 18). The realization of the threat to the cathedral is recorded by Dugdale: "the . . . Scaffolds [used in Charles I's repairs were] assigned to Colonel Jephson's Regiment, for [money] due thereto from the said *Parliament*, and in Arrear. For the better Disposal of the Timber . . . much of it was sawed up in the Church, Pits being digg'd for that Purpose . . . Since which Time, the Body of the Church was frequently converted to a *Horse-quarter* for Soldiers. . . ." (*History of St. Paul's*, pp. 146–148).

24–25. Cp. Ben Jonson, *Epigramme* IV, "To King James"; see note to "A" text, lines 19–20.

Some to undo, and some to be undone;
While luxury, and wealth, like war and peace,
Are each the others ruine, and increase;
As Rivers lost in Seas some secret vein   35
Thence reconveighs, there to be lost again.
Oh happiness of sweet retir'd content!
To be at once secure, and innocent.
Windsor the next (where *Mars* with *Venus* dwells.   *Windsor.*
Beauty with strength) above the Valley swells   40
Into my eye, and doth it self present
With such an easie and unforc't ascent,
That no stupendious precipice denies
Access, no horror turns away our eyes:
But such a Rise, as doth at once invite   45
A pleasure, and a reverence from the sight.
Thy mighty Masters Embleme, in whose face
Sate meekness, heightned with Majestick Grace
Such seems thy gentle height, made only proud
To be the basis of that pompous load,   50

---

35 vein] veine *1655*
36 reconveighs] recon-
    veys *1671*
37 happiness] happinesse
    1655

39 dwells.] dwells, *1655,*
    1671
40 Valley] valley *1655*
43 denies] denyes *1655*
44 Access . . . turns] Ac-
    cesse . . . turnes *1655*

47 Embleme] Emblem
    1671
48 meekness . . . Grace]
    meeknesse . . . Grace.
    1655
49 only] onely *1655*

33–34. A proverbial succession: see note to "A" text, lines 37–38.
35–36. See note to "A" text, lines 39–40; cp. *Georgic* IV.362 ff. and *Aeneid* VI.658–659.
39. *Windsor*] See note to "A" text, line 49.
39–40. *Mars* with *Venus*] A Renaissance emblem of harmony. See note to "A" text,
lines 49–50. See also E. Panofsky, *Studies in Iconology* (New York, 1939; 2d ed., rev., 1962),
pp. 161–165; see esp. Plates LXIV, LXVI, and text illus. p. 129.
47. Masters Embleme] See note to "A" text, line 61.
48. Sate] Use of the past tense in this reference to Charles strengthens the probability
that Denham carried out the "B" text revision during his 1653–54 interval at Wilton, that
is, after the execution of the King. The "A" text also employs a past tense — "I saw" — but
does so under the pressure of rhyme. But though the "A" text poet *saw* the King, what he
saw — "Majestie and love" — still "appeare" at the time of writing (see "A" text, lines
61–64).

141

Than which, a nobler weight no Mountain bears,
But *Atlas* only that supports the Sphears.
When Natures hand this ground did thus advance,
'Twas guided by a wiser power than Chance;
Mark't out for such a use, as if 'twere meant   55
T'invite the builder, and his choice prevent.
Nor can we call it choice, when what we chuse,
Folly, or blindness only could refuse.
A Crown of such Majestick towrs doth Grace
The Gods great Mother, when her heavenly race   60
Do homage to her, yet she cannot boast
Amongst that numerous, and Celestial host,
More *Hero's* than can *Windsor*, nor doth Fames
Immortal book record more noble names.
Not to look back so far, to whom this Isle   65
Owes the first Glory of so brave a pile,
Whether to *Caesar*, *Albanact*, or *Brute*,
The Brittish *Arthur*, or the Danish *Knute*,
(Though this of old no less contest did move,
Then when for *Homers* birth seven Cities strove)   70
(Like him in birth, thou should'st be like in fame,
As thine his fate, if mine had been his Flame)
But whosoere it was, Nature design'd

---

51 Than . . . nobler . . . bears] Then . . . Nobler . . . Bears *1655*	Tow'rs . . . grace *1671*	65 Isle] Ile *1655*
	61 Do] Doe *1655*	66 Glory of so] Glory so *1655*
54 than] then *1655*	62 Celestial host] Celestiall hoast *1655*	68 Brittish] British *1671*
58 blindness] blindnes *1655*		69 less] lesse *1655*
59 towrs . . . Grace]	64 Immortal book] Immortall booke *1655*	71 fame] Fame *1655*
		73 whosoere] whosoe're *1671*

59. A Crown] Also a specifically "B" text innovation (see line 15, above).
60. The Gods great Mother] Cybele, whose name appears through drafts I–III, though sometimes garbled in manuscripts (see note to "A" text, line 76). The printed "A" text shoulder note "The Mother of the Gods" has now become part of the text.
65–66. Imitated from Waller (see note to "A" text, lines 81–82).
67–68. See note to "A" text, lines 83–84.
71–72. Imitated by Pope, *Windsor Forest*, lines 9–10 (see note to "A" text, lines 87–88).

First a brave place, and then as brave a mind.
Not to recount those several Kings, to whom   75
It gave a Cradle, or to whom a Tombe,
But thee (great *Edward*) and thy greater son,   *Edward* the third, and the *Black Prince.*
(The lillies which his Father wore, he won)
And thy *Bellona*, who the Consort came   Queen *Philip.*
Not only to thy Bed, but to thy Fame,   80
She to thy Triumph led one Captive King,   The Kings of *France* and *Scotland.*
And brought that son, which did the second bring.
Then didst thou found that Order (whither love
Or victory thy Royal thoughts did move)
Each was a noble cause, and nothing less,   85
Than the design, has been the great success:
Which forraign Kings, and Emperors esteem

---

74 mind] minde *1655*
75 several] severall *1655*
76 Tombe] Tomb *1671*
77 son] sonne *1655*
   Shoulder] Edward the 3. and the black Prince. *1655* Edv. 3. *Lat.*
78 lillies . . . won] lillies . . . wonne *1655* Lillies . . . won *1671* *Shoulder*] Princip. Cognom. Nigrum. *Lat.*

79 *Shoulder*] Queene *Philip. 1655* Phillippam Reginam. *Lat.*
80 only] onely *1655*
81 *Shoulder*] *The Kings of France & Scotland. 1655* Joannes Gallorum. *Lat.*
82 son] sonne *1655* *Shoulder*] Davide Scotorum. *Lat.*
83 whither love] whither love, *1655* whether love *1671*

84 Royal] Royall *1655*
85 less,] lesse, *1655* less *1671*
86 Than . . . design . . . success] Then . . . designe . . . successe *1655*
87 forraign . . . Emperors esteem] forraigne . . . Emperors esteeme *1655* foreign . . . Emperours esteem *1671*

78. lillies] Emblem of France (see note to "A" text, line 94).
79. *Bellona*] See note to "A" text, line 95.
   Shoulder] Philippa of Hainault, consort of Edward III.
81. one Captive King] David II of Scotland, captured in 1346 at Neville's Cross, while Edward III and the Black Prince were both in France, was popularly supposed to have been captured by Queen Philippa herself (see notes to "A" text, lines 96, 97).
82. the second] Jean le Bon, king of France, captured at Poitiers by the Black Prince in 1356 (see notes to "A" text, lines 94, 96).
83. that Order] The Order of the Garter, founded by Edward III probably in 1349.
83 ff. See note to "A" text, lines 101 ff.
85. See note to "A" text, line 103.
87–88. See note to "A" text, lines 107–108.

143

The second honour to their Diadem.
Had thy great Destiny but given thee skill,
To know as well, as power to act her will,   90
That from those Kings, who then thy captives were,
In after-times should spring a Royal pair
Who should possess all that thy mighty power,
Or thy desires more mighty, did devour;
To whom their better Fate reserves what ere   95
The Victor hopes for, or the Vanquisht fear;
That bloud, which thou and thy great Grandsire shed,
And all that since these sister Nations bled,
Had been unspilt, had happy *Edward* known
That all the bloud he spilt, had been his own.   100
When he that Patron chose, in whom are joyn'd
Souldier and Martyr, and his arms confin'd
Within the Azure Circle, he did seem
But to foretell, and prophesie of him,

---

88 honour] Honour *1655*
89 Destiny . . . given]
    destiny . . . given
    1655   Destiny . . .
    giv'n *1671*
91 captives] Captives
    1671
92 Royal pair] Royall

paire, *1655*
Shoulder] Car. Jac. 6.
F. Maria Hen. Mag.
F. *Lat.*
93 possess] possesse *1655*
94 devour] devoure *1655*
95 ere] e're *1671*
96 fear] feare *1655*

97 bloud] blood *1655*
99 been] bin *1655*
100 bloud] blood *1655*
101 *Shoulder*] Divum
    Georg. Cappad. *Lat.*
104 foretell . . . prophe-
    sie] foretel . . .
    prophecie *1655*

92. a Royal pair] Charles I, of the Scottish royal house, and Henrietta Maria, of the house of Bourbon. The shoulder note of *Coopers Hill Latine Redditum* expanded reads: *Carolus Jacobi 6ti Filius, Maria Henrici Magni Filia* (Charles, son of James VI [of Scotland], Maria, daughter of Henri [IV] the Great [of France]) (see note to "A" text, line 112).
97. thy great Grandsire] Edward I, grandfather of Edward III (see note to "A" text, line 117). The anomalous logic here, which would have Edward III's knowledge influencing the actions of Edward I, is harshly ridiculed by John Scott in *Critical Essays on Some of the Poems of Several English Poets* (London, 1785).
101. that Patron] St. George of Cappadocia (see note to "A" text, lines 125–126).
102. his arms] A red cross on a white shield, the same device as that borne by Spenser's Red Cross Knight. It is the ensign of England.
103. Azure Circle] The blue garter, bearing the words *honi soit quy mal y pense*, which, surrounding the shield of St. George, constitutes the emblem of the Order of the Garter (see note to "A" text, lines 127–129).
104. him] Denham certainly intends this primarily as a reference to Charles I (see note to "A" text, lines 130–134).

144

Who to his Realms that Azure round hath joyn'd,   105
Which Nature for their bound at first design'd.
That bound, which to the Worlds extreamest ends,
Endless it self, its liquid arms extends;
Nor doth he need those Emblemes which we paint,
But is himself the Souldier and the Saint.   110
Here should my wonder dwell, & here my praise,
But my fixt thoughts my wandring eye betrays,
Viewing a neighbouring hill, whose top of late
A Chappel crown'd, till in the Common Fate,
The adjoyning Abby fell: (may no such storm   115
Fall on our times, where ruine must reform.)

---

108 Endless . . . self]   Nor doth he need   113 neighbouring]
     Endlesse . . . selfe   those Emblems *1671*   neighboring *1655*
     1655   He, who not needs   115 storm] storme *1655*
109 Nor doth he need   that Embleme *1655*
     those Emblemes]   111 &] and *1655*

105–106. An improvement over the garbled lines 131–132 of the "A" text which can appropriately apply only to James I. The "B" text lines may be construed as a reference to Charles I's shipbuilding program (for which he resorted to the levying of "ship-money" and "tonnage and poundage"). By a twist of fate Denham was perhaps not unconscious of, British naval dominance was a good deal more evident under Cromwell than it had been under Charles I. While Denham was revising *Coopers Hill*, Edmund Waller had turned his coat and was complacently remarking, in *A Panegyrick to my Lord Protector* (1654), that

> The Sea's our own, and now all Nations greet
> With bending Sails, each Vessel of our Fleet.
> Your Pow'r extends as far as Winds can blow,
> Or swelling Sails upon the Globe may go.

109–110. A condensation of six lines of the "A" text (lines 135–140).
109. See note to "A" text, lines 135–136.
110. King Charles had validated his claim to soldiership in the civil wars, to sainthood by his "martyrdom" in 1649; the two aspects of the King, his "fortitude" in "this Order" and his future sainthood (through present piety) in "that sacred Order" have been united through his execution. History has conspired to justify and simplify Denham's poetic task. One of several curious coincidences in the "B" text is that the undoubted soldier Oliver Cromwell in the parlance of his own religious faction was also a "Saint" (see also notes to "A" text, lines 137–140, 139–140).
113. a neighbouring hill] St. Anne's Hill, southeastward of Cooper's Hill, in Chertsey, Surrey.
114. A Chappel crown'd] Unchanged from the "A" text, but "crown'd" now repeats the same motif from St. Paul's and Windsor.
115. The adjoyning Abby] Chertsey Abbey, a Benedictine foundation of the seventh century.

145

Tell me (my Muse) what monstrous dire offence,
What crime could any Christian King incense
To such a rage? was't Luxury, or Lust?
Was he so temperate, so chast, so just?   120
Were these their crimes? they were his own much more:
But wealth is Crime enough to him that's poor,
Who having spent the Treasures of his Crown,
Condemns their Luxury to feed his own.
And yet this Act, to varnish o're the shame   125
Of sacriledge, must bear devotions name.
No Crime so bold, but would be understood
A real, or at least a seeming good.
Who fears not to do ill, yet fears the Name,
And free from Conscience, is a slave to Fame.   130
Thus he the Church at once protects, & spoils:
But Princes swords are sharper than their stiles.
And thus to th'ages past he makes amends,

---

117 offence] Offence *1655*	Lust] Was't Luxury? or lust *1655*	*1655* and spoils *1671*
118 Christian King incense] Christian incense *1655*	125 o're] or'e *1655*	132 than . . . stiles] then . . . styles *1655*
	127 Crime] crime *1671*	
119 was't Luxury, or	128 real] reall *1655*	
	131 & spoils] and spoyles	

118. Christian King] Henry VIII. "Most Christian King" was a title of the kings of France coveted by Henry (see note to "A" text, line 152).

122. A generalization, replacing the specific reference to Henry VIII in the "A" text (line 156).

127. Another generalization, replacing "And he might thinke it just . . ." of the "A" text (lines 161–163).

129–130. A generalization having no equivalent in the "A" text.

131–132. Replaces the "Pen and Sword" couplet of the "A" text (see notes to "A" text, lines 165, 166). The "A" text couplet refers exclusively to Henry VIII, but line 132 here again generalizes.

132. Cp. *The Destruction of Troy*, line 48: "Their swords less danger carry than their gifts."

stiles] A pun (on *stile*, "pen," and *stile*, "title"). Cp. the act of 35 Henry VIII (1544) to the effect that "The King's Stile of King of England, France *and* Ireland, *Defender of the Faith; and of the Church of* England, *and also, of* Ireland, *in Earth, the* Supreme Head, shall be united and annexed for ever unto the Imperial Crown of this Realm of England."

Their Charity destroys, their Faith defends.
Then did Religion in a lazy Cell,   135
In empty, airy contemplations dwell;
And like the block, unmoved lay: but ours,
As much too active, like the stork devours.
Is there no temperate Region can be known,
Betwixt their Frigid, and our Torrid Zone?   140
Could we not wake from that Lethargick dream,
But to be restless in a worse extream?
And for that Lethargy was there no cure,
But to be cast into a Calenture?
Can knowledge have no bound, but must advance   145
So far, to make us wish for ignorance?
And rather in the dark to grope our way,
Than led by a false guide to erre by day?

---

134 destroys] destroyes   139 known] knowne   142 restless . . . extream]
    1655   *1655*   restlesse . . . ex-
135 lazy] lazie *1655*   141 Lethargick dream]   treame *1655*
136 airy] airie *1655*   Lethargicke Dreame   146 far] farre *1655*
138 stork] storke *1655*   *1655*   147 dark] darke *1655*
                                                                148 Than] Then *1655*

But for "protects . . . stiles" cp. also Article I of the *Instrument of Government* which
vested supreme authority over the Commonwealth in "one person" (Oliver Cromwell):
"the style of which person shall be the Lord Protector." The *Instrument* was promulgated
on December 16, 1653, in the middle of Denham's period of retirement at Wilton during
which the "B" text revision was effected. "Prince" was a common designation for the
protector.
    Denham was apparently experimenting with a version of this pun in 1652: cp. the open-
ing of his published verse on Davenant's *Gondibert*, "I am old *Davenant* with my Fustian
quill," with the opening of one of his unpublished companion pieces (in the Osborn-Denham
copy of *1668*), "As I came from Lombardy with my fustian Style."
    134. Faith defends]   Allusion to Henry VIII's style, *Fidei Defensor*, "Defender of the
Faith" (see line 132 and note), conferred by Pope Leo X for Henry's *Assertio Septem Sacramentorum adversus Martinum Lutherum* (1521) (see notes to "A" Text, lines 165, 168).
    137–138. block . . . stork]   An allusion to Aesop's fable (see note to "A" text, lines
171–172.
    139. temperate]   harmoniously balanced between extremes.
    143–144. Lethargy . . . Calenture]   chills and fever, in disease.
    145–146. Cp. Denham's "Of Prudence" (1667), lines 103–104 (see note to "A" text,
lines 179–180).

147

Who sees these dismal heaps, but would demand
What barbarous Invader sackt the land?   150
But when he hears, no Goth, no Turk did bring
This desolation, but a Christian King;
When nothing, but the Name of Zeal, appears
'Twixt our best actions and the worst of theirs,
What does he think our Sacriledge would spare,   155
When such th'effects of our devotions are?
Parting from thence 'twixt anger, shame, & fear,
Those for whats past, & this for whats too near:
My eye descending from the Hill, surveys
Where *Thames* amongst the wanton vallies strays.   *Thames.*   160

---

149 dismal . . . demand]   appeares *1655*   . . . what's . . . neare
     dismall . . . demand,   157 & fear] and feare   *1655*   what's . . .
     1655   *1655*   and fear   & . . . what's . . .
150 Invader] Jnvader   *1671*   near *1671*
     1655   158 whats . . . & . . .   159 surveys] survaies
151 hears] heares *1655*   whats . . . near]   *1655*
153 Zeal, appears] Zeale,   what's . . . . and   160 strays] strayes *1655*

149–156. A "B" text innovation. From the specific ruins of the chapel on St. Anne's Hill, or the remains of Chertsey Abbey, Denham in this revision has turned to a mental panorama of England, which he sees as a "desolation" of "dismal heaps" sufficient to suggest a general devastation by barbarian and heathen invaders.

153. the Name of Zeal] Henry VIII made little claim to "zeal" in his religious depredations. What Denham really has in mind may perhaps be suggested in a passage of similar import but of more recent historical bearing in Bishop Henry King's *An Elegy Upon the most Incomparable K. Charls the I*, dated March 11, 1648 (i.e., 1649):

> Reputing it Rebellions fittest Pay
> To take both *God's* and *Cesar's* dues away
> The tenor of which execrable vote
> Your over-active Zelots so promote,
> That neither *Tomb* nor *Temple* could escape
> Nor *Dead* nor *Living* your Licentious Rape.

Thereupon follow more than two pages detailing Puritan outrages against churches and cathedrals all over England, compared with the activities of various notorious historical heretics, persecutors, vandals, and pillagers of churches. Those instanced include Basing Chapel, Winchester, Winchcomb in Gloucestershire, the royal chapels at both Whitehall and Windsor, and

> Churches unbuilt by order, others burn'd;
> Whilst *Pauls* and *Lincoln* are to Stables turn'd.

See note to line 22, above.

Thames, the most lov'd of all the Oceans sons,
By his old Sire to his embraces runs,
Hasting to pay his tribute to the Sea,
Like mortal life to meet Eternity.
Though with those streams he no resemblance hold,   165
Whose foam is Amber, and their Gravel Gold;
His genuine, and less guilty wealth t'explore,
Search not his bottom, but survey his shore;
Ore which he kindly spreads his spacious wing,
And hatches plenty for th'ensuing Spring.   170
Nor then destroys it with too fond a stay,
Like Mothers which their Infants overlay.
Nor with a sudden and impetuous wave,
Like profuse Kings, resumes the wealth he gave.
No unexpected inundations spoyl   175

---

161 sons] sonnes *1655*
162 Sire to . . . embraces
     runs] Sire, to . . .
     imbraces runnes *1655*
164 mortal] mortall *1655*

165 streams] streames
     1655
166 foam . . . Gravel]
     foame . . . Gravell
     1655
167 less] lesse *1655*

169 Ore] O're *1671*
171 destroys] destroyes
     1655
173 sudden] suddain
     1655
175 spoyl] spoyle *1655*

158. Those] anger and shame.
     this] fear.
163. See note to "A" text, line 189.
165–166. The "A" text had specifically instanced Tagus and Pactolus, rivers both noted in antiquity for their golden sands (see note to "A" text, line 192), but neither for amber. *Coopers Hill Latine Redditum*, which is a translation of *1655*, gratuitously supplies the names "Tagus Eridanusque." According to Ovid, *Metamorphoses* II, Phaeton's sisters the Heliades were transformed into poplar trees weeping tears of amber beside the Eridanus (Po). Cp. Pope, *Pastorals: Spring*, lines 61–64:

> O'er Golden Sands let rich *Pactolus* flow,
> And Trees weep Amber on the Banks of *Po*;
> Blest *Thames's* Shores the brightest Beauties yield,
> Feed here my Lambs, I'll seek no distant Field.

167. guilty wealth] See note to "A" text, line 193.
171–172. A "B" text innovation. Cp. Waller, *The Battle of the Summer Islands*, Canto II, lines 21–22:

> As careless dames whom wine and sleep betray
> To frantic dreams their infants overlay.

175–176. See note to "A" text, lines 199–200. During his Wilton sojourn, while Den-

The mowers hopes, nor mock the plowmans toyl:
But God-like his unwearied Bounty flows;
First loves to do, then loves the Good he does.
Nor are his Blessings to his banks confin'd,
But free, and common, as the Sea or Wind;   180
When he to boast, or to disperse his stores
Full of the tributes of his grateful shores,
Visits the world, and in his flying towers
Brings home to us, and makes both *Indies* ours;
Finds wealth where 'tis, bestows it where it wants   185
Cities in deserts, woods in Cities plants.
So that to us no thing, no place is strange,
While his fair bosom is the worlds exchange.
[Rome only conquerd halfe the world, but trade
One commonwealth of that and her hath made
And though the sunn his beame extends to all
Yet to his neighbour sheds most liberall
Least God and Nature partiall should appeare
Commerse makes everything grow everywhere]
O could I flow like thee, and make thy stream

---

176   toyl] toyle *1655*   183   world] World *1655*   188   fair   bosom]   fayre
177   God-like] Godlike   185   wants] wants, *1655*   bosome *1655*
      1655, 1671   186   Cities in] Citties in   189   stream] streame *1655*
182   grateful] gratefull   *1655*
      1655

ham probably was revising *Coopers Hill*, he added the "plowman" phrase to his partial
translation of *Aeneid* II: *The Destruction of Troy* (1656). Elsewhere I have argued that by
so doing Denham retrospectively labels *Coopers Hill* a georgic poem ("Vergil's First *Georgic*
and Denham's *Coopers Hill*," *PQ*, XLII [1963], 542–547).

177 ff. God-like] This simile replaces the lover–wise king similes of the "A" text
(lines 201 ff.).

183–184. The "flying towers" couplet, rewritten, has been transposed to a relatively
more advanced position than it occupied in the "A" text (lines 215–216).

188. his] See note to "A" text, line 218.

Between 188 and 189] These six lines were added in holograph by Denham to his own
copy of *1668*, now in the possession of Mr. James M. Osborn; contractions and abbreviations
have been expanded. In the second line "that" presumably is "the world," and "her" presumably "Rome."

189–192. The "Thames couplets," praised by Dryden, upon which the eighteenth-

My great example, as it is my theme!   190
Though deep, yet clear, though gentle, yet not dull,
Strong without rage, without ore-flowing full.
Heaven her *Eridanus* no more shall boast,
Whose fame in thine, like lesser Currents lost,
Thy Nobler streams shall visit Jove's aboads,   195
To shine amongst the Stars, and bath the Gods.
Here Nature, whether more intent to please   The Forrest.
Us or her self, with strange varieties,
(For things of wonder give no less delight
To the wise Maker's, than beholders sight.   200
Though these delights from several causes move
For so our children, thus our friends we love)
Wisely she knew, the harmony of things,
As well as that of sounds, from discords springs.
Such was the discord, which did first disperse   205
Form, order, beauty through the Universe;

---

191 clear . . . gentle]
    cleare . . . Gentle
    1655
192 ore-flowing] 'ore-
    flowing *1655* o're-
    flowing *1671*
193–196 *not in 1655*

195 aboads] abodes *1671*
197 *Shoulder*] Forest
    1671 *not in 1655*
198 Us or . . . self] Us,
    or . . . selfe *1655*
199 less] lesse *1655*

200 than beholders] then
    beholder's *1655*
201 several . . . move]
    severall . . . move,
    1655 several . . .
    move; *1671*
206 Form] Forme *1655*

century reputation of *Coopers Hill* largely depended, first appeared in J. B.'s "B" text edition of 1655. Yet the poem was manifestly famous before these lines were added to it. Despite their success, these couplets distort the symbolic valences of the poem. Whereas in the "A" text a harmonious balance of wooded hillside and stream had constituted the emblematic Thames used as a natural hieroglyph of harmony, these couplets present that natural harmonious balance as resident in the stream — the water of the river — alone. A consequence is that the following scene, which reverts to the "A" text conception of the Thames as a composed arrangement of hill and stream (see note to "A" text, lines 235–249), in the "B" context seems to involve an unmotivated redefinition of the stream image from an autonomous emblem to a mere component of one.

193–196. A rewriting of "A" text, lines 219–222, replaced by the Thames couplets. Not in J. B.'s text, they are perhaps a genuine afterthought added to *1668*, where they supplement, not repeat, the content of the "deep yet clear" lines.

193. *Eridanus*]   The Milky Way; also the Po (see note to "A" text, line 221).

197–212. See note to "A" text, lines 223–238.

While driness moysture, coldness heat resists
All that we have, and that we are, subsists.
While the steep horrid roughness of the Wood
Strives with the gentle calmness of the flood.　210
Such huge extreams when Nature doth unite,
Wonder from thence results, from thence delight
The stream is so transparent, pure, and clear,
That had the self-enamour'd youth gaz'd here,　*Narcissus.*
So fatally deceiv'd he had not been,　215
While he the bottom, not his face had seen.
But his proud head the aery Mountain hides
Among the Clouds; his shoulders, and his sides
A shady mantle cloaths; his curled brows
Frown on the gentle stream, which calmly flows,　220
While winds and storms his lofty forehead beat:
The common fate of all that's high or great.
Low at his foot a spacious plain is plac't,

---

207 driness . . . coldness . . . resists] drynesse . . . coldnesse . . . resists, *1655* driness . . . coldness . . . resists, *1671*
209 steep . . . roughness] steepe . . . roughnesse *1655*
210 calmness] calmenesse *1655*
211 extreams] extreames *1655*
212 delight] delight. *1655, 1671*
213 stream . . . clear] streame . . . cleare *1655*
214 self-enamour'd] selfe-enamour'd *1655*
216 bottom . . . seen] bottome . . . seene *1655*
217 aery Mountain] aery Mountaine *1655*
220 Frown . . . gentle stream] Frowne . . . Gentle streame *1655*
221 storms . . . forehead] stormes . . . forhead *1655*
222 high or] high, or *1655*
223 plain] plaine *1655*

207. driness moysture, coldness heat] Empedocles' "roots" of all things (see note to "A" text, line 233).
209–222. An emblematic concept of the Thames as including both stream and wooded hill, as in the "A" text (see note to "A" text, lines 235–249), although the "Thames couplets" (lines 189–192, above) had redefined the stream as in itself a complete image of harmony.
222. A sympathetic view of the tribulations of the politically eminent, in marked contrast with the critical view of "our surly supercilious Lords" in the "A" text (lines 245–248).
223. a spacious plain] Egham Mead (Runnymede and Long Meadow), as the "A" text shoulder notes make clear.

Between the mountain and the stream embrac't:
Which shade and shelter from the Hill derives,   225
While the kind river wealth and beauty gives;
And in the mixture of all these appears
Variety, which all the rest indears.
This scene had some bold Greek, or Brittish Bard
Beheld of old, what stories had we heard,   230
Of Fairies, Satyrs, and the Nymphs their Dames,
Their feasts, their revels, & their amorous flames
'Tis still the same, although their aery shape
All but a quick Poetick sight escape.
There *Faunus* and *Sylvanus* keep their Courts   235
And thither all the horned hoast resorts,
To graze the ranker mead, that noble heard
On whose sublime and shady fronts is rear'd

---

224 mountain . . . stream   revells, and . . .   *Sylvanus* keep . . .
     embrac't] mountaine   flames! *1655*   rev-   Courts, *1671*
     . . . streame imbrac't   els, & . . . flames? *1671*   236 hoast resorts,] host
     1655   233 aery] ayery *1655*   resorts *1671*
227 appears] appeares   235 *Faunus . . . Sylvanus*   237 ranker mead . . .
     1655   keep . . . Courts]   heard] rancker
229 Brittish] British *1671*   Faunus . . . Sylvanus   meade . . . heard,
231 Fairies] Faries *1655*   keepe . . . Courts,   *1655*
232 revels, & . . . flames]   *1655*   *Faunus . . .*   238 rear'd] reard *1655*

225–226. The plain here seems to be an emblem of a harmonious commonwealth, receiving wealth and beauty from the river (perhaps harmonious living, as the "Thames
couplets" suggest; perhaps an orderly political constitution, as the end of the poem suggests;
perhaps both interpretations are compatible), "shade and shelter" from the ruler, who takes
upon himself the buffets of adversity.
228. Variety] Probably to be understood as composed of paired contrasts. Pope declared "variety" to be "included mostly in the contrasts" (Joseph Spence, *Observations,
Anecdotes and Characters of Books and Men*, ed. James M. Osborn [Oxford, 1966], I, 254,
no. 612). Cp. *Windsor Forest*, lines 15–16:

> Where Order in Variety we see,
> And where, tho' all things differ, all agree.

229–234. In rewriting the "A" text to produce these lines Denham has lost sight of
their original function. Now "this scene" is presented merely as one that might have inspired some ancient poet to mythological fabling, but why a "quick Poetick sight" should
now bother to see "Fairies, Satyrs, and the Nymphs" is not established. The dryads and
naiads of the "A" text performed a genuine function in defining the nature of poetic vision;
the present lines are essentially irrelevant (see note to "A" text, lines 249–254).

Natures great Master-piece; to shew how soon
Great things are made, but sooner are undone.   240
Here have I seen the King, when great affairs
Give leave to slacken, and unbend his cares,
Attended to the Chase by all the flower
Of youth, whose hopes a Nobler prey devour:
Pleasure with Praise, & danger, they would buy,   245
And wish a foe that would not only fly.
The stagg now conscious of his fatal Growth,
At once indulgent to his fear and sloth,
To some dark covert his retreat had made,
Where nor mans eye, nor heavens should invade   250
His soft repose; when th'unexpected sound
Of dogs, and men, his wakeful ear doth wound.
Rouz'd with the noise, he scarce believes his ear,
Willing to think th'illusions of his fear
Had given this false Alarm, but straight his view   255

---

239 Master-piece . . . soon] Masterpeece . . . soone *1655* master-piece . . . soon *1671*
241 seen . . . affairs] seene . . . affaires *1655*
242 Give] Gave *1671*

244 devour] devoure *1655*
245 &] and *1655*
246 fly] flye *1671*
247 stagg . . . fatal] stagg . . . fatall *1655* stag . . . fatal *1671*
248 fear] feare *1655*
249 dark] darke *1655*
252 dogs . . . wakeful

ear . . . wound.] doggs . . . wakefull eare . . . wound. *1655* dogs . . . wakeful ear wound: *1671*
253 noise . . . scarce . . . ear] noyse . . . scarse . . . eare *1655*
254 fear] feare *1655*
255 Alarm] Alar'm *1655*

241–322. These 82 lines describing the stag hunt replace 38 lines of the "A" text (lines 263–300).

241. the King] Suppression of the "A" text's "our *Charles*" here is both typical of the "B" text generalization of particulars and a product of circumstances in 1653–54. Charles I had been dead for more than five years; Charles II was officially, in England, "Charles Stuart, a tall black man" who had been a fugitive after Worcester fight (September 1651). A revaluation of the "Allegory of the Royall Stag" would also have motivated deletion of the King's name.

242. Give] The 1671 alteration to "Gave" perhaps represents Denham's actual intention for the "B" text; the change of tense is appropriate and consistent with other changes of a like nature.

243–262. Twenty lines replacing four in the "A" text (lines 265–268).

246. Cp. Sir Robert Howard, *The Duel of the Stags*, line 212: "And only fear'd his Enemy should fly."

Confirms, that more than all he fears is true.
Betray'd in all his strengths, the wood beset,
All instruments, all Arts of ruine met;
He calls to mind his strength, and then his speed,
His winged heels, and then his armed head;   260
With these t'avoid, with that his Fate to meet:
But fear prevails, and bids him trust his feet.
So fast he flyes, that his reviewing eye
Has lost the chasers, and his ear the cry;
Exulting, till he finds, their Nobler sense   265
Their disproportion'd speed does recompense.
Then curses his conspiring feet, whose scent
Betrays that safety which their swiftness lent.
Then tries his friends, among the baser herd,
Where he so lately was obey'd, and feard,   270
His safety seeks: the herd, unkindly wise,
Or chases him from thence, or from him flies.
Like a declining States-man, left forlorn
To his friends pity, and pursuers scorn,
With shame remembers, while himself was one   275

---

256 Confirms . . . fears]   268 Betrays . . . swift-   273 States-man . . . for-
     Confirmes . . .   ness] Betrayes . . .   lorn] Statesman . . .
     feares 1655   swiftnesse 1655   forlorne 1655
260 heels] heeles 1655   269 tries . . . herd] tryes 274 pity . . . scorn] pitty
261 avoid] avoyd 1655   . . . heard 1655   . . . scorne 1655
262 fear] feare 1655   270 feard] fear'd 1655   275 himself] himsefe
263 flyes] flies 1671   271 herd] heard 1655   1655
264 ear] eare 1655   272 flies] flyes 1655

263–268. Six lines replacing two in the "A" text (lines 269–270).
269–274. Six lines retained almost intact from the "A" text, where they had been among
the lines most warrantably interpreted as support for the hypothesis that the stag hunt was
an allegory of Strafford's death. But in English minds after 1649 the end of the Earl would
be overshadowed by the much more consequential execution of the King.
271. unkindly] Contrary to what is natural to their species (i.e., to herd together).
Perhaps "unkindly-wise": in a manner alien to their species.
272. See note to "A" text, line 274.
275–276. A "B" text innovation. Charles I regarded his acquiescence in the death of
Strafford as the moral origin of his own calamity. On the scaffold he stated: "God forbid
that I should be so ill a Christian, as not to say, that Gods Judgments are just upon me. . . .

Of the same herd, himself the same had done.
Thence to the coverts, & the conscious Groves,
The scenes of his past triumphs, and his loves;
Sadly surveying where he rang'd alone
Prince of the soyl, and all the herd his own;   280
And like a bold Knight Errant did proclaim
Combat to all, and bore away the Dame;
And taught the woods to eccho to the stream
His dreadful challenge, and his clashing beam.
Yet faintly now declines the fatal strife;   285
So much his love was dearer than his life.
Now every leaf, and every moving breath

276 herd, himself] heard, himselfe *1655*	heard . . . owne *1655*	284 dreadful . . . beam] dreadfull . . . beame *1655*
277 &] and *1655, 1671*	281 proclaim] proclaime *1655*	285 fatal] fatall *1655*
280 soyl . . . herd . . . own] soyle . . .	283 stream] streame *1655*	286 than] then *1655*
		287 leaf] leafe *1655*

That unjust Sentence that I suffered to take effect, is punished by an unjust Sentence upon me." Bishop King, in his *Elegy on Charles I*, also associates Charles's death with Strafford's:

    you did enforce
His Hand against His Reason to divorce
Brave Strafford's Life.

Within a few lines of this passage King likens Charles to a hunted beast of the chase:

The Royal Game dislodg'd and under Chase
Your hot Pursute dogs Him from place to place.

277–288. A "B" text addition having no equivalent in the "A" text.
278. Charles I was taken to be executed through a window of the banqueting hall at Whitehall to a scaffold set up immediately outside. The banqueting hall had been the scene of the last masque put on at Charles's court—Davenant's *Salmacida Spolia*, an allegory of the King's stilling furies of discord and rebellion, in which Charles himself had played the central role of Philogenes, lover of his people (Christmas 1639)—and its ceiling was decorated with Rubens' allegorical "Triumphs" of James I and Charles I. As George Bates saw the matter, "they agree it will suffice, that he lose his head upon a Scaffold to be erected before the Banquetting-House of *White-hall*, that from the same place where he used to mount the Throne, and appear in the sacred pomp of *Majesty*, he might pass to the Block, and cast off the Ornaments of *Royalty*, where he commonly put them on" (*Elenchus Motuum Nuperorum in Anglia* [1685], p. 151).
280. A probable allusion to Charles I.
281–282. Charles I was painted by Rubens as St. George, rescuing Henrietta Marie from a dragon (see note to "A" text, lines 135–136).

Presents a foe, and every foe a death.
Wearied, forsaken, and pursu'd, at last
All safety in despair of safety plac'd,   290
Courage he thence resumes, resolv'd to bear
All their assaults, since 'tis in vain to fear.
And now too late he wishes for the fight
That strength he wasted in Ignoble flight:
But when he sees the eager chase renew'd,   295
Himself by dogs, the dogs by men pursu'd:
He straight revokes his bold resolve, and more
Repents his courage, than his fear before;
Finds that uncertain waies unsafest are,
And Doubt a greater mischief than Despair.   300
Then to the stream, when neither friends, nor force,
Nor speed, nor Art avail, he shapes his course;
Thinks not their rage so desperate t'assay

---

290 despair] despaire   . . . dogs] Himselfe   300 mischief than De-
     1655   . . . doggs . . . doggs   spair] mischiefe then
291 bear] beare *1655*   *1655*   Despaire *1655*
292 vain . . . fear] vaine   298 than . . . fear] then   301 stream] streame *1655*
     . . . feare *1655*   . . . feare *1655*   302 avail] availe *1655*
294 Ignoble] ignoble   299 uncertain waies] un-   303 assay] assay, *1655*
     1671   certaine waies *1655*
296 Himself . . . dogs   uncertain ways *1671*

289–292. Retained from "A" text, lines 277–280.
293–294. A "B" text addition.
295–296. Retained from "A" text, lines 281–282.
297–300. A "B" text addition, perhaps alluding to Charles's irresolution and contradictory policies throughout the Civil War and especially afterward, from 1646 until his execution: negotiating separately with the Scots and with the Army, ineffectively hoping to deceive both, then rashly fleeing to the Isle of Wight. Cp. Marvell's *An Horatian Ode upon Cromwell's Return*, lines 49–52:

> Where, twining subtile fears with hope,
> He wove a Net of such a scope,
>   That *Charles* himself might chase
>   To *Caresbrooks* narrow case.

301–306. A rewriting of "A" text, lines 283–288.
301. friends] Cp. King's *Elegy on Charles I:*

> Wearied by faithlesse Friends and restlesse Foes,
> To certain hazard doth his Life Expose:

An Element more merciless than they.
But fearless they pursue, nor can the floud   305
Quench their dire thirst; alas, they thirst for bloud.
So towards a Ship the oarefin'd Gallies ply,
Which wanting Sea to ride, or wind to fly,
Stands but to fall reveng'd on those that dare
Tempt the last fury of extream despair.   310
So fares the Stagg among th'enraged Hounds,
Repels their force, and wounds returns for wounds.
And as a Hero, whom his baser foes
In troops surround, now these assails, now those,
Though prodigal of life, disdains to die   315
By common hands; but if he can descry
Some nobler foes approach, to him he calls,
And begs his Fate, and then contented falls.
So when the King a mortal shaft lets fly

---

304 merciless than] mer-   311 Stagg . . . th'enraged   . . . die] prodigall
   cilesse then *1655*   Hounds] Stagg . . .   . . . disdaines . . .
305 fearless . . . floud]   th'inraged hounds   dy *1655*
   feareless . . . flood   *1655*   Stag . . . the   318 begs] beggs *1655*
   1655   enraged Hounds   319 mortal . . . fly] mor-
306 bloud] blood *1655*   *1671*   tall . . . fly *1655*
307 Gallies] Gallyes *1655*   312 Repels] Repells *1655*   mortal . . . flye *1671*
310 extream despair] ex-   314 assails] assailes *1655*
   treame despayre *1655*   315 prodigal . . . disdains

         When through your Quarters in a mean disguise
         He to His Country-men for succour flies . . .
         Whick back to you their Rendred *Master* sends
         To tell how *He was us'd among his friends.*

   307–310. A revival of the drafts I and II ship simile, drastically rewritten and condensed
from six to four lines.
   311–312. Lines transposed from the end of the hero simile in the "A" text (lines 295–
296) in order to complete the sense of the ship simile.
   313–318. Lines essentially retained from the "A" text, lines 289–294; the hero simile,
personalizing the end of the stag.
   316. common hands] The "A" text reads "vulgar hands," making a distinction between *vulgar* and *noble* (or *royal*). The distinction now would be between *common* and
uncommon hands, not necessarily noble or royal.
   319–322. A marked revision of "A" text, lines 297–300.
   319. the King] Replaces *"Charles"* of the "A" text, as in line 241, above.

From his unerring hand, then glad to dy.   320
Proud of the wound, to it resigns his bloud,
And stains the Crystal with a Purple floud.
This a more Innocent, and happy chase,
Than when of old, but in the self-same place,
Fair liberty pursu'd, and meant a Prey   325
To lawless power, here turn'd, and stood at bay.
When in that remedy all hope was plac't
Which was, or should have been at least, the last.

Runny Mead where that great Charter was first sealed.

---

320 dy.] dy, *1655*   ... floud] staines   323 happy] hapyy *1671*
     dye, *1671*   ... Chyrstall ...   324 Than ... self-same]
321 bloud] blood *1655,*   flood *1655* stains   Then ... selfe-same
     1671   ... Crystal ...   *1655*
322 stains ... Crystal   flood *1671*   325 Fair] Faire *1655*

322. Deletion of the "A" text "quibble" on *dying* and *dyeing* adds dignity to the stag's death. For a description of the destruction of Charles I as a hunt, cp. King's *Elegy on Charles I*:

> The Royal Game dislodg'd and under Chase,
> Your hot Pursute dogs Him from place to place:
> Not *Saul* with greater fury or disdain
> Did flying *David* from *Jeshimon's* plain
> Unto the barren Wildernesse pursue,
> Than Cours'd and Hunted is the King by you.
> The *Mountain Partridge* or the *Chased Roe*
> Might now for Emblemes of His Fortune go.
> And since all other May-games of the Town
> (Save those your selves should make) were Voted down,
> The Clam'rous Pulpit Hollaes in resort,
> Inviting men to your *King-catching* Sport.

In the same year (1649) Denham himself had compared the fallen King to a stag, in "An Elegie Upon the Death of the Lord Hastings," lines 27–32:

> But as the Leader of the Herd fell first,
> A Sacrifice to quench the raging thirst
> Of inflam'd Vengeance for past Crimes: so none
> But this white fatted Youngling could atone,
> By his untimely Fate, that impious Stroke
> That sullied Earth, and did Heaven's pity choke.

326. lawless power] Replaces "tyranny" of the "A" text (line 304). Although in either case the historical allusion must be to King John, the "A" text specifies an abuse of *monarchy*, whereas the "B" text suggests the reverse. King Charles, denying the claim of the tribunal that tried him to be a court of law, asserted "I find that I am before a Power."

Between 328 and 329] Here the "A" text had included six lines reluctantly opening to consideration the proposition that success might justify the actions of "armed subjects" against their princes (like those of the barons against King John) (see note to "A" text,

Here was that Charter seal'd, wherein the Crown   *Magna Charta.*
All marks of Arbitrary power lays down: 330
Tyrant and slave, those names of hate and fear,
The happier stile of King and Subject bear:
Happy, when both to the same Center move,
When Kings give liberty, and Subjects love.
Therefore not long in force this Charter stood;   335
Wanting that seal, it must be seal'd in bloud.
The Subjects arm'd, the more their Princes gave,
Th'advantage only took the more to crave:
Till Kings by giving, give themselves away,
And even that power, that should deny, betray.   340
"Who gives constrain'd, but his own fear reviles
"Not thank't, but scorn'd; nor are they gifts, but spoils.
Thus Kings, by grasping more than they could hold,

---

329 Crown] Crowne *1655*	331 fear] feare *1655*	338 took the more] took more *1655*
Shoulder] *Magna Carta 1655, 1671*	332 bear] beare *1655*	341 constrain'd . . . own fear reviles] con-
330 marks . . . lays down] markes . . . layes downe *1655*	333 same Center] samCenter *1655*	straiu'd . . . owne feare reviles, *1655*
	336 seal . . . bloud] seale . . . blood *1655* seal . . . blood *1671*	342 spoils] spoyles *1655*

lines 307–312). In the "B" text leaving such a question moot would be to take a neutral stand on the King's execution, wherefore the excision of those lines.

329–340. Essentially retained from "A" text, lines 313–326.

331–334. See note to "A" text, lines 315–318.

336. that seal] Love.

341–342. See note to "A" text, lines 325–326.

342–343. In the "A" text these lines (respectively "A," 326, and "A," 343) are separated by an interval of sixteen lines. This passage contains two sequences: six lines ("A," 327–332) on the conspiracies to strip the King of power, ending with a comparison of the King to Antaeus, to the effect that he will gather strength from adversity; that comparison serves as transition to the description of a river in flood ("A," 333–342) which, in context, can symbolize only the dire consequences of provoked royalty. In the "B" text the first sequence is dropped entirely as no longer valid in view of the obliteration of the kingship in England. The second sequence is postponed to the end of the poem where, without the contextual control provided by the preceding sequence in the "A" text, it serves as an image only of disorder and anarchy.

343 ff. See note to "A" text, lines 331 ff. The ending of the "B" text does not deny the dialectical view of English history implicit in the ending of the "A" text, but recognizes that the alternating process has taken a different turn from what Denham anticipated in

First made their Subjects by oppression bold:
And popular sway, by forcing Kings to give   345
More than was fit for Subjects to receive,
Ran to the same extreams; and one excess
Made both, by striving to be greater, less.
When a calm River rais'd with sudden rains,
Or Snows dissolv'd, oreflows th'adjoyning Plains,   350

---

343 than] then *1655*   348 less] lesse *1655*   . . . o're flowes . . .
346 than] then *1655*   349 calm . . . rains]   Plaines *1655*
347 to the same extreams   calme . . . raines   Snows . . . o'reflows
     . . . excess] to same   *1655*   . . . Plains *1671*
     extreames . . . ex-   350 Snows . . . oreflows
     cesse, *1655*   . . . Plains] Snowes

1642. The earlier part of English history remains the same: monarchical dominance from William I to John; baronial dominance from John until the Tudors; monarchical dominance from Henry VIII until the Stuarts; popular reaction increasing under Charles I. At one time in the past a harmonious balance was attained — under Edward III. Charles I had been a potential Edward III, but his subjects had not contributed their share toward the harmonizing of the state. In 1642 Denham had been warning that Charles might be forced, in effect, into tyranny. Events had proved him a bad prophet, and in the interim popular rage had swollen into a deluge that had wiped away all order and harmony in the state and had utterly destroyed the King. The end of *Coopers Hill* "B," then, is not the admonition on behalf of harmony which had concluded the "A" text: lines 349–354 of the "A" text are dropped entirely, and the new text is made to end with a picture of chaotic flooding, a picture of mere anarchy which is the product of "popular" victory in the civil wars.

343–348. These lines have been transposed from a position immediately following the river-flood passage in the "A" text to their present position as an induction to that passage. By coincidence the line numbers remain the same ("A," 343–348).

343. Alluding the King John and to the expropriations of Henry VIII.

345 ff. Cp. King's *Elegy on Charles I*:

> For when by easie Grants the Kings Assent
> Did your desires in greater things prevent,
> When He did yield faster than You intreat
> And more than Modesty dares well repeat;
> Yet not content with this, without all sense,
> Or of *His Honor* or *His Conscience,*
> Still you prest on, till you too late descry'd,
> 'Twas now lesse safe to stay than be deny'd,
> For like a Flood broke loose the Armed Rout . . .

349–358. Transposed from "A" text, lines 333–342. This ending also omits "A" text, lines 349–354, an admonition to subjects and princes to reconcile their differences, with its implied promise that order and harmony will be restored. After 1649 that promise is void: "the bounded waters / . . . lift their bosoms higher than the shores, / And make a sop of all this solid globe." Yet in the "A" text this river flood had been an emblem of princely resurgence, and in Denham's historical dialectic popular excess should be countered by mo-

The Husbandmen with high-rais'd banks secure
Their greedy hopes, and this he can endure. #
But if with Bays and Dams they strive to force
His channel to a new, or narrow course;
No longer then within his banks he dwells,   355
First to a Torrent, then a Deluge swells:
Stronger, and fiercer by restraint he roars, #
And knows no bound, but makes his power his shores.

---

352 #greedy . . . can]
graedy . . . cau *1668*
353 Bays . . . Dams]
bayes . . . Dammes
1655
354 channel] channell
1655

355 dwells] dwels *1655*
356 to a Torrent . . .
swells] to Torrent
. . . swels *1655*
357 Stronger, and . . .
roars] Stronger, and
. . . roares *1655*

Stronger and . . .
roars *1671*
#restraint] testraint
1668

narchical force. Perhaps Cromwell was the real fulfillment of Denham's false prophecy of 1642. The image was used with direct application to Cromwell by Waller, *Epitaph* (on Charles Cavendish), lines 33–34:

> So when the Bank neglected is o'erthrown,
> The boundless Torrent does the Country drown.

See note to "A" text, lines 333–342.
  353. Bays] Embankments or levees. See note to "A" text, line 337.

CRITICAL READINGS OF *COOPERS HILL*

The Balance of Opposites

As a PRELIMINARY to the following attempts to provide brief critical readings of the separate drafts of *Coopers Hill*, it is necessary to state, in somewhat dogmatic fashion, the outlines of a particular world view — both a means of interpreting and an assumption about the nature of the apprehensible universe — which controlled Denham's writing. This view, or assumption, or doctrine, is that least understood classical and Renaissance cosmological principle of "balanced opposition" or *concors discordia*. Recent scholarship has been elucidating the operations of that principle in the works of Pope, and has also pointed to its presence in *Coopers Hill*.[1] But though evidence of the pervasiveness of the concept in seventeenth- and eighteenth-century thought has been accumulating, together with the signs of its presence in earlier Renaissance and in classical cosmographical speculation, the doctrine itself appears not to be well understood. Doubtless one reason for this is that no grand formulation of the doctrine was ever put forward at any time during the millennia when it flourished in men's minds. Another is that the doctrine is emotional rather than intellectual; like the doctrine of the great chain of being, it is not susceptible of rigorous analysis or capable of strict logical exposition. As a philosophical explanation of the nature of the universe, it is quite incapable of standing up to comparison with the philosophical systems of Aristotle or any of the Schoolmen, nor can it meet on equal terms the

---

1. For various discussions and documentation of the principle, see Earl R. Wasserman, *The Subtler Language* (Baltimore, 1959), pp. 3–168, and Pope's *Epistle to Bathurst* (Baltimore, 1960), pp. 11–55; Maynard Mack, *An Essay on Man*, Twickenham Edition of the Works of Alexander Pope, Vol. III, part i (London and New Haven, 1947), introduction and notes; F. W. Bateson, *Epistles to Several Persons [Moral Essays]*, Twickenham Edition, Vol. III, part ii (London and New Haven, 1951), introduction and notes.

intellectual constructs of Descartes, Hobbes, Locke, Newton, Leibniz, or Berkeley, thinkers who flourished contemporaneously with major poetic incorporations of the doctrine. Like the great chain of being also, the doctrine of *concors discordia* depends for its exposition and demonstration on analogy, and therefore on the intuitive, poetic, and imaginative functions of the mind, rather than on the logical, algebraic, and geometric. Attempts to expound the doctrine of balanced opposites as a serious explanation of the way the world is constituted and of the way it works are bound to become entangled in unresolvable ambiguities, self-contradictions, and sheer logical muddle, and must in the end retreat on dogmatic assertion. A third reason for the present obscurity of the doctrine is its relative complexity as compared with so similar a doctrine as that of the great chain, and the readiness with which it could accommodate itself to that other imaginative (rather than intellectual) philosophy. A typical result is that, especially since the great work of Arthur Lovejoy, the world is well aware of the shaping influence on such a poem as Pope's *Essay on Man* of the great chain of being, but remains in general either unconvinced or ignorant of the fact that balance of opposites, in several of its corollaries, is a far more important doctrine in the shaping of that very poem.

There is, then, no one author or philosopher to whom the inquiring reader can be sent for a clear exposition of the doctrine of balanced opposition. On the contrary, the doctrine must be synthesized from the writings and remarks of a thousand authors. For my purpose here this fact presents another embarrassment: to elucidate the doctrine fully those thousand writings and remarks must be sifted, compared, and analyzed, a task that obviously requires a whole book to its purpose, rather than these few paragraphs prefixed to the examination of Denham's relatively short poem.[2] Consequently what follows is supported with relatively little documentation, and the

---

2. My unpublished doctoral dissertation attempts to deal fully with the doctrine: Brendan P. O Hehir, "Balanced Opposites in the Poetry of Pope, and the Historical Evolution of the Concept," Johns Hopkins University, Baltimore, 1959.

reader must be requested to grant faith to whatever he finds not proved.

Although Renaissance and even classical writers on the subject of the balance of opposites as a matter of course invoke the name of Heraclitus as the progenitor of the doctrine, independent recourse to the fragments of Heraclitus may well confuse as well as disappoint the seeker.[3] Some aspects of the doctrine are older than Heraclitus, others later, but the gnomic quality of Heraclitus' utterings, and the analogizing, parabolic shape of his thought — his images of rivers, roads, smoke, fire, bows, and lyres — held an immeasurable attraction for the poetic as well as for the mysticizing mind which accounts in some degree for the influence of the doctrine attached to his name. The historical development of the doctrine among the Greeks, however, owed as much to Empedocles as to Heraclitus, and the tables of opposites that became fundamental to later manifestations of the doctrine were drawn up independently of either by the "so-called Pythagoreans."

The basic assumption of the doctrine of balanced opposites is the essentially dyadic nature of the universe. The primal Chaos as conceived of by Empedocles contained the four *rhizomata*, consisting of antagonistic pairs: hot, cold; moist, dry. The orderly four elements of Cosmos were composed of the *rhizomata* conjoined in nonantagonistic pairs and hierarchically arranged so that neutral buffers are interposed between warring pairs:

hot + dry   fire
hot + moist   air
cold + most   water
cold + dry   earth.[4]

---

3. But any student would be well advised to approach Heraclitus through the extremely sound study of G. S. Kirk, *Heraclitus: The Cosmic Fragments* (Cambridge [England], 1954).

4. It is the circular interconnections of the elements, here schematized, which Heraclitus undoubtedly has in mind in fragment 76: "Fire lives the death of earth, and air lives the death of fire; water lives the death of air, earth that of water," and in fragment 126: "Cold things grow hot, hot things grow cold, the wet dries, the parched is moistened" (translations from Kathleen Freeman, *Ancilla to the Pre-Socratic Philosophers* [Cambridge, Mass., 1957]).

Among the elements themselves, fire and water, for instance, are mutual antagonists, but air interposed between them preserves them from all but occasional skirmishes. The collision of all-fire with all-water would, however, reduce Cosmos to Chaos once more — hence the emotional attachment to all forms of hierarchy noticeable in, for example, Renaissance thought.

All material things in the universe are made of combinations of the elements, and so necessarily of combinations of basic opposites. The stability of any material thing therefore depends upon the *temperament,* or due balance and reconciliation, of the opposites that compose it. In the grand scheme of the Cosmos, each major force or entity, material or quasi-material, must be offset somehow by its own opposite, and yet the two opposites must not be allowed to meet in head-on clash. In what may be termed, for the purposes of a distinction that will presently become clear, God's system, the most usual method of effecting a net balance of the opposites is that of alternation. Day and night follow each other successively, as do winter and summer; sometimes equilibrium is achieved by spatial rather than by temporal alternation. As John Ray writes of the vicissitudes of weather, "yet are they so ordered by the wise Providence of the Almighty . . . as nearly to balance one another, and to keep all things in an *Aequilibrium* . . . a long Drought in one Place is compensated probably at the same time by as long a Rain in another. . . . The same may be said of violent and continuing Heats and Colds in several places, that they have the like Vicissitudes and Changes, whereby in the whole they so balance and counterpoise one another, that neither prevails over other, but continue and carry on the World. . . ."[5] It is to the same divine economy that Pope is referring in the *Epistle to Bathurst* (lines 163–170):[6]

"Extremes in Nature equal good produce,
"Extremes in Man concur to gen'ral use."

---

5. *Three Physico-Theological Discourses* (1693), pp. 280–281, Discourse III.
6. Twickenham Edition text (line numbers vary in other editions).

Ask we what makes one keep, and one bestow?
That POW'R who bids the Ocean ebb and flow,
Bids seed-time, harvest, equal course maintain,
Thro' reconcil'd extremes of drought and rain,
Builds Life on Death, on Change Duration founds,
And gives th'eternal wheels to know their rounds.

The first of these couplets Pope had published two months earlier than this *Epistle*, in *Essay on Man*, II, 205–206, but the context there had been different. In that part of the *Essay on Man* he had been concerned to show the equivalence between man's passions and the elements, and *Epistle* II emphasizes the dyadic structure of man's mind, built on the same pattern of yoked opposites as general nature: see especially lines 53–54, 83, 87, 111–112, 117–120, and 203–210. But *Epistle* I of the *Essay on Man* refers to the same alternation of the seasons invoked in the *Epistle to Bathurst* to make a somewhat different point:

As much [the great] end a constant course requires
Of show'rs and sun-shine, as of Man's desires;
As much eternal springs and cloudless skies,
As Men for ever temp'rate, calm, and wise.
If plagues or earthquakes break not Heav'n's design,
Why then a Borgia, or a Catiline?
Who knows but he, whose hand the light'ning forms,
Who heaves old Ocean, and who wings the storms,
Pours fierce Ambition in a Caesar's mind,
Or turns young Ammon loose to scourge mankind?

(lines 151–160)

Because Pope insists in this epistle that a Borgia or a Catiline conforms to Heaven's design, he has been accused of inconsistency for his condemnation of such extremists elsewhere in the *Essay*. Accusations of that kind result entirely from failure to undertand the full scope of the concept of balanced opposites. In the same *Epistle* I Pope writes, with regard to the Borgias and Catilines:

169

The gen'ral ORDER, since the whole began,
Is kept in Nature, and is kept in Man.

(lines 171–172)

Pope here says explicitly "the *general* Order," and *Epistle* I adver-
tises itself specifically as treating "Of the Nature and State of Man,
with respect to the UNIVERSE." In that heading the operative word
is "UNIVERSE," and in the quoted couplet it is the verb: "is kept."
The three later epistles of the *Essay on Man* deal with man relative
to his own affairs, not to the universe, and not to "the general Order."
As Pope had clearly explained in a note attached to the separate first
edition of *Epistle* I: "This, which we first give the Reader, treats of
the *Nature and State of Man*, with Respect to the *Universal System*;
the rest will treat of him with Respect to *his Own System*."

In a world governed by Almighty God it is madness to dream that
the rebellion of a part can overthrow the whole; that is both an obvious truism and the reiterated message of *Epistles* II to IV of the
Essay on Man. Yet critical attention to the great chain of being as
the chief structural principle of the *Essay* has led to disregard of that
message, and to the assumption that Pope really feared for the stability
of the chain. What he actually feared for, in those epistles, is the
stability of what he called man's "Own System," and that system
is a concept derived from the notion of balanced opposites. For embraced within God's system of achieving equilibrium between
opposites by reciprocal alternation lies man's own narrower system,
through which equilibrium may be attained by the preferable method
of *harmonizing* the opposites. To harmonize the opposites is difficult, but it is the method especially available within man's system,
and so is essentially the method of morality rather than of Nature, of
the spirit rather than of the fallen world. Any failure of harmony
within man's order causes the destruction only of that order; the laws
of God's order are immutable and will prevail whenever man's order
is breached. What could be construed as a formulation of this relationship between orders had been delivered long before Denham's or

170

Pope's time, by Philosophy to Boethius: "Ordo enim quidam cuncta complectitur, ut quod ab assignata ordinis ratione discesserit, hoc licet in alium, tamen in ordinem relabatur, ne quid in regno providentiae liceat temeritati."[7]

Man's system of harmonies is not capable of reconciling "extremes of drought and rain"; it can have no part with extremes, which fall exclusively under the jurisdiction of God's system. Extremes can be reconciled only by alternation, and alternation is God's business; he will see to it that extremes do alternate, that the "general Order" *is kept*. But extremes are often violent and uncomfortable to man, and it is to man's interest to see to it that everything that can be harmonized is harmonized. In morality, for instance, all extremes are vices, as Pope remarked to Joseph Spence: "We should not speak against one large vice without speaking against its contrary. As to the general design of Providence, the two extremes of a vice serve like two opposite biases to keep up the balance of things. Avarice lays up (what would be hurtful); Prodigality scatters abroad (what may be useful in other hands). The middle [is] the point for virtue."[8] For harmony, extremes must be reduced to means, or middle points, and then dyadically united.

The word "harmony" itself, from Greek *harmonia*, is in this context often misunderstood.[9] Aside from its technical musical senses, the word in modern languages on the whole is taken to mean something like "concord," the unison of many voices. But the Greek application of the word *harmonia* to music was originally a metaphor, drawn probably from handicrafts, for the fundamental meaning of the word, as it is used by Homer, Hesiod, and other early writers, is *a*

---

7. *De Consolatione Philosophiae* IV, Prosa vi.

8. Joseph Spence, *Observations, Anecdotes and Characters of Books and Men*, ed. James M. Osborn (Oxford, 1966), I, 130–131, no. 297.

9. What has often been cited as the richest modern account of the concept — Leo Spitzer's "Classical and Christian Ideas of World Harmony," *Traditio*, II (1944), 409–464, III (1945), 307–364 — is in my estimation sadly vitiated by a failure to recognize the basically dyadic nature of the classical idea of harmony, and the continuance of a dyadic sense into Christian thought on the topic.

means of connection between two things.[10] In the context of the doctrine under present discussion, the word *harmonia* in Greek *always* denotes a means of connection between *a pair of opposites*, not a general agreement among many diverse things. As a result, even in non-Greek discourse on the topic, down to the time of Pope, the word "harmony" and its substitutes, including "concord" and "variety," usually imply a dyadic, not a multiple, agreement. The word "harmony," then, denotes equally (1) that which connects the opposed members of a dyad; (2) the union of the opposites, or the composed dyad itself; (3) a product of the unity of the opposites. All three meanings are represented in Hesiod's assertion that Harmonia is the daughter of the marriage of Ares and Aphrodite.[11]

As Pope has asserted that avarice and prodigality are vices, extremes of the same continuum the center of which is the residence of virtue, so in poetry he demonstrates their reconciliation through alternation. The miser is "This year a Reservoir, to keep and spare,/ The next a Fountain, spouting thro' his Heir" (*Bathurst*, lines 175–176), and the point is elaborated in the same poem through the parable of Cotta and Cotta's son. But Pope hardly approves of this violent method, and insists, for instance, that Cotta's spendthrift son "mistook reverse of wrong for right." But the median area where virtue lies must include a reciprocal connection with a matter that cannot be dissociated from either the impulse to avarice or to prodigality, namely, the wealth that is either hoarded or squandered. Pope's poetic discussion of these extremes takes place, after all, in the course of a moral essay, "On the Use of Riches." The virtuous course is

To balance Fortune by a just expence,
Join with Œconomy, Magnificence.

(*Bathurst*, lines 223–224)

---

10. This fact is succinctly demonstrated by Kirk in his discussion of the Heraclitean fragment 51: *The Cosmic Fragments*, pp. 203–221.

11. *Theogony*, 937, 976; Hesiod's tradition is distinct from the Homeric myth that has Aphrodite married to Hephaestus, her union with Ares an adulterous one (according to Hesiod Hephaestus was married to Aglaia [*Theogony*, 945]).

Therefore, it appears, each virtue, like each vice, is joined in a dyadic union with some reciprocal quality. The destitute man cannot squander wealth, but destitution, or fear of destitution, can stimulate avarice. It is the hoarded wealth accumulated by avarice which can tempt the miser's heir, mistaking reverse of wrong for right, to spendthrift squandering, the ultimate effect of which can be only his genuine destitution. Therefore, in the mechanics of God's system, the alternation of avarice and prodigality is linked with a reciprocal alternation of destitution and hoarded excess. But man has available to him the milder laws of his own system, the system of harmonious balance, if he has but sense enough to take advantage of them.

To recapitulate then, each "good" mean is flanked by two "bad" extremes, forming a triad: extreme-mean-extreme, or bad-good-bad. Yet each triad is accompanied by a reciprocal triad, making a sequence of possible dyads, the extremes of which will be governed by God's laws of alternation, the means by a balanced harmony. In schematic form, the triple dyads would have a relationship like this:

$$+ \text{Extreme A} \quad \text{Mean A} \quad - \text{Extreme A}$$
$$- \text{Extreme B} \quad \text{Mean B} \quad + \text{Extreme B.}$$

The dyad $+$Extreme A$/-$Extreme B would be subject to perpetual vicissitude or alternation with the dyad $-$Extreme A$/+$Extreme B, in the pattern of Pope's cycle of avarice-excess-prodigality-destitution-avarice and so on. Only the union of means can hope for stability.

In the world of *Coopers Hill* the laws of extremes and means, of God's order and man's own, operate as fully as they do in the conceptual world of Pope. The operation of God's laws of extremes is exemplified throughout the discourse of Denham's poem in all its drafts, and a plea for the attainment of harmony at the means is consistently reiterated. From Draft II onward, for instance, early in the text London is described as the place

Where Luxury and Wealth, like war and peace,
Are each the others ruine, and increase.

This is a formulation that, like Pope's treatment of avarice and prodigality, recognizes the cyclical nature of the operation of God's law of alternating extremes. The formulation had been made in English before Denham's time by George Puttenham,[12] among others, and was to be made again, as in the doggerel printed in Mary Clarke's almanac, alluded to by Swift in the opening of *The Battle of the Books*:

> War begets Poverty,
>   Poverty Peace;
> Peace maketh Riches flow,
>   (Fate ne'er doth cease:)
> Riches produceth Pride,
>   Pride is War's ground,
> War begets Poverty, &c.
>   (The World) goes round.

Quite literally, this kind of sequence could be regarded as a vicious circle, and Denham sees English history as a cycle of reciprocating vices, in which only now and again has the opportunity opened up for harmonious settlement between means.

One such important occasion was the agreement embodied in Magna Charta. As a result of that charter, a harmony was achieved to replace a dyad of extremes:

Tyrant and Slave, those names of hate and feare,
The happier stile of King and Subject beare.

Thus the achievement was stated baldly in drafts I and II; in draft III Denham added a glossing couplet that highlights the operation of the law of harmony:

Happy when both to the same Center move;
When Kings give Liberty, and Subjects love.

The "mean" dyad king/subject, in other words, has replaced the "extreme" dyad tyrant/slave, and should have a hope of surviving,

---

12. See "A" text, note to lines 37–38, p. 112, above.

whereas the extreme dyad *will inevitably be replaced* by its opposite extreme.

Any political state, whatever the details of its constitution, is at bottom a dyadic structure of ruler and ruled. As the doctrine of opposites conceived the matter, only three forms of such a structure are possible—combinations of the respective extremes and means of ruler and ruled—and of the three possibilities Denham mentions two. The extreme forms of a ruler are the despot, or as Denham says, tyrant, and the extremely weak ruler, nonking, or *roi fainéant* (to whom Denham seems to refer a few lines later: "Who gives constrain'd, but his owne feare reviles"). A particularly bad ruler may even vacillate between one extreme and the other, like Nero in Bacon's essay *Of Empire*: "in Government, sometimes he used to winde the pins too high, sometimes to let them downe too low." The mean form of a ruler Denham calls a king, and John Dryden later, with more experience and more sophistication, a "sober Prince." As for the ruled, they may be at one extreme, as Denham indicates, slaves; at the mean, subjects. At the other extreme they would be an anarchic mob, what Dryden termed "the dregs of a democracy." Certain dyadic combinations are obviously impossible: a state composed of tyrant and rebellious mob would simply explode; one composed of *roi fainéant* and slaves would freeze into paralysis. These are the respective states of calenture and lethargy which Denham finds in the history of the English church. A political state, then, may take only one of these three possible shapes:

tyrant	king	nonking
slaves	subjects	mob

The ideal constitution is the median one; either of the extremes will fall under God's law of alternation and will be succeeded by the opposite extreme until the cycle is broken. Denham reviews the process of alternation quite explicitly, in explaining the failure of Magna Charta:

The Subjects arm'd, the more theire princes gave,
But this advantage tooke the more to crave: . . .

Thus Kings by grasping more then they could hold,
First made their Subjects by oppression bold,
And popular sway by forcing Kings to give,
More then was fitt for Subjects to receave,
Ranne to the same extreame, and one excesse,
Made both by striving to be greater, lesse.[13]

Denham's final attitude toward the possibility of a contemporary English attainment of that desirable middle state of harmony and virtue changed between the pre–Civil War time of the composition of the "A" text of *Coopers Hill* and the post–Civil War time of the revision that produced the "B" text. But the abandonment of hope for the attainment of political harmony which distinguishes the "B" text from the "A" may also have been the motivation for the personal dedication to the harmoniously dyadic mean expressed in the most famous lines of the "B" text:

O could I flow like thee, and make thy stream
My great example, as it is my theme!
Though deep, yet clear, though gentle, yet not dull,
Strong without rage, without ore-flowing full.

---

13. These lines, excerpted here from the conclusion of *Coopers Hill* and reproduced in approximately the wording of Draft I, are to be found little changed in all four drafts.

Separate Interpretations

THE "A" TEXT, DRAFT I

DRAFT I OF *Coopers Hill* is, comparatively speaking, a rather simple poem, with a structure and organization simpler than that of any of the later drafts. For one thing, it really lacks one whole sequence common in various forms to the other drafts and therefore has a less complex interplay among its several parts. To facilitate discussion of the whole poem and mutual comparisons among the four drafts it has been an easy matter to regard all texts of the poem as being composed of eight principal sections. The first section in all versions of *Coopers Hill* is an invocation of the hill itself. The second section is a meditation on London and St. Paul's Cathedral, and this second section Draft I essentially lacks. Lines 17–26 of Draft I do in fact mention both Paul's and London, but an accurate approach to Draft I recognizes that it lacks the complicated consideration of the City usual in later drafts, and that in fact lines 1–26 of Draft I constitute a single section, a prolonged invocation to Cooper's Hill.

If the opening twenty-six lines of Draft I of *Coopers Hill* be regarded as constituting a single section of the poem, it is a section that might be adequately titled "Cooper's Hill." And this section is composed of three subsections: the invocation (lines 1–8); a statement of the merits of the hill (lines 9–16); a statement of revulsion from London (lines 17–26). This final subsection, which in other drafts becomes an independent expatiation on London and the cathedral, is here merely a form of negative support for the preceding subsection. London is, after all, at a considerable distance from Cooper's Hill, and in the composition of Draft I Denham remained pretty actively aware of the topographical facts. Whereas in the later drafts one of the advantages of Cooper's Hill is that it is an auspicious place from which to contemplate London, in Draft I the situation is almost the reverse. The poet appears to be congratulating himself on not being in London, on having a scene and a landscape to read which are removed from London. It is true that from Cooper's Hill the poet can look down on Paul's, just as from the tower of Paul's men can look down "unto the Towne" (lines 17–18), but he makes no claim that the town is really discernible from the hill. Mind and eye in this opening are dissociated from each other: the poet's mind is "up-pon the Tumult & the Crowde"; his eye sees St. Paul's, and the city "wrapt in a more dusky Cloud / Of busines, then of Smoke" (lines 19–20). Denham's reaction to his troubled thoughts and obscured view of London is uncomplicated aversion. This epening section of Draft I ends with perfect appropriateness on a note of what amounts to self-congratulation:

Oh happiness of Sweete retyr'd content
To be at once Secure, and Innocent.

(I, 25–26)

This opening, that is to say, is a fairly conventional restatement of traditional poetic preference of the innocent simplicity of the coun-try over the vain and soul-destroying turmoil and trade of the city. The City of London, in other words, enters this version of the poem only as a negative contrast to the rural felicity of Cooper's Hill and its environs. There is no hint of destructive threat in the activities of the Londoners, vain and self-defeating though they may be, either to the rustic peace of Egham and the Thames Valley, or to the peace and general well-being of the commonweal. Although St. Paul's Cathedral is mentioned, it is mentioned only for very obvious and nontendentious reasons. As the tallest building in London it was the one most distinctly discernible at a distance: its crossing tower, the butt of its former spire, no doubt rose high above the urban haze. Moreover, as the highest building in London, it was the viewpoint from which the sightseer usually looked down on the city; the still happier viewpoint of Cooper's Hill afforded the opportunity to look down on St. Paul's. Although at the time he made this draft of *Coopers Hill* Denham was already acquainted with Waller's poem *Upon His Majesties repairing of Pauls*, this draft contains not the faintest touch of Waller's iconographical interpretation of the cathedral, or of Waller's presentation of it as an emblem of the "modesty and greatness" of King Charles's mind or as an earnest of the virtues of the King's church policies. In Draft I of *Coopers Hill* St. Paul's Cathedral is the tallest building and most prominent landmark in London, neither more nor less.

If the passage on London and Paul's in Draft I is merely a conventional device to emphasize the happiness of sweet retired contentment — the life of the country rather than that of the city — it is only one such device in an entire opening which is an elaboration of conventions. Lines 1–8, for instance, have many Roman imperial age precedents in rejecting the Greek Muses. Horace, Tibullus, Propertius, Ovid, Manilius, Seneca, and others find various substitutes for the Muses. Vergil, by invoking Caesar as the Muse of his *Georgics*, established a precedent of encomium which was perhaps not far distant from Denham's mind. The opening of *Coopers Hill* appears to be specifically modeled, however, on Persius' rejection of the Muses in the prologue to his first *Satire*.[14] There Persius presents himself as a half rustic bearing verses uninspired by dreaming upon Parnassus or by tasting the fountain of Hippocrene. In Persius this attitude is partly a satirist's pose of uncouthness, partly a genuine contempt for degenerate poetry, and demonstrates his independence of the sterile rhetorical tradition. Denham follows Persius' words closely, but changes their tenor completely. There is no affectation of modesty in his assertion that poetry makes Parnassus, and not the other way around. He does not come forward as a "semipaganus," but as a poet on equal terms with all other poets if his *poetry* will stand up to comparison. Denham therefore genuinely adds something new to what

---

14. See "A" text, note to lines 1–4, p. 109, above.

otherwise might well be considered but one more repetition of a re-jection-of-the-Muses topos. For latent in his lines on the true na-ture of poetic inspiration lies a conception of poetic vision funda-mental to *Coopers Hill*: the poetic sight is that which can see that a hill in Egham is Parnassus. This is to imply neither the facile concept that the inspiration afforded by the Greek Parnassus is "mere mythol-ogy," nor the chauvinistic one that any English hill is a match for any in Greece, nor yet the purely pragmatic one that any hill a bard labors up becomes his private Parnassus. Rather it is to recognize that poetry is a peculiar mode of discourse as well as a peculiar mode of intellection, that it can deal, and does deal, with serious matters, with *reality*. The Parnassus quality of Cooper's Hill is not imposed on it by the poet; the relationship between poet and hill is reciprocal, is mu-tual:

if I can bee to thee
A Poet, thou Pernassus art to me,
Whose topp when I ascend, I seeme more high
More boundlesse in my Fancy then myne Eye.

(I, 7–10)

The poet must accept from the hill the inspiration it has to offer, and the same mutual reciprocity must be established between him and all the details in the landscape he is to examine.

The second eight lines of Draft I establish an equivalence between elevation of body and of thought, either of which can place an ob-server above the elements. The context of weather prognostication is reminiscent of Vergil's *Georgics*, especially of the first, and probably can be directly associated with that source. As in the *Georgics*, one kind of prognostic power is equated with others, so that the poet, aloof on the summit of Cooper's Hill, becomes a kind of meteorolo-gist, able impartially to view and to predict storms or any other sorts of dire events. This subsection is the center of the Draft I opening, and the "dusky Cloud" of London in the next subsection subserves the meteorological imagery in this: London is merely one kind of cloud that can be seen from Cooper's Hill. The poet, therefore, in these twenty-six lines is shown as a detached observer of places or events, secure and innocent on the inspirational high ground of his hill. London he has nothing much to do with — it is no more than an unpleasant smudge on the distant horizon. From the summit of Cooper's Hill the poet views a more circumscribed landscape, and in Draft I of *Coopers Hill* it is effectively to that circumscribed landscape that he confines his attention.

To his west, in the near distance from Cooper's Hill, the poet has a clear view of Windsor Castle, rising on its low hill from the wooded valley; this edifice will be his first object of attention. To his east, approximately, St. Anne's Hill in nearby Chertsey raises its head, no longer crowned by its chapel which the expropriation of the monasteries had doomed. At the foot of St. Anne's Hill flows the Thames, on its way to London, having passed previously in turn both Windsor Castle and Cooper's Hill. To the west the Thames flows past Windsor Forest; directly below Cooper's Hill it glides by the washland of Runnymede and Long Meadow, at the eastern end of which the flood-controlling causeway marches toward Staines. This is the whole of the landscape examined or discussed in *Coopers Hill* Draft I. It is a landscape entirely rustic, and little in the conventional praise of rural retirement which constitutes the opening of Draft I gives any hint that the inordinate and perverse values of the City will more and more dominate like an incubus the structural balance of the subsequent drafts of the poem.

Only one such possible hint present in Draft I requires direct consideration. In the fifth line of Draft I, as of all the other drafts, occurs what Earl Wasserman has interpreted as a topical allusion to contemporary political issues. Denham asserts that "Courts make not Kings, but Kings the Court," and Wasserman sees in this statement a rejection of the parliamentary thesis that the king owes his power to election by the people. "In mid-1642, moreover, Charles had removed from London to York and was enticing members of Parliament to join him," Wasserman continues. "Parliament — the 'high *Court* of

Parliament'—insistently demanded his return to London in order that the parliamentary monarchy might function."[15] But events of mid-1642 could hardly have entered even Draft III of *Coopers Hill*, in print by August 5, 1642, still less the text of Draft I; and Wasserman's specific identification of a topicality must be rejected as impossible. Perhaps it would be as well to allow the line no topicality beyond its patent sense: that a circle of courtiers does not engender the king in their midst, but that the presence of the king constitutes his companions into a "court." The parallel to the relation between poet and Parnassus is plain enough. But just that obviousness of the simile makes it suspect—it is a little too much, redundant.

Denham borrows his opening, as has been said, from Persius, but line 5 has no equivalent in Persius, and so is Denham's separate insertion. Moreover, despite Wasserman's anachronism in relating the line to the parliamentary dispute of 1642, the fact remains true that Parliament during the seventeenth century was frequently, or customarily, referred to as a "court." But of even greater significance is the fact that to say in England, at any time from the winter of 1640–41 until the termination of the civil wars, that "Kings make Courts," was to make a highly charged partisan political affirmation. For regardless of the application of the word "court" to Parliament, the word was certainly applied to courts of law. Ever after the barons of the King's Bench had ruled in favor of the King in Hampden's ship-money case (1638–39) that court itself had been under attack. In the infancy of the Long Parliament two men who were later to become eminent Royalists led massive attacks on the entire royal judiciary system. In the Lords, Lucius Cary, Viscount Falkland, led the assault on the court of King's Bench, accusing the seven majority judges, including Lord Keeper Finch, of having accepted bribes to pronounce ship money legal. Although Finch repudiated the charges with dignity, and asserted that he had interpreted the law faithfully as he understood it, he nevertheless fled (on December 22, 1640) to the

---

15. *The Subtler Language*, p. 49 and n. 3.

Netherlands. Meanwhile in the Commons Edward Hyde, future chancellor of Charles II, was the eloquent spokesman for a majority who demanded abolition of the prerogative courts. The possible relevance of these attacks to Denham's line 5 of *Coopers Hill* may be deduced from this analysis of the situation by a modern historian:

By accusing the judges, Parliament implied that it alone could decide the validity of laws: that Parliament, and not the King, was the fountain of justice. It followed logically from this that the prerogative courts must go; if the King was not, in his proper person, the fountain of justice, no court could function by his authority alone. The High Court of Parliament remained; it could indeed prosecute and try men — as it would shortly do Strafford — because it embodied the King's justice. King-in-Parliament was the source of law, not the King alone.[16]

As a barrister himself, Denham could scarcely fail to be alive to the sense of these attacks on the courts, nor could he easily write such a line as line 5 of *Coopers Hill* without awareness that his words willy-nilly embodied a doctrine hostile to that of the Parliament, identical with that of the King and his supporters. If Denham is to be found thus on the King's side earlier than either Falkland or Hyde, the fact is less surprising than it may seem. Because Denham's father, one of the barons of the King's Bench, had ruled with the minority in the ship-money case, it does not follow that either he or his son would welcome parliamentary attacks on the integrity of the court. The senior Denham had in fact ruled for the Crown in earlier litigation on ship money, and perhaps the fact that five members in all of the twelve-man court had ruled in favor of Hampden may indicate that none of the judges was bribed. When in February 1642 the leading minority judge, George Croke, died, Denham wrote an elegy praising him not for his staunchness on behalf of Hampden, but for his steadfastness during the recent "zealous" attacks on the court. To at-

16. C. V. Wedgwood, *The Great Rebellion: The King's Peace 1637–1641* (New York, 1956), p. 383.

tribute the rulings of the King's Bench judges to partisanship is misleading; twelve judges may very honestly divide seven to five on a disputed point of law, and the minority react with indignation to intemperate outside attacks on the majority, and on the integrity of the court itself. Certainly when the High Court of Parliament, which began proceedings against Strafford in November 1640, concluded by legislating his death in May 1641, Denham showed no sympathy with its pretensions or its acts in his poem "On Strafford's Tryal and Death."

With regard to line 5 of *Coopers Hill*, then, this much definite may be said: If Denham wrote the line with no external reference in mind, he must have been extraordinarily insensitive to events that his own and his father's profession would have induced him to be deeply concerned with, and which, moreover, two others of his poems show that he *was* concerned with. If, on the other hand, Denham wrote in awareness of the implications of his line, the fact would suggest two things, the first of which is in any event highly probable. They are: that *Coopers Hill* was first written at approximately the time of Strafford's trial, that is, from the winter of 1640–41 to mid-1641; and that Denham at the time was already committed, on some issues at least, to the King's side.

If a proroyal bias is hidden in the opening of Draft I of *Coopers Hill*, in line 5, a very explicit encomium of the King appears in the subsequent section on Windsor Castle (section 3 in the overall comparative analysis of the drafts). This long section (lines 27–118 in Draft I), one of the most stable sections throughout the successive revisions of the poem, is divisible into three subsections: the castle itself; its foundation and embellishment, especially by Edward III; and the establishment there of the Order of the Garter.

Windsor Castle, a warlike fortification settled securely on a femininely rounded hill, strikes the poet at once as a typification of the union of Mars and Venus, "Beauty with Strength." Here we see the peculiar quality of Denham's poetic vision beginning to work. Mars and Venus are less pagan deities than they are stock terms from the language of poetry; but the poet can manipulate even stock terms so as to produce fresh poetic meaning. It is the poet's eye that can look at the setting of Windsor Castle and see the presence of Mars and Venus, just as he can recognize Parnassus in Cooper's Hill, but what he sees must be found valid in the parallel realms of poetry and reality. Mars and Venus are not just an accidental or random conjunction: they are a god and goddess who in the well-known Homeric myth were adulterous lovers, but who were according to Hesiod husband and wife, and parents of the goddess Harmonia. The union of beauty and strength, warlikeness and amiability, produces harmony, so that what Denham sees at Windsor is a harmonious composition. Renaissance iconography had developed the custom of painting rulers and their consorts as Mars and Venus, betokening the harmony that resulted from their union, so that the *appearance* of conjoined Mars and Venus which Denham discerns in Windsor Castle is confirmed or reinforced by the *reality* that the castle is the residence of the king and queen, Charles and Henrietta Maria, England's royal Mars and Venus. But what the King and Queen represent conjointly, the harmony of warlikeness and love, is contained absolutely in the King himself, ultimately the realm's sole fountainhead of harmony. Windsor Castle therefore, in its setting, is his particular emblem, or one of his emblems:

Thy Masters Embleme in whose face I saw
A frendlike sweetnes & a Kinglike Awe
Where Majesty & love soe mixt appeare
Both gently kinde, both Royally Severe.

(I, 39–42)

Having entered upon the discussion of emblems, a hieroglyphic language analogous to the language of poetry, Denham is then able to call upon still a higher validation of his interpretations. The foundation of Windsor Castle, and its erection upon its particular hill, was no accident, but an apt and proper response to a correct reading of

185

one of God's hieroglyphics inscribed upon the expansed manuscript of his Book of Works:

Nature this Mount soe fitly did advaunce
Wee might conclude then nothinge is by Chance
Soe plac't as if shee did on purpose rayse
The Hill to Robbe the builder of his praise.

(I, 47–50)

The actual building of the castle was no more than the endorsement by an intelligent reader of a prepared document presented to him. And even that reader-builder himself was arranged for by Providence, so that the manmade Windsor Castle is not merely an emblem of the King, but as completely valid a divine hieroglyph as the hill on which it was built:

whosoere it was, Nature design'd
First a brave place, & then as brave a mynde.

(I, 67–68)

If the Mars and Venus balance of opposites evident in Windsor Castle is a visible emblem of Charles I, and if the castle itself on its hill is a divine hieroglyphic of harmony, the validation of the emblem by the hieroglyphic is still not quite established. Other kings have been masters of Windsor, not all of whom have been harmonious combinations of majesty and love. But Denham, viewing the castle, cannot but be struck by the crownlike round tower, which calls to mind not only King Arthur's Round Table legendarily associated with it, but especially the real builder or renovator of that tower, the King most closely associated with Windsor — Edward III. Windsor Castle certainly can justly be recognized as an expression of the person of Edward III — his creation — and therefore his own written hieroglyph. And four at least of the acts of Edward's reign prove upon inspection to be foreshadowings of the reign and person of Charles I.

First, Edward had united in England the crowns of France and Scotland. This he had accomplished by holding prisoner at the same time both King John of France and King David II of Scotland. In a happier sense the same effect had been accomplished in the reign of Charles I. Charles was the lineal descendant of the Scottish kings, and was in fact himself king of Scots. Queen Henrietta Maria, on the other hand, was a Bourbon, daughter of King Henri IV of France. The union that Edward had accomplished by bloodshed (Mars) had been more temperately accomplished by Charles through love (Venus).

Second, Edward had founded the Order of the Garter, and had made Windsor its seat. Two separate respectable traditions ascribed his motivation in so doing respectively to love and to victory. The whole matter of the founding of the Garter had recently been canvassed by Peter Heylyn, a man with whom Denham was to be associated in Royalist Oxford during the Civil War.[17] Heylyn had rejected the legend concerning the Countess of Salisbury's garter as a vain and idle romance, but his account gave countenance to both theories: that the device of the garter had been chosen because of some use as a token or password at the victory of Crécy; and that it was to be a symbol of the "fast tie of amitie and concord" among the Knights: "so by their Garter, as a bond of love and unitie, they might bee kept in minde to effect each other."[18] This balance of love (Venus) and victory (Mars) at the origin of the Garter is therefore another unconscious prediction of the Venus-Mars combination achieved by Charles I. Heylyn's book, in fact, in almost every detail anticipates Denham in *Coopers Hill*, and provides the most cogent and detailed commentary possible on this section of Denham's poem. The frontispiece of Heylyn's first edition (1631), for instance, con-

---

17. THE / HISTORIE / OF / That most famous Saint and Soldier / of *CHRIST IESUS*; / S^t. GEORGE / OF / CAPPADOCIA / *Asserted from the Fictions, of the middle / Ages of the* CHURCH; *and opposition, / of the present.* / The Institution of the most Noble ORDER of / S^t. *GEORGE,* named the GARTER. / . . . Printed for HENRY SEYLE . . . 1631. A *"second Edition, corrected and enlarged"* was published in 1633. It is impossible to escape the conviction that the "Garter" section of *Coopers Hill* arose out of Denham's reading of Heylyn's book. Heylyn became chief writer and editor of *Mercurius Aulicus*, the Royalist newssheet produced at Oxford during the Civil War. See p. 63, above, for discussion of the relevance of the April 1643 publication of Heylyn's *Theeves, Theeves* to solution of the problem of dating the 1643 Oxford issue of *Coopers Hill*.

18. *Historie of . . . St. George*, 2d ed., pp. 322, 323.

nects Edward III with Charles I through the Order of the Garter, displaying in one corner a portrait of the former king subscribed "Instituit EDWARDUS," and in the corner across from it one of Charles subscribed "Adornavit CAROLUS." The plate also illustrates Denham's line about Edward's wearing of "the Lillies," showing Edward's shield of the English leopards and France Ancient quarterly.[19] Charles's arms are also shown, displaying his "better Fate," Edward's arms quartered additionally with Scotland and Ireland.

Edward's third significant act was his choice as his own patron, patron of the Garter, and patron of England, of St. George of Cappadocia, "In whome the Martyre & the Souldier ioyne." Heylyn's title page had already described St. George as "That most famous Saint and Souldier." St. George therefore is a kind of christianized or baptized combination of Mars and Venus, and as such alone a prototype of Charles I. But Denham has no hesitation in asserting that in Charles's "Heroicke face I see the Saint / Better exprest then in the livelyest paint." This is slightly ambiguous; it is not entirely clear whether the saint Denham sees in the King's face is St. George — that is, the King is the liveliest possible portrait of that saint — or in fact St. Charles. Similarly in the next two lines,

That fortitude which made him famous heere,
That heavenly Piety which Saints him there,

(I, 115–116)

the application is equally to George and to Charles. But the next couplet restricts the application entirely to the King:

Whoe when this Order he forsakes may hee
Companion of that Sacred Order bee.

(I, 117–118)

"This Order" is both the Order of the Garter and what that order has come to represent: the earthly kingdom of England, the order of

---

19. "France Ancient" is the conventional heraldic term for the blazon: "A field azure, semé of fleurs-de-lys or." It is distinguished from "France Modern": "On a field azure, three fleurs-de-lys or."

man's own harmonious system, the order of this world. "That Sacred Order" is God's heavenly order, which is at the same time the order of the knights of sainthood, of which Charles is destined to become a companion, a fellow of St. George.

But the fourth of Edward's acts is the one that guarantees that Denham is not mistaken in his identification of Charles with St. George. That act was Edward's selection of an *emblem*, the device of the garter. An emblem exists within the proper realm of emblems, which is the same world as the world of poetic discourse. Edward's designation as the emblem of his order of the blue garter surrounding the red-cross shield of England (and St. George) was a direct prophecy of Charles I:

And when thou didst within the Azure Rounde,
(Who Evill thinkes may Evill him confound)
The English Armes incircle, thou didst seeme
But to foretell, & prophesie of him
Who has within that Azure Round confin'd,
Those Realmes which nature for their bounds design'd.

(1, 105–110)

In several ways Denham's wording here is not felicitous, but his intention is obvious. Under the Stuarts the union of the crowns of England and Scotland had made the encircling seas the only boundary of the kingdoms that shared the island of Great Britain. It is true also, as early readers of *Coopers Hill* recognized, that it was James I rather than Charles who had effected the union of the crowns.[20] In fact the conceit implicit in the circling seas had already

---

20. The scribe of Draft I MS EL 8899 so misrecognized the allusion, adding the shoulder note "K: James." Waller's *Upon His Majesties repairing of Pauls* unites both Stuarts:

the first Monarch of this happy Isle
Mov'd with the ruine of so brave a pile,
This work of cost and piety begun
To be accomplish't by his glorious Son.

It is curious that the first of these couplets should be the earliest echo of Waller's poem in *Coopers Hill*, being present even in Draft I (lines 59–60).

been exploited by Ben Jonson in his *Epigramme* "On the Union," directed to King James.[21] But Charles was the only one of the two Stuarts of England to whom "heavenly Piety" might be ascribed without seeming to provoke a thunderbolt from on high, and only he of the two had any pretense to being a soldier. James had loathed war, but Charles had even by the time of Draft I of *Coopers Hill* conducted his two abortive Bishops' Wars against the Scots. Only he, too, had taken a serious interest in the seas that bounded his realms. Although Englishmen might complain of their naval impotence which allowed Dutch and Spanish ships not merely to fight battles within English territorial waters, but to land men and fight skirmishes on English soil, Charles did exert himself, through ship money and other levies, to build up the English fleet. In 1637 he had added to his navy the great ship "Sovereign of the Seas," 254 feet long, armed with 144 guns; the name had been chosen by the Earl of Northumberland as a compliment to the King himself. That ship, like most deliberate creations of King Charles, existed in a state somewhere along the fluid boundary between reality and allegory. *Coopers Hill* exists in roughly the same state, but it is a poem, the creation of a poet, not a king, and therefore appropriately unfolds itself in symbols.

The royal citadel of Windsor is then, to him who reads aright, a hieroglyphic inscription conjointly inscribed by God and man upon the landscape of England, which is a page of God's Book of Works. In little it signifies much: it speaks of British imperial greatness, of the superiority of peace to strife, of the divine warrant of the British monarchy. It reveals the history of English kingship to have been in sum a preamble to and prediction of the potential harmony now within reach of actualization in the Stuart reign. Of greatest importance, it is an emblem of Charles I, bequeathed to him by his predecessors, particularly by his great prototype, Edward III, and authenticated to him by God. Conversely, Charles is a king who exemplifies

---

21. See p. 17, above, and "A" text, note to lines 130–134.

the meanings of his own emblem: in himself he combines the virtuous dyads, majesty and love, friendship and awesomeness, strength and beauty. He offers harmony to his people, he is himself a model of harmony. In contemplating Windsor Englishmen may contemplate their king. If they pattern themselves and their commonwealth on his example political harmony will ensue. Unless they follow his example harmony cannot ensue, for he is a living representative of what harmony is.

But the history of the English kings to whom Windsor had given a cradle or a tomb was not an unbroken display of harmoniously balanced opposites. One of the kings buried there is brought soon to Denham's mind when his eye has become satiated with Windsor. Although his "wonder" could remain fixed at Windsor, his less steady eye begins to stray, until its attention is caught by "an emulous hill" — St. Anne's Hill — eastward from his standpoint. St. Anne's Hill is emulous not merely in that it rises in rivalry to Windsor, or seeks to distract attention jealously from Windsor to itself, but in that it contains or represents qualities seemingly emulative of those of Windsor. If the towers of Windsor are like "the Towers which the holy temples grace / Of Cibele," that is, her turreted crown, in former days at least St. Anne's Hill was by "A Chappell crown'd." (The poet's viewing of the dissolution of Chertsey Abbey as a "storm," such as he prays will not fall on his own times, is another formal gesture toward the georgic motif of weather prognostication.) And whereas Windsor was crowned by a monarch, St. Anne's Hill was uncrowned by one.

Denham refrains from naming Henry VIII, but alludes to that king (who is entombed at Windsor) in several pointed ways. The enormity of the monasteries' having been destroyed by "any Christian King" calls to mind the style of "Most Christian King" traditionally held by the kings of France, but which Henry coveted and sought to have transferred from Louis XII to himself. Henry moved against the monasteries ostensibly because of their moral corruption, but, as Denham points out, the crimes of which the monks were accused were precisely those for which Henry was himself most notorious: luxury and lust. Had he been temperate he might with justice have attempted to curb luxury; had he been chaste, to curb lust. Being neither, he was also unjust in purporting to restore balance when he also was violating balance. The punctuation of the next line (Draft I, line 133) varies from exemplar to exemplar, so that it is difficult to be sure of the grammatical mood intended by Denham in the clause "Were these their Crimes" — interrogative or subjunctive. In either case he refrains from accepting Henry's charges against the monasteries as true. From Henry, at any rate, those charges are irrelevant, but Denham will offer some more judicious charges of his own against the former ecclesiastical establishment. Henry's real motivation, however, he asserts, was simple cupidity: "they alas were rich & he was poore," so that he "Condemne[d] their Luxury to feede his owne."

But the desolation on St. Anne's Hill which first moved Denham to his dismayed questioning he realizes can within its proper context be understood, and even Henry's despoliation be viewed with some degree of sympathy. Henry's attack on the monastic system, glossed over with "devotions name," was not entirely an act of bold and shocking hypocrisy; Henry, like every other criminal, needed to justify his act to himself. Every crime requires a colorable justification, and Henry had not far to seek to cover his. He had grasped some sense of the necessity for balancing opposites, but in the circumstances of his times he was tempted into making his balancing efforts a sort of parody of God's system: reciprocal alternations of extremes rather than temperate harmonizing of means. The king who wished to be known as "Most Christian" had "reformed" the church by ruining it, had rid the church of luxury by absorbing the means of luxury to himself. In his quest for the coveted title he had written a tract in defense of the unreformed sacramental system of the unreformed church, *Assertio Septem Sacramentorum adversus Martinum Lutherum*, for which he had been granted the still more grandiose title of "Defender of the Faith." The Latinity of his tract had been praised at Rome, and in thus exercising his pen Henry was playing part of the role of the ideal Renaissance prince: harmonizing the pen with the civil sword. But where Henry should have reconciled his antithetical instruments and made his sword and pen into mutual supports, he instead alternated their use. Instead of his pen's defense of the church being seconded by his sword, his sword replaced and confuted his pen. In the final couplet on Henry a number of ironies are compact:

Thus to the Ages past he makes amends,
Their charity destroyes their faith defends.

(I, 145–146)

The defender of faith is the destroyer of charity, disregardful of St. Paul's words: "though I have all faith, so that I could remove mountains, and have not charity, I am nothing." [22] In the most mundane sense of the word "charity," the Defender of the Faith in suppressing the monasteries destroyed all that existed in England up to that time of a public welfare system, a method of disbursing "charity" to the poor. Being himself "poor" he aggrandized all the national resources of charity to feed his own luxury. But also by destroying charity he destroyed his own defense of the faith against Martin Luther. For Luther, too, had deemphasized charity in preaching his doctrine of salvation by faith alone; Henry, the adversary of Luther, had himself become a kind of grossly distorted Lutheran.

The true faults of the church that Henry had destroyed were not those he had accused it of, but apathy, frigidity, idleness; its virtue was entirely fugitive and cloistered. It had been in fact, as Denham saw it, a distempered church, to which the post-Henrician state of religion in England was a reaction. One extreme breeds its opposite extreme until or unless a harmonious union of means can be achieved, and Denham compares the pre-Reformation with the pres-

---

22. I Corinthians 13:2.

ent church in England by a series of three similes: the block and the stork in Aesop's fable of the frogs who desired a king; the frigid and torrid zones of the globe; and the pathological medical states of lethargy and calenture. Medical health resides in a mean temperature, healthful and pleasing climate in a temperate zone between pole and tropics. Only as between the block king and the stork king does Denham fail in this passage to suggest a happy medium — perhaps because the whole preceding section of the poem, on Windsor, had been an elaboration on the characteristics of just such a king, all incarnate in Charles I.

Both Henry VIII and Charles I are associated with English church policy, and both, interestingly, as uniters of the antithetical Christian traditions of conservative Catholicism and innovating Protestantism. Henry had "balanced" the two as he had balanced his pen and his sword — by alternation. First he defended the traditional church with his pen, then extirpated it with his sword and replaced it by a form of Protestantism. By his actions he plunged the national religious body from a torpor into a fever. Charles, on the other hand, through Laud's ecclesiastical refinements, was seeking at one and the same time to preserve and defend "the true protestant religion" and to preserve and retain for the church the beauty of holiness in the decency and formality of ritual and observance handed down from the past.

In this section Denham, without explicitly naming either Charles or Archbishop Laud, and without expounding their church policy except by way of the rhetorical question, "Is there no temperate Region can be knowne?" nevertheless takes a firm stand with their party. He deplores the torpor of the medieval church, and sees in it grounds for Henry to deceive himself into attacking it: "And he might thinke it iust, the cause & time / Considered well." But Denham is also clear that contemporary fiery Puritanism, which opposed Charles's and Laud's policies as a return to Popery, is "a worse extreame." Therefore his remarks on the appearance of good which every crime requires as a condition for its committing have a contemporary as well as a historical force. If every crime must be cloaked in the appearance of good, an appearance of good will always be evident whenever a crime is being committed. Therefore the indication of an ostensible good as its end is no valid proof that any act is not a crime. Consequently, for instance, the cloaking of Puritan demands on either the king or the church in the language whether of "the ancient rights of Englishmen" or "a thorough godly reformation" should not deceive; in either case the acts contemplated or committed are criminal.

In the Draft I version of this sequence all specific naming is suppressed, as if to avoid exacerbation of sensibilities. Henry VIII is never named, although he is unambiguously labeled and described. Charles I is not named, and even in the preceding section on Windsor his religious policies are rather hinted at than stated; in this draft they are nowhere else in the poem emphasized. Similarly the Puritans are not named, even by way of the telltale word "zeal," the instances of which multiply in later drafts; in Draft I it occurs not at all. Nonetheless the transitional lines to the next section make explicit that in the desecrated St. Anne's Hill Denham sees an omen of a new religious despoliation now threatening:

Partinge from thence twixt Anger Shame & fearre
Those for what's past, & this for what's too neere . . .

(I, 161–162)

His anger and shame are for the ruin King Henry has brought to St. Anne's Chapel; his fear for the church ruin he feels is impending, which will not be wreaked by the King, for King Charles is seeking a temperate mean.[23]

Denham, standing atop Cooper's Hill, continues to be guided in his understanding by the wandering of his eye. To his left he had seen Windsor, and recognized it as a hieroglyph of balanced order; to his right the "emulous" St. Anne's Hill had unfolded to him a story

---

23. In the autumn of 1641, pursuant to Parliamentary ordinances, began the removal or obliteration of all "remnants of Popery" in parish churches — rapidly in Puritan districts, against recalcitrance in others.

of disharmony, of mismanaged extremes following cyclically upon each other. Now his eye leads his mind to contemplation of the Thames, flowing in its valley, past Windsor, Cooper's Hill, and St. Anne's Hill, hastening toward London and ultimately the sea. In his first attempt to decipher the hieroglyphic of the Thames Denham sees it as an emblem of mortal life, hastening to meet the sea of eternity. But if the river can be read as a symbol of mortal life it must therefore symbolize man's world of life, and the system by which opposites can be harmoniously balanced. Since man pursues his earthly ends always in states and commonwealths, the river can reveal something of what God has written in his Book of Works on the true nature of a commonwealth. Since a commonwealth based on the divine model, namely, a kingdom, should be summarized in its king, the river reveals also the qualities of a good king.

The wealth that Thames produces does not take the form of the guilty dross of gold such as that found in the fabled sands of the Tagus or the Pactolus, but rather is to be found on its shores. There are two ways in which Thames confers wealth on its shores, and in describing both ways Denham perceives the river's actions to be those of a good king. The first is by the fertilization, through annual and regular flooding, of the agricultural lands on its banks. In this flooding the Thames is moderate and predictable; it never by angry, unruly, or unexpected inundations destroys the wealth it has fostered: it is not a king of the type of Henry VIII. The second way is by providing an avenue of commerce and trade, both domestically within England and between England and the outside world, the Far East and the Far West. In this activity likewise the Thames is compared to a "wise king," and again, though without emphasis in the poem, its activity is contrary to the disruptive activity of Henry VIII. Whereas Henry had driven affairs belonging to man's proper province of harmonized means recklessly out into the harsh world of reciprocal justice by alternation of extremes, King Thames draws some of God's extremes inward to the happier sphere of harmony. An often-expressed corollary of the notion of opposites was that mutual extremes were ultimately identical (the life of unspending avarice is identical with that of penury). One favorite illustration of this thesis was the identity of extreme East and extreme West. A very well-known example of a conceit based on this occurs in Donne's "Hymne to God my God, in my Sicknesse":

As West and East
In all flatt Maps (and I am one) are one,
So death doth touch the Resurrection.

But these extremes are nonetheless reduced to means and harmonized in England by the shipping on the Thames. Other opposites are equally and creatively harmonized. Where God has allowed one extreme in one place to be offset by the contrary extreme in another, the Thames harmoniously equalizes conditions:

Findes wealth where tis, & gives it where it wants,
Citties in deserts, woods in Citties plants.

(I, 195–196)

With this last set of reconciliations may be compared King Henry's creation of a desert on the summit of St. Anne's Hill.

The Thames remains the most complex hieroglyphic within Denham's ken, and his difficulties in extracting fully and fully expressing its meanings remained one of the strongest motivations for his continuing revisions of the poem. The Thames sums up within itself the emblematic meanings of all the other hieroglyphics in the landscape that Denham attempts to interpret, and his struggles to explicate it completely reach at best a provisional final success. In Draft I he concludes his direct interrogation of the river, which he has seen as simultaneously the emblem of man's mortal life and the fullest emblem of harmony of opposites in the state and in the king, by invoking the power of the river as a Muse that should possess and be expressed in all poetry:

O could my lines fully & smoothly flow,
As thy pure flood: heaven should noe longer knowe

197

Her ould Eridanus, thy purer Streame,
Should bathe the God's & be the Poets Theame.

(I, 199–202)

Denham could not rest satisfied with this desperate formulation. In time, nevertheless, questing for the exact explication of the hieroglyphic meaning of the Thames which continued to elude him, he would attain the lines upon which his most lasting fame has been founded.

Following the line of the Thames westward through the landscape to Windsor Forest, Denham finds the river in its valley taking on a further, though not contradictory, hieroglyphical configuration. In the confrontation of the "horrid roughnes of the wood" and the "gentle Calmenes" of the water he recognizes a clear and simple emblem of *concors discordia*, the harmony of opposites. He treats this confrontation openly as a hieroglyphic, and his reading of it is explicit. The scene is pleasing to the eye because of its "variety," but if it is so, it is so because it is an outward and visible manifestation of the composition of the Cosmos itself by the harmonization of chaotic opposites. The universe is order, order is form, form beauty; in this beautiful scene the form and order of the universe are displayed. The meaning too is obvious; if all subsists by nature's uniting of discords, then a concordant state must be organized on similar principles — which happen to be the principles earlier seen displayed by King Charles at Windsor. The partly manmade emblem of Windsor is now seen to be wholly endorsed in its meanings and suggestions by the completely natural emblem of the Thames at Windsor Forest.

The combination of musical and material harmony at Windsor Forest may be, in an oblique way, a reference to the circumstances of the trial and execution of the Earl of Strafford. While to a certain extent the fact that the language used here is rather reminiscent of language used by Strafford in his own defense may be discounted, on the ground that both Denham and Strafford are appealing to a common body of notions and imagery, another factor connects the two more closely. On April 13, 1641, Strafford spoke for two hours in his own defense. The safety of the commonweal, he argued, depended neither on the destruction of the prerogative nor on the excessive use of it, but on the harmony and balance between the King's authority and the subject's liberty:

The prerogative of the Crown and the propriety of the subject have such mutual relations that this took protection from that, that foundation and nourishment from this; and as on the lute if anything be too high or too low wound up, you have lost the harmony, so here the excess of a prerogative is oppression, of a pretended liberty in the subject disorder and anarchy. The prerogative must be used as God doth his omnipotency, at extraordinary occasions; the laws . . . must have place at all other times, and yet there must be a prerogative if there must be extraordinary occasions.[24]

The special factor connecting this with *Coopers Hill* has to do with the fact that on May 2, 1641, in the atmosphere of royal gloom preceding the execution of Strafford, the King's daughter was nevertheless married to the son of the Prince of Orange. William Cartwright wrote a poem on the occasion, in which he sought to evoke a harmony from the circumambient anxiety and strife. His language reflects that of both Strafford and Denham:

Thus while cold things with hot did jar,
And dry with moist made mutual war,
Love from the Mass did leap;
And what was but an heap
Rude and ungathered, swift as thought was hurled
Into the Beauty of an Ordered World.[25]

---

24. Reproduced by Wedgwood, *The King's Peace*, pp. 414–415. Strafford's analysis of governmental harmony parallels that presented by Denham in *Coopers Hill*. The king's prerogative, for use like God's omnipotence on extraordinary occasions, allows the king excursions outside man's system of harmonized opposites without disaster — a privilege exclusively his. Strafford's defense of the prerogative may bear on Denham's line about kings' making courts, but it is the conclusion of *Coopers Hill* which seems especially to parallel Strafford's statements (see below, p. 209 and n. 32).

25. Cartwright's poem and the circumstances of its composition are noted by C. V. Wedgwood, *Poetry and Politics under the Stuarts* (Cambridge [England], 1960), p. 68.

The parallel of this to Denham's lines adds to the cumulative suggestions that *Coopers Hill* came to life first in Denham's mind during the crisis about Strafford.

What remained then to Denham, having conceived of the unity of this hieroglyph, was to dissect it, to see in what way its parts pertain to the political state. In attempting this he encountered another muddle of significances which he was never quite able, through successive revisions, to work out in a manner completely satisfactory. The images he evokes from the water of the stream and from the wooded hillside are lucid, but their meanings evasive.

What, for instance, is the significance of the fact that the clarity of the Thames will not reflect deceptive illusions? *Coopers Hill* is not a poem organized in such a manner as to encourage belief that the Narcissus image has no other function than to emphasize the naturalistic fact that the water of the river is very clear. Up to this point in the poem, the river has been treated as an emblem of life, of poetry, of the state, of harmonious kingship. Consequently one thinks at once of other images in seventeenth-century political poetry of the deceptiveness of reflections in water; for example, this from Dryden's *Astraea Redux*:

That sun, which we beheld with cozen'd eyes
Within the water, mov'd along the skies.

(lines 61–62)

Here the reference is unambiguously to true sovereignty, which Englishmen during the interregnum sought in false substitutes for God's true anointed, Charles II. Denham's Thames would not have permitted the sort of error Dryden refers to, permitting only a clear view of its bottom instead of the delusive and alluring surfaces that betrayed Narcissus and Parliamentary England. In Latin literature the *overflowing* of a river became something of a topos portending civil disorders; it reappears in the Renaissance and comes to be fully exploited later in *Coopers Hill*.[26] Here Denham may perhaps be credited

---

26. See Wasserman, *The Subtler Language*, p. 80 nn. 37, 38, and p. 81. See also the present discussion below, and n. 31.

with initiating an obverse topos which gained some later currency in the seventeenth century: the temperate and regular river as a symbol of the well-regulated state, or perhaps specifically, of the well-harmonized *kingdom*.[27]

Denham's isolation and examination of the other half of the harmony at Windsor Forest are even more unsatisfactory than the Narcissus image. The roughness of the hill conjures up the presence of Diana and Mars, counterpart deities in Renaissance iconography, and especially in later seventeenth-century political poetry: war and hunting are variant manifestations of the same impulse.[28] But here war / hunting is not counterpoised explicitly by any detail of the stream, nor, having been introduced, are Diana and Mars used to any obvious further end. True, this section is immediately followed by the description of a stag hunt, over which Diana may be presumed to preside, but she does not do so openly. The end of the poem, likewise, is filled with wars and rumors of wars, but it is only ex post facto that these can be retrospectively connected with Mars. The poem never really incorporates these figures, and it is not surprising that Denham in his ultimate revision excluded them.

Similarly it is hard to know what to make of the comparison of the hill to "our angry supercilious Lords." Who are these lords? They can hardly be meant to include either Charles I or the Earl of Strafford, and it is difficult, though not impossible, to imagine that by them Denham intends a reference to the Parliamentary leaders. One may perhaps conjecture in the simile a kind of reminiscence of the derogatory picture of Henry VIII derived from contemplation of St. Anne's Hill; perhaps Denham was thinking by anticipation of King John and his tyrannous predecessors. But what more than any-

---

27. See *ibid.*, p. 80 n. 37, and App. E, below. Some connection may also subsist between the visibility of the Thames's bottom in *Coopers Hill* and a couplet employed by Denham in his "Elegy on the Death of Judge Crooke," written in February 1642, or thereafter, and therefore certainly later than Draft I at least of *Coopers Hill*: "He was the first who happily did sound / Unfathomd Royalty and felt the Ground."

28. See Pope's *Windsor Forest*; Dryden's *Secular Masque*; *Paradise Lost*, XII, 24–61; also Wasserman, *The Subtler Language*, pp. 117–143, and Jay Arnold Levine, "John Dryden's Epistle to John Driden," *JEGP*, LXIII (1964), esp. 468–471.

thing else puzzles about this simile is that, while the "Lords" are viewed in anything but a flattering light, the hill to which they are compared is none other than Cooper's Hill itself.

Now by a piece of poetic legerdemain the scene of the poem shifts slightly. The contemplative segregation of hillside and stream at Windsor Forest has conceptually opened a gap between them, and the conceptual gap becomes now objectified merely by shifting attention slightly downstream from Windsor Forest. At the edge of Egham a grassy plain intervenes between Cooper's Hill and the Thames — Egham Mead, composed of the Long Meadow and Runnymede. And in the contemplation of this "firtile greene" Denham's peculiar poetic vision once more triumphantly asserts itself:

Where from the woods the Dryades oft meete
The Nayades, & with their nimble feete
Soft dances leade; although their Ayry Shape
All but a quicke poeticke sight escape.

(I, 231–234)

These lines make a statement about the nature of poetry consonant with the discussion of poetic inspiration in the invocation of Cooper's Hill as Parnassus. The naiads and the dryads are not mere figures from an outworn mythology, but a potential mode of discourse for realizing in language the relationship between water and woods; the harmonious balance of the constituents of the landscape, already spoken of in the terminology of musical harmony, can be represented as a "soft dance." It is the "quicke poeticke sight" that establishes the existence of the nymphs, just as it establishes the reality of Parnassus in the Thames Valley.

On Egham Mead herds of deer sometimes come to browse, and with the first consideration of the herds a new quality invests the language of the poem. Whereas hitherto it has dealt with details of the landscape present and visible to the poet's eye — Windsor, St. Anne's Hill, the Thames, Windsor Forest, Egham Mead — now it deals with temporal events, *sometimes* visible from Cooper's Hill, although not asserted to be taking place in the poem's present time. With the change in the status of the objects of description occurs a change in the language: events are not emblems or hieroglyphics inscribed in the landscape. Their meaning is of a different sort, for which an adequate terminology is lacking. The events are not allegorical, but quasi-allegorical: they parallel other events, or resemble other events in details, or obliquely refer to them. The transition from one kind of language to the other is made by means of an actual emblem, but one not physically present to the observer on Cooper's Hill. The antlers of the stags are

Natures greate Masterpeece to shew how soone
Greate things are made, but sooner farre undone.

(I, 241–242)

Like most of God's hieroglyphics, this one has a didactic intention, though its specific application in *Coopers Hill* may not be at all clear. Yet within the referential ambience of *Coopers Hill* a signal instance of greatness rapidly made but sooner far undone comes very readily to mind. In 1639 Thomas Wentworth, Viscount Wentworth, became the principal adviser of Charles I; in January 1640 he was created Earl of Strafford and lord lieutenant in Ireland; in May 1640 he offered to lead an Irish army on the King's behalf against the covenanting Scots, but Pym and the Parliamentary sympathizers with the Scots, recognizing Strafford as the one strong obstacle to their victory over the King's policies, set about to undermine his position; on September 13, 1640, in a splendid ceremony at York, Charles bestowed on Strafford the Order of the Garter; shortly thereafter Charles swore to Strafford, on the word of a king, that Strafford should not suffer in life or fortune from his Parliamentary enemies; in November 1640 the Commons moved to impeach Strafford and he was committed to the Tower; on March 22, 1641, his trial commenced in Westminster Hall, but Strafford's skillful defense reduced his opponents to abandon due process, and on May 9 a bill of attainder was presented to King Charles who, urged thereto by the casuistical sophistry of the Bishop of Lincoln and the politic advice of Strafford himself, signed the bill on the 10th, with tears in his eyes; on May 12, 1641, sixteen months after he had been created Earl and eight months almost to the day since he had been inducted companion of the Garter, Strafford was beheaded. Great men in Charles's reign soon were made, but sooner far undone.

Whatever the contemporary emblematic applicability of the stag's antlers, it is immediately after their mention that King Charles first appears in his proper person in *Coopers Hill*, although in less dismal circumstances than those in which he signed the bill for Strafford's death. At Egham Mead the poet has sometimes observed him:

Here have I seene our Charles (when greate affaires
Give leave to slacken & unbend his Cares)
Chasing the Royall Stagge . . .

(I, 243–245)

Each draft of *Coopers Hill* contains some version of the stag hunt, but in the Draft I version it extends over only thirty-eight lines (lines 243–280). There is little remarkable in the details of the hunt, but some observations about the stag may have tangential bearings on the world outside the poem:

He tryes his frends amongst the lesser heard,
Where he but lately was obey'd & fear'd:
Safety he seekes, the heard unkindly wise:
Or chases him from thence, or from him flyes;
(Like a declyning Statesman left forlorne
To his frinds pitty & pursuers scorne) . . .

(I, 251–256)

No forcing is required to see that the stag's situation at least parallels that of Strafford, with the exception that Strafford was not *like* a declining statesman; he *was* one. What is simile for the stag was actuality for the Earl. In fact the simile can be said to point directly at Strafford: the poem says in effect that the stag's fate was very like

Strafford's. And the final end of the stag is also very like that of Strafford:

As in a Calme the Oare-fynn'd Galleys creepe,
About a winde bound, & unweildy Shipp;
Which lyes unmov'd, but those that come too neere
Strikes with her thunder, & the rest with feare,
Till through her many leakes the Sea shee drinkes
Nor yealds at last but still resisting sinks:
So stands the stagg among the lesser hounds,
Repells their force & wounds returnes for wounds,
Till Charles from his unerring hand letts fly,
A mortall shaft, then glad & proud to die
By such a wound, he falls. . . .

(I, 269–279)

So Strafford for seven weeks fought off his accusers with a fortitude, patience, and ability that moved, alarmed, and dismayed them. But then at last he gracefully accepted death through Charles's assent to the bill of attainder: "To a willing man," he wrote to the King, "there is no injury done . . . to you I can give the life of this world with all the cheerfulness imaginable." [29]

Even if Denham incontestably does have the fall of Strafford in mind in his depiction of the stag hunt in *Coopers Hill*, there can be nothing of the "outrageous" in his characterization of the hunt as "a more Innocent & happie chase" (line 281) than the danger to which liberty was subject from tyranny before the signing of Magna Charta.[30] Whatever its tangential implications, a stag hunt is still a

---

29. Wasserman prints Strafford's letter to the King at greater length (*The Subtler Language*, p. 75). The suggestion that the stag hunt in *Coopers Hill* bears some relationship to the end of Strafford was first advanced by Wasserman, and remains convincing despite Wasserman's entanglement among the several drafts of the poem.

30. Ruth Nevo (*The Dial of Virtue* [Princeton, 1963], p. 36) finds necessary a defense of *Coopers Hill* from this charge by viewing the comparison between the situation prior to Magna Charta and "the most tragic *cause célèbre* of Charles's reign" as "the fruit of a considered historical judgment." But she is looking right through the surface of the stag hunt and seeing only what she accepts as its allegorical content.

stag hunt and so of much less consequence than the pursuit of liberty by tyranny. But though the poetic justification for considering Magna Charta in juxtaposition with the royal stag hunt is that the stag hunt takes place at Runnymede, "the selfe same place" at which Magna Charta was signed, on the referential level of the poem the two events are also connected. On May 12, 1641, the day of Strafford's death, the Commons authorized, as a deliberate celebration of that death, the publication of the late Sir Edward Coke's *Second Part of the Institutes of the Laws of England*, a work that had been forbidden publication by the King twelve years before. The *Second Part of the Institutes* contained chiefly Coke's commentary on Magna Charta, a particular application of the general terms of that charter to the instances of the present, defending common law against the royal prerogative.

Denham's attitude toward the circumstances under which Magna Charta was granted is equivocal, although his approval of the document itself marches level with his antipathy to tyranny. What disturbs him is that the charter was extorted from King John by "Armed Subiects," and approval of their action comes perilously close to approval of conceivable future armed action against the King. The latter possibility Denham abhors, so that he spends six lines trying to formulate his highly limited and conditioned acceptance of the barons' actions. Ultimately he canceled these lines in revision as a way of escaping the dilemma entirely.

Magna Charta as Denham sees it was not quite the revolutionary or antimonarchical document the triumphant Commons found in Coke's commentary, but an instrument of *concors discordia*, harmonious balance of mean opposites:

Tyrant, & Slave, those names of hate & feare,
The happier Stile of King, & Subiect beare.

(I, 295–296)

But the recent history of England revealed all too depressingly that the harmony promised in Magna Charta had not been realized. Although Denham nowhere considers the relationship between king

206

and subject in the reign of Edward III, one gathers from the Windsor Castle section of *Coopers Hill* that he was prepared to accept that reign as a harmonious one. But if from William I to John tyrannous kings had prevailed in England, certainly for a long time after Edward III a baronial anarchy had largely prevailed and replaced the tyranny. That period had been ended by the advent of the Tudors, and the St. Anne's Hill section of the poem had clearly presented Henry VIII as a tyrant. A certain pattern therefore has been observable in English history since Magna Charta: continued pressure from the armed subjects has successively weakened kings (as in the Wars of the Roses) until kings rebound with recovered strength (like that of Henry VIII). In the present time the pattern seems to be repeating: King Charles is being shorn of power by his persistent subjects, and he by yielding — as in acceding to Strafford's death, or to Pym's bill prohibiting the dissolution of the Parliament without its own consent, which he passed on the same day — seems to be conspiring with his enemies. But sooner or later, all should realize, he will rebound with terrible strength:

The Subiects Arm'd, the more theire princes gave,
But this advantage tooke the more to crave:
And as by giving the Kings power growes les,
So by receaving, their demands increase;
To limitt Regall greatnes all Conspire,
While each forgets to lymitt his desire,
Till kings (like ould Anteus) by their fall
Reinforc't, their courrage from dispaire recall.

(I, 299–306)

At this point in Draft I occurs a significant image which will recur in each later draft of *Coopers Hill*. The image of a river in flood, as has been remarked earlier, had attained some classical and Renaissance standing as a topos portending civil disorders.[31] But earlier in *Coopers Hill* Denham had established the calm and regular Thames

---

31. See Horace, *Odes* I.ii; Vergil, *Georgics* I, 481–483; Shakespeare, *Troilus and Cressida*, I, iii, 109–113; Bacon, "Of Vicissitude."

as a type of the orderly harmonious kingdom (or kingship) of England. Now he presents the picture of a calm river in flood — an image directly related to his former depiction of the Thames and probably suggested by the sight of the causeway that still protects the low-lying parts of Egham from the annual floods — as a parable of the history he has just been recounting:

When a Calme River rais'd with suddaine Raines,
Or Snowes dissolv'd, oreflowes the adioyning plaines;
The husbandmen with high rais'd banks secure
Their greedy hopes, & this hee can endure:
But if with Bays, & Dams they strive to force
His current to a new or narrow Course,
No longer then within his banks he dwells,
First to a torrent then a deluge swells:
Stronger & fercer by restraint he Roares,
And knowes no bound, but makes his power his shores.

(I, 307–316)

This passage is purely in the georgic tradition. It gives practical advice to husbandmen — the mower and the plowman of the Thames Valley — as to what is feasible and what is not in attempting to preserve crops from inundation. Defensive action against such a river as the Thames can be quite successful, but aggressive attempts to divert the river, to alter or narrow its channel, can result only in disaster. But, as in Vergil's *Georgics*, the real purport of the agrarian advice is political: the river is a type of the royal power. Self-protection against attempted kingly tyranny will be successful, as Magna Charta was successfully won from King John, perhaps even as some legitimate concessions have been drawn from King Charles. But attempts to subject royal power entirely to the popular will can lead only to devastating reaction, as the fifteenth-century anarchy had eventuated in the oppressive monarchy of King Henry.

The next eight lines of Draft I (lines 317–324) in effect repeat in a generalized way the history of political dialectic previously set forth, and make the direct application of the flooded-river image. The final four lines attempt to inculcate a lesson for the contemporary situation. In this the direct significance of the river image is precisely defined. The flowing waters of the river — its power — stand for the princely powers; its usual course or channel for the laws and customs by which temperate princely power is usually bounded. An overflowing river is therefore an excessive exercise of princely power beyond customary limits. In retrospect then the evenly flowing Thames can be seen as the type of Charles I's temperate kingship: any royal excess will be mild at worst, and can easily be guarded against and induced to return to its normal bounds. But attempts to coerce the king into following completely new courses, and to bind his power into new arbitrary limits, will result in his eventual overflow of all limits, and the exertion of his "boundles power" without restraint.[32] Denham's final word is an admonition to King Charles's turbulent and provocative subjects:

Therefore their boundles power lett princes draw
Within the Chanell & the shoares of Lawe:
And may that Law which teaches Kings to sway
Their Septers, teach their subjects to obey.

(I, 325–328)

It is rather amazing that critics of *Coopers Hill* ever since Gosse, including the intelligent ones, have come customarily to regard the "A" text of *Coopers Hill* as more "neutral" toward the issues of the impending civil war than is the "B" text. If anything, the reverse is true. Although Denham was not a rabid Royalist, who regarded the King's actions, in all respects and on all occasions, as necessarily and absolutely correct, Draft I is a poem extremely sympathetic to Charles I. It presents the King's policies, through the hieroglyphic of Windsor Castle, as the very essence and model of harmony, and as

---

32. The entire analysis of political harmony in the conclusion of *Coopers Hill* bears an obvious parallel to the analysis presented by Strafford in his defense speech. The special privilege on the king's side only of overflowing the bounds of law without necessarily creating universal disorder reflects Strafford's distinction of the royal prerogative for use on "extraordinary occasions."

the necessary issue of his own harmonious character and person. It assumes his residual powers to be limitless, and in no way complains at that assumption. It comes closest to criticizing the King in suggesting that he has been too pliable to demands made on him, and it glosses over his shameful part in the destruction of Strafford, which must nevertheless have been the most important incident precipitating Denham's composition of *Coopers Hill*. Draft I of *Coopers Hill* is a Royalist poem, drafts II and III were to become even more committedly Royalist. Only with Draft IV—the "B" text—in fact, does a quality resembling neutralism enter the poem, and for very sufficient reasons. This fact, if not the reasons for it, was fully appreciated by Joseph Spence, whose analysis of the revisions that converted the "A" text into the "B" later critics would have done well to pay more attention to. Among the lines already present in Draft I which were canceled during the final drastic revision of *Coopers Hill* are lines 287–292 (the lines on the dubious justification of armed opposition to princes); lines 303–306 (on the conspiracy to limit regal greatness and the predictable kingly reaction); and lines 325–328 (the admonitory conclusion). Spence does not mistake these for neutralist lines; on the contrary, he classifies all, with perfect accuracy, as "party lines omitted," that is, as lines compounded wholly of partisan Royalist sentiments.[33]

Draft I of *Coopers Hill*, then, in its 328 lines, having established Cooper's Hill as a fit standpoint from which to read the hieroglyphics expansed in the Thames Valley, proceeds at once to the analytical comparison of the meanings of the two neighboring hills, one on each side. Windsor reveals the nature of royal harmony and balance, St. Anne's Hill the nature of royal disharmony and unbalance. One hill is the emblem of Charles I, the other of Henry VIII. Henry's despoliation of the monasteries recalls to mind the present threat of despoliation of the church by contrary forces, the popular extreme reaction

---

33. Spence, *Observations, Anecdotes, and Characters*, ed. Osborn, I, 194–195, no. 454.

to such a royal extreme as Henry's. As the law of balanced opposites recognizes, the effects of one extreme are usually indistinguishable from those of its opposite. Averting his attention from the impending danger that St. Anne's Hill hints at, however, just as he had earlier hastily averted his attention from the distant cloud of London, the poet turns to examine the most enigmatic and densely meaningful hieroglyphic of the entire landscape, the Thames winding calmly past all three hills — Windsor, Cooper's, St. Anne's — on its way to London and the sea. Among the significances to be extracted from the Thames are its symbolizing of human life, of poetry, of an orderly commonweal, of a wise and temperate kingly power. At Windsor Forest the harmonious contrast of river and wooded hillside creates an image of the universal harmony, but the poet fails in his attempt to wrest from the scene all the significance he feels is there. Denham's confusion at this point is eloquent testimony to the fact that the emblematic "reading" of a landscape is not simply the self-deceptive imposition of preconceived ideas on the scene. The meanings that Denham is able to extract from this junction of wood and water are obscure and inconsistent, but he presents them as he finds them, although in later drafts of the poem he will make still further attempts at their decipherment.

In the course of his unsatisfactory struggle to read fully the emblem presented by the Thames at Windsor Forest, the poet allows his eye to drift downstream to Egham Mead. There the nature of his approach to the landscape alters. In retrospect the scene becomes peopled: first by classical mythological divinities created by the poetic eye out of the water and the woods; next by herds of deer; at last by King Charles, engaged in a stag hunt that bears several overtones reverbatory of the fall of the Earl of Strafford. When the hunt is concluded the scene is recognized as Runnymede, the place where King John was forced to grant Magna Charta to his subjects. But this leads to the reflection that Magna Charta did not bring, as it had promised, harmony between king and subjects. Subjects pressing for unlimited concessions from the king must in time expect a violent reaction, an inordinate reassertion of kingly power. The river, earlier seen as an emblem of harmony and temperate kingship, is now seen, under constraint, violently overflowing its banks. This violent reaction is typical of the way kingly power will behave when rash subjects attempt to constrain it beyond reason.

The lesson is obvious. Charles I is a model king, but his mildness should not mislead anyone into thinking that the kingship is an office without immense power — look at the devastation Henry VIII was able to effect. Charles has no intention of behaving like Henry, but if Pym, Haslerig, Hampden, Holles, and the rest think that Charles can be endlessly constrained with impunity they are vastly mistaken. They have gone too far, they will one day find, when they are overwhelmed in the royal deluge. Unprovoked, Charles will be restrained; to establish harmony in the kingdom what is required is for his subjects *to obey*.

Only perhaps because of Charles's ill success in the eventual civil war has there been difficulty in apprehending the final message of the "A" text of *Coopers Hill*. But hindsight should not be allowed to obscure the fact that *before* the civil war Denham could envision the outcome of armed conflict between the King and his subjects as total and devastating victory for the former, utter subjugation and defeat for the latter. What has been taken for "neutralism" in the early versions of the poem is only his warning to the King's opponents of the dire consequences that may be in store for them from an aroused and no longer self-restrained royal wrath, a tyranny the King might be forced into in response to his subjects' refusal to enter with him a modulated harmonious union.

THE "A" TEXT, DRAFT II

Although Draft II of *Coopers Hill* differs from Draft I in few essential ways, in one important particular at least its basic structure has been fundamentally altered. The first sixteen lines in each draft remain identical, but thereafter the configuration of the poem becomes quite different. Whereas the invocational opening of Draft I had in effect extended over the first twenty-six lines of the poem, in Draft II the invocation ends with line 16, and the next line begins what will in all subsequent drafts constitute a distinct second section of the poem.

Yet the wording of lines 17–18 in Draft II is only minimally different from the wording of the same lines in Draft I, the statement made is apparently identical. In both drafts the poet, from the summit of Cooper's Hill, asserts that he can look down on St. Paul's Cathedral as men from St. Paul's can look down upon London. But then follow six lines (19–24) without equivalent in Draft I, which totally requalify the reference to the cathedral. Denham appears certainly to have been acquainted with Waller's poem *Upon His Majesties repairing of Pauls* even before his composition of Draft I of *Coopers Hill,* but only in Draft II does Waller's poem significantly affect Denham's. Waller's poem had set a precedent for *Coopers Hill,* in that, whereas Denham had interpreted hieroglyphically such features of the landscape as Windsor Castle and St. Anne's Hill, Waller had previously interpreted the renovated St. Paul's as both an emblem of the "modesty, and greatnesse" of King Charles's mind — harmoniously combined opposite attributes such as Denham found at Windsor — and "an earnest of his grand designe / To frame no new Church, but the old refine."[34] This last contrasts markedly with the "storm" of Henry VIII, and the threatening Puritan storm that Denham feared, "where ruine must reforme."

When Denham revised *Coopers Hill* to make Draft II he reconsidered the relevance of *On the repairing of Pauls* to his own work, and the fruit of his reconsideration was an altered treatment of the presence of London in his poem. What had been a dark cloud from which the poet in his rustic retreat had hastily averted his attention

34. See App. B, below.

became instead an object of deliberate attention, with Waller's emblematized St. Paul's in its midst. The six lines on St. Paul's first introduced into Draft II are in that draft still detectably a separate insertion into the older fabric of the poem:

Pauls' the late theame of such a Muse whose flight
Hath bravely reacht & soar'd above thy height,
Now shalt thou stand, though time or sword or fire
Or zeale more feirce then they thy fall conspire,
Secure, while thee the best of Poetts sings
Preserv'd from ruine by the best of Kings.

(II, 19–24)

Time and *fire* had already attacked the cathedral, but as yet neither *sword* nor *zeal*. The last word, now first introduced into a text of *Coopers Hill*, was, of course, something of a shibboleth in the early seventeenth century. To Anglicans and Royalists the very word denoted Puritanism; in a less dire way everything that Denham dwells on in his contemplation of London was already summed up in the name of Ben Jonson's Zeal-of-the-Land Busy. Ben Jonson in fact is not distant from the inspiration of this passage: the formulas "best of Poets" and "best of Kings" had already been used by him in his *Epigramme* "To King James." And the Puritan threat to St. Paul's was real and active; the rebuilding of the cathedral was associated with the hated "Prelaty" of Archbishop Laud, and the King's enemies as well as his supporters interpreted Charles's activity on behalf of Paul's as an earnest of his ecclesiastical designs. Denham, therefore, by this addition to *Coopers Hill* is accepting Waller's emblematic interpretation of St. Paul's and incorporating it into the sequence of hieroglyphics he is attempting to read from the summit of Cooper's Hill.

Insertion of the allusion to Waller's emblematic poem required some slight adjustment of the ensuing lines. Whereas in Draft I the poet had been aware of the distant pall surrounding London and Paul's both, now from Cooper's Hill he sees first Paul's,

Then London where my eye, the place, the crowd
My minde surveyes wrapt in a thicker cloud
Of businesse then of smoake. . . .

(II, 25–27)

The eye/mind contrast, presented earlier in Draft I, is here postponed
to this point. These lines are somewhat elliptical, and slightly obscured
by the punctuation, but their sense is something like this: "Then London—where my eye [surveys] the place [wrapped in a cloud of
smoke]; my mind surveys the crowd wrapped in a thicker cloud of
business." Here Denham is once more insisting on the correlation
of what the mind apprehends with what the eye beholds. The cloud
of smoke surrounding London is in sober fact an emanation of the
cloud of busyness which surrounds the lives of the Londoners. Poetic
and physical perceptions are parallel, and in the final resort unitary.

Having engaged upon interpretation of the activities of the Londoners, Denham must now be more precise than he needed be in
merely alluding to them in Draft I. In that draft he had seen in the
City "men like Ants / Preying on others to supply their wants."
However depressing and distasteful this activity, it seems no more
than an unhappy necessity inherent in the nature of urban life. Upon
reconsideration, however, Denham finds that the "men like Ants /
Toyle to prevent imaginary wants"—their acts now are seen, not as
the products of necessity, but of sheer perversity. After the comment
on the uselessness of this toil, expressed in a couplet retained from
Draft I, Denham in Draft II proceeds to an eight-line catalogue of
self-defeating City activities, set off by universalizing similes expressive of the violated doctrine of *concors discordia*:

As food to unsound bodies, though it please
The appetite, feedes only the disease.
Where with like hast, though sev'rall wayes they run,
Some to undoe, & some to be undon.
Where Luxury & wealth like warre & peace
Are each the others ruine & increase:

215

As rivers lost in Seas, some secret vaine
Thence reconveyes, there to be lost againe.

(II, 31–38)

Only at this point in the new draft does Denham place the transitional couplet, which in Draft I had borne almost the entire significance of the brief allusion to London:

Oh happinesse of sweete retir'd content
To be at once secure & Innocent.

(II, 39–40)

The remodeled *Coopers Hill*, then, has broken up a former twenty-six line opening section, on Cooper's Hill and rural retirement, into two sections, so that for the first time the full eight-part structure of *Coopers Hill* becomes apparent. Section 1 is reduced to the sixteen lines invoking the auspicious qualities of Cooper's Hill; the remaining ten lines of the former opening are absorbed into the new section 2, on St. Paul's and London, which with the addition of fourteen new lines attains an independent length of twenty-four lines, almost as long as the former inclusive first section which has now been divided in two. But the rearrangement of lines and sections is of less significance than the substantial alteration made to the shape of the entire poem.

The view from Cooper's Hill in Draft I had chiefly included, besides the Thames Valley, two hills of opposite significance, Windsor and St. Anne's. Windsor, as the first examined, set the tone of equipoise with which St. Anne's Hill could be contrasted, and with which all other objects surveyed could be compared. In Draft II the key position is held by St. Paul's and London, and the grand tableau of the poem has become tripartite: St. Paul's-London; Windsor; St. Anne's. In one sense like a prologue or an overture, St. Paul's-London makes a preliminary statement of the themes of the two hills: St. Paul's the harmony of Windsor; London the destructive and vain vicissitudes of St. Anne's. In another sense it is coequal with the other hills: against the monarchical harmonious balance of Windsor are set on the one hand the *monarchic* extreme exemplified at St. Anne's Hill, on the other the *popular* extreme, equal and opposite, exemplified in London. But these separate senses of St. Paul's-London to some degree run counter to each other, and one of the problems confronting Denham in his future revisions of the poem will be the satisfactory accommodation of his afterthought to the overall structure of his poem. Nevertheless, the inclusion in *Coopers Hill* of London and St. Paul's on a hieroglyphical par with Windsor Castle and St. Anne's Hill must be recognized as belonging to a fairly early stage in the development of the poem — Draft II was very likely completed in 1641. The tripartite tableau has been a part of the structure of *Coopers Hill* in all the versions of the poem known ever since, except to an infinitesimal minority of readers.

Beyond whatever modulation or warping of the reader's apprehension results from the prior presentation of St. Paul's Cathedral and London, the next two sections of *Coopers Hill* — Windsor Castle, and St. Anne's Hill — are unaltered in Draft II from their condition in Draft I. Lines 27–118 of Draft I are retained intact as lines 41–132 of Draft II, and lines 119–160 become new lines 133–174. Only in section 5, on the Thames, does Draft II effect a few slight alterations from the text of Draft I. An inconsequential but grotesque eight-line simile in Draft I (lines 179–186) is replaced in Draft II by a somewhat more restrained, but still essentially inconsequential, four-line simile (lines 193–196). A few lines later Draft II introduces a new couplet in which Denham strains after a new significance for the Thames; he attempts to interpret the river as a kind of Noah's ark:

And on thy streames as many nations floate
As when mankinde all soiourn'd in one boate.

(II, 209–210)

But this reading of the river advances the development of *Coopers Hill* in no way, nor does it contribute anything of value to the hieroglyphic quality of the Thames. The couplet is best regarded as a will-

217

o'-the-wisp which tempted the poet into momentary aberrancy; it occurs only in Draft II, the later revisions returning it to the aboriginal darkness from whence it briefly arose.

The remaining three sections of *Coopers Hill* — on Windsor Forest; on Egham Mead, the hunt, and Magna Charta; and the conclusion — are identical in Draft II to their originals in Draft I (except that each line occurs relatively twelve lines later in the poem). Naturally the two drafts differ in their readings of a number of words, but the variants hardly affect the critical interpretations of the texts.

Overall, then, a critical reading of Draft II of *Coopers Hill* does not differ drastically from a critical reading of Draft I. But one radical structural difference does set the two drafts apart, to make the net reading of the second differ from that of the first. That is, Draft I contains two prominent emblematic loci, Windsor Castle and St. Anne's Hill, and Draft II contains three, London (with St. Paul's), Windsor Castle, and St. Anne's Hill. The Thames flows equally by all three places, and, as far as the Thames is the really dominant emblem of the poem, the slight amount of tampering to which its presentation is subjected affects its significance not in the least.

THE "A" TEXT, DRAFT III

Draft III of *Coopers Hill* appears to have been prepared deliberately for the press, for not only is it the first draft of the poem to be printed, but all evidence suggests that it never had any manuscript circulation. With Draft III, therefore, Denham was preparing to expose his poem to the judgment of the undifferentiated general public, and so could be expected to put on it the glossiest finish he was capable of. The revision that converted Draft II into Draft III was then a thorough one, and in many respects the resulting text of the poem is the most satisfactory and cohesive of all four drafts. Draft IV has its special moments of high particular beauty or felicity, but Draft III may well be on the whole a better poem.

The first marked difference between Draft III and Draft II occurs after only eight lines. Both texts share the opening direct invocation of Cooper's Hill as the poet's Parnassus, but thereafter alterations multiply. The rather prosaic and homely line 9 of Draft II is in effect replaced by three more adventurous lines in Draft III, in which Cooper's Hill is for the first time characterized as an "auspicious height," and the physical elevation of the hill equated with its advantages as an intellectual prospective point. By the elimination of the intervening six lines of georgic material on weather prognostication (II, 11–16), Draft III brings together into immediate sequence the section 1 remarks on the contest between the fancy and the eye and the initial statement of section 2 about looking down on Paul's. The structural effect of this elimination is to reduce the Draft III opening to a mere twelve lines, scarcely more than the actual invocation of Cooper's Hill.

Section 2, on Paul's and London, begins now with line 13, and the ensuing allusion to Waller's poem on the cathedral is introduced this time without the air of afterthought and digression it wears in Draft II. On the contrary, a very slight rewording of line 17 of Draft II ("Soe to this height exalted I looke downe) on its way to becoming line 13 of Draft III has the effect of making the introduction of St. Paul's seem part of the aboriginal intention of the poem:

Exalted to this height, I first looke downe
On *Pauls*, as men from thence upon the towne.

As a consequence of this, the Waller allusion — "*Pauls*, the late Theme of such a Muse . . ." — seems the most natural continuation in the world.

By an extremely adroit move, the six lines of georgic weather-prognosticating material which had been eliminated from the opening section of Draft III, instead of being dropped entirely, were transposed to section 2, following the remarks on St. Paul's. The effect of this transposition is to make the prediction or observation of storms irrelevant to St. Paul's, but immediately relevant to London, the discourse on which now follows directly upon the weather lines. The eye-mind contrast in the apprehension of London, by which the cloud of smoke over the city is seen as emblematic of the cloud of useless busyness over the Londoners, is thus assimilated to the georgic theme of weather forecasting. The cloud of busyness and smoke becomes also, therefore, a storm cloud, and Denham has managed at this point to fuse his particular emblematic mode of vision with the georgic tradition in which he also attempted to conduct his poem:

As those who rais'd in body, or in thought
Above the Earth, or the Aires middle Vault,
Behold how winds, and stormes, and Meteors grow,
How clouds condense to raine, congeale to snow,
And see the Thunder form'd, before it teare
The aire, secure from danger and from feare;
So rais'd above the tumult and the crowd
I see the City in a thicker cloud
Of businesse, then of smoake. . . .

(III, 21-29)

Twelve lines then follow, substantially identical with their predecessors of Draft II, on the self-defeating activities of the citizens. But these are followed by another six lines, on men making and unmaking plots, which are unique to Draft III. In fact only the first two of these lines mention plots, and the rest may be taken almost indifferently either as specific continuations of the lines on the plots, or as general continuations of the preceding catalogue of forms of futile busyness, violative of the proper harmony of opposites:

Some study plots, and some those plots t'undoe,
Others to make 'em, and undoe 'em too,
False to their hopes, affraid to be secure,
Thos mischiefes onely which they make, endure,
Blinded with light, and sicke of being well,
In tumults seeke their peace, their heaven in hell.

(III, 41-46)

220

Not to add to the mass of vain words written on these lines, the fact need only be noted that, if they have any topical bearing whatever, they may refer, like so much else in the "A" text of *Coopers Hill*, to events of about the time of Strafford's trial. During the proceedings against Strafford a number of men, including Denham's future associate, Ashburnham, indicated to the King their willingness to support him in a military counterstroke. Although no evidence connects Denham to this group, *Coopers Hill* indicates his sympathy with their aims. At the same time Harry Jermyn, the Queen's master of the horse, involved the poets Suckling and Davenant together with Colonel George Goring in a parallel plot. Goring lost his nerve and betrayed the plot to Pym. On May 5 the Parliament summoned the officers it believed implicated in Jermyn's plot—now known as the Army Plot—and most of them fled the country or went into hiding. Thus not only Goring but also his less treacherous fellow conspirators busied themselves as much in undoing their own plot as in making it. Further disclosures and treachery in June revealed the existence of the solider Royalist plot and forced the exile of its leader, Harry Percy, brother of the Earl of Northumberland. From a sober Royalist viewpoint, therefore, the Army Plot was utterly deplorable, especially as it weakened rather than strengthened the situation of the King. As for reasons why Denham should choose to drop these lines again in the course of making Draft IV ample numbers may be found. What is harder is to justify his inserting them into Draft III in the first place, since they had not formed part of the original conception of *Coopers Hill*, nor of the first extended contemplation of London, in Draft II. Perhaps the explanation is that now, with his full attention devoted to the examination of London and St. Paul's as an autonomous section of *Coopers Hill*, and having segregated within that section the treatment of St. Paul's from the treatment of the City, Denham was simply overeager for material with which to fill out the discussion.

One result of the rearrangement of the first two sections of *Coopers Hill* between Draft II and Draft III is that section 1 has been reduced to a bare twelve lines, against the sixteen of Draft II, and section 2 expanded to thirty-six lines in contrast with twenty-four in Draft II. Consequently section 3 of Draft III opens at line 49, eight later than the opening of the same section in Draft II. And section 2 is distinctly at home in Draft III, no longer the patched-in after-thought it seemed in Draft II.

The next two sections of the poem, on Windsor Castle and St. Anne's Hill, pass intact from Draft II into Draft III, just as they had passed intact from Draft I to Draft II. The fifth section, on the Thames, is also virtually unchanged. One alteration is the cancellation of the misconceived Noah's ark couplet which had first appeared only in Draft II (lines 209–210). Essentially in replacement of that couplet, but at a slightly earlier position, a new couplet appears, embodying more successfully what Denham had attempted to say about the universalizing capability of Thames shipping. The canceled couplet would have occurred between Draft III lines 218 and 219; the new couplet appears after line 214:

Rounds the whole Globe, and with his flying towers
Brings home to us, and makes both Indies ours.

(III, 215–216)

These lines accomplish what the earlier venture had not: they place the Thames, with its shipping, directly in the pattern of harmonious balancing of opposites that the neighboring images establish. The "flying towers" of the ships are a kind of oxymoron, yet they associate the ships with the crown of towers at Windsor; they are also something like the "Cities in Desarts, woods in Cities" of the preceding line. The return of both Indies — "of spice and mine" — to London is also both a commonplace conceit and a further instance of the harmonizing of extremes, East and West, at a middle point for virtue. In the next revision Denham retained this newly achieved couplet, although in Draft IV it suffers some displacement. In Draft III the net effect on the Thames section is to leave it the same length, forty-two lines, as in Draft II, but of a much comelier shape.

The next section of *Coopers Hill* — the sixth, on Windsor Forest — is substantially unaltered between Draft II and Draft III. Likewise unchanged are the first thirty-nine lines of the seventh section of the poem. These include the entire thirteen-line description of Egham Mead and the bulk of the narrative of the stag hunt — twenty-six of its thirty-eight lines. The most striking alteration occurs at the end of the hunt. There, in lines 281–292 of Draft II, the death of the stag was described, as it had been in Draft I, by the simile of a slowly sinking warship, fighting off to the last the creeping attacks of galleys. In Draft III that simile vanishes, to be replaced by one entirely different, although to a similar effect:

As some brave *Hero*, whom his baser foes
In troops surround, now these assaile, now those,
Though prodigall of life, disdaines to die
By vulgar hands, but if he can descry
Some Nobler foe's approach, to him he cals
And begs his fate, and then contented fals:
So the talle Stagge, amids the lesser hounds
Repels their force, and wounds returnes for wounds,
Till *Charles* from his unerring hand lets flie
A mortall shaft, then glad and proud to dye
By such a wound, he fals . . .

(III, 289–299)

The first six of these lines are new to Draft III, the remainder carried over from drafts I and II. Obviously the two sides of the simile are much more closely integrated here than they were when the stag was compared to a ship: in each case now it is a single sentient being that dies. Moreover, the hero falls by the hand of "Some Nobler foe," as the stag falls by the hand of the King, whereas the ship merely sank into the sea. But strangest of all, the stag's former somewhat hyperbolical pleasure and pride in his fatal wound is ratified by the simile, which insists that the hero requests his death and is contented to receive it. At the very minimum this simile serves as a reminder that a voluntary death is really possible. Exactly such a voluntary death at the hands of Charles had recently been sought by a hero beset by baser foes; during 1641 Strafford's letter to Charles on the bill of attainder against himself was widely circulated: "to set your Majesty's conscience at Liberty, I do most humbly beseech your Majesty, for prevention of evils, which may happen by your refusal,—to pass this Bill, and by this means to remove (praised be to God) I cannot say this accursed (but I confess, this unfortunate) thing forth of the way towards that blessed agreement, which God, I trust, shall ever establish between you and your subjects." Whatever Denham's implications in the stag hunt he described in drafts I and II, there can here be hardly any question that in Draft III he wishes it to point toward Strafford's death. The result is not to make the hunt an allegory—Charles, after all, did not hunt down the Earl as he did hunt down the poetic stag—but to set up within its discourse a constant system of allusions to Strafford, just as *Coopers Hill* as a whole sets up a constant system of allusions or references to contemporary religious and political affairs.

The alterations that Denham effected in the stag hunt for Draft III—that is, the substitution of the hero simile for the ship simile—should probably not be construed as an alteration of the significance of the episode. Most of the changes made between Draft II and Draft III, especially those toward the end of the poem, seem to have been made in the interest of clarity, to sharpen the reader's awareness of the significant implications. The stag hunt then is immediately a royal stag hunt—"a more Innocent, and happy chase" than the pursuit of liberty by tyranny in the time of King John, although happening "in the selfe-same place," Runnymede. But even to the extent that the larger setting of the two acts was England, and the more recent act the King's dooming of Strafford, the latter was "more Innocent" than the former because its intention was Strafford's intention, to reestablish a "blessed agreement" between the King and his subjects.

Denham's turning at that point to consider Magna Charta and its failure is therefore fully warranted: it was the failure of that first attempted settlement which created the necessity for the new settlement on behalf of which Strafford willingly sacrificed his life. The subsection of the poem on Magna Charta remains substantially the same in Draft III as it had been even in Draft I, but the one significant new addition is also by way of clarification. In Draft I Denham had already construed Magna Charta as a potential means of harmonizing the relationship between ruler and ruled so that the extremes of tyrant and slave are reduced to the means of king and subject. In Draft III he adds a couplet that makes not only this meaning, but the doctrine of *concors discordia*, explicit:

Happy when both to the same Center move;
When Kings give liberty, and Subjects love.

(III, 317–318)

These lines constitute a successful addition to the poem, which will survive into the final draft, as they also help to clarify the dialectics of alternation and vicissitude of tyranny and anarchy Denham expounds in the following section.

Near the beginning of the concluding section of *Coopers Hill* in Draft III Denham makes some final adjustments, involving in all eight lines of verse. One couplet of Draft II (lines 313–314) is canceled. It had stated succinctly a general law of unbalance: the first line had merely expressed the truism that the more a king concedes the weaker he becomes; the second line had made the slightly less obvious point that the receivers of concessions do not become satiated, but more demanding, with each access.[35] In Draft III this couplet is replaced by six lines which read like much more pointed advice to King Charles to refuse further concessions:

. . . Kings by giving, give themselves away,
And even that power, that should deny, betray.

---

35. This point was also made with direct contemporary reference by Dr. George Bates, *Elenchus Motuum Nuperorum in Anglia* (1685), p. 30: "[the King's] Concessions so far from satisfying [his opponents], increased onely their thirst, and made them insolent in demanding more."

"Who gives constrain'd, but his owne feare reviles,
"Not thank't, but scorned, nor are they gifts, but spoyles,
And they, whom no denyall can withstand,
Seeme but to aske, while they indeed command.[36]

(III, 323–328)

The reason for the quotation marks at lines 325 and 326 has never been discovered, but the marks occur not only in all three surviving printings of Draft III, but also in the printings of Draft IV, to which the lines also descended. The sentiments, however, are those of the Royalist ultras who began to gather around Charles in 1642 as the actual outbreak of war approached. Since Denham was probably preparing this draft in the summer of 1642 (it was first printed in the first week of August), and since in October he was appointed Royalist sheriff of Surrey, it is not difficult to imagine that these were sentiments he heard often expressed in the circles he must have been frequenting. This Royalist attitude was indeed never abandoned once the war came really to bloodshed, and in the end it became an ideological cage for the King in which he was still imprisoned when he was summoned to the scaffold.

The final twenty-six lines of *Coopers Hill*, Draft III, remain the same as the final twenty-six lines of Draft II, and their message remains the same. As civil war was actually erupting in England, Denham continued to warn his fellow subjects that they had provoked excessively their mild and moderate king. Royal power, he warned, in its occasional mild overflowings of the normal bounds of law is easily guarded against; but royal power provoked and rashly constrained beyond precedent is a terrible thing. In reaction it will sweep away all opposition and inundate the land with fierce and arbitrary

---

36. Two sentences from Wedgwood, *The King's Peace*, may serve as apt though unintentional commentary on these lines: "The monarchy, which had now for a hundred and fifty years remained stable against all shocks, had become so abject that the King had consented to the disgrace and death of ministers whom he trusted, to the reversal of his acts of justice and the destruction of his own power. Educated men could refer to history and note with interest or dismay that nothing like this had happened since the Wars of the Roses" (p. 454).

rule. That such is the nature of royal power is not the King's fault — Charles would much rather cooperate in harmony with his subjects — it is simply inherent in the natural laws of government. Therefore those who oppose and provoke the King are rash and evil; the only end they can promote is chaos, tyranny, and their own destruction. As the only way to avert calamity he prays them to abandon their reckless courses, and to follow in their own proper sphere the moderate example of King Charles in his:

And may that Law, which teaches Kings to sway
Their Scepters, teach their Subjects to obey.

(III, 353–354)

There is little to wonder at in the fact that despite the exigencies of the wartime press in Royalist Oxford, and the desperate scarcity of paper, the necessary effort was made to issue *Coopers Hill*, Draft III, from that capital in the spring of 1643.

THE "B" TEXT, DRAFT IV

The revision that altered Draft III of *Coopers Hill*, the only printed form of the "A" text, into Draft IV, or the "B" text, was undertaken under circumstances far different from those under which the poem was first conceived or the first two sets of revisions carried out. The revision itself was radical and massive; not a single section of the poem, not even a single subsection, remained unaltered and unaffected. To understand the revision, it is necessary to appreciate what the differences in the circumstances actually were.

Coopers Hill was first written, and drafts I to III successively issued, in a time reverberating with the echoes of Strafford's trial and death, and resonant with the bugle calls of impending civil war. Denham wrote as a Royalist, and his poem in effect predicted the ultimate victory of the King. But Draft IV was created in 1653 or 1654, after the Civil War, the Royalist defeat, the King's execution, and the legal abolition of the English monarchy. Denham himself had returned impoverished from exile to live as a pensioner of the Earl of Pembroke, one of the pillars of the new regime. *Coopers Hill* had been originally composed as a tract for the times, but the times had drastically changed. A pressing question indeed is why Denham revised the poem at all, and did not let it lie forgotten among the political ephemera of the beginning of the war; in Cowley's phrase, "Laurels for the vanquished" are absurd.

To this question answers are manifold. Although *Coopers Hill* may have been written as a tract for the times, it had also been intended as a statement of universal truths; and, though in its premature awards of laurels it had proved mistaken, the truths it expressed remained true and universal. So others besides Denham apparently felt, for *Coopers Hill* was not forgotten. By 1653 the "A" text had been printed three, or possibly four, times, and the poem was already celebrated. Herrick had published a poem dedicated "To M. Denham on his Prospective Poem"; Joshua Poole had probably already rifled it for his book of quotations; in 1654 William Godolphin at Oxford would plagiarize several sequences from *Coopers Hill*.[37] And Denham had both the artistic conscience and now, perforce, the leisure to make his poem into a fit monument for its own reputation, although part of its original *raison d'être* had dissolved.

Yet in revising *Coopers Hill* Denham needed to face certain realities which imposed conditions and stipulations on his re-creating of the poem. The first and most obvious of these was that he could not ignore the outcome of the Civil War. A second was that he must recognize that the trial and execution of Strafford was no longer a lively event in the public mind. A third was that extended encomia on Charles I were no longer timely. Here there was no necessary question of loyalty; even the most devoted Royalist could acknowledge that Charles I was no longer in control of anything in this world, and that consequently his emblematic example could have little but historical relevance. Almost a corollary of this fact is the need to sup-

---

37. See App. C, D, E, below.

press such overt expressions as "our Charles." Setting aside the present political inexpediency of such remarks, the fact remained that for even the most loyal monarchist "our Charles" was now the exiled Charles II, who had never hunted at Egham Mead.

A fifth condition that Denham had to keep in mind was a consequence of the first. A few months after Denham's return from exile in 1653 Oliver Cromwell had become lord protector of the Commonwealth. The Earl of Pembroke, with whom Denham was taking shelter when he worked on the revision of *Coopers Hill*, was a member of the Protector's Council of State. Regardless of Denham's private feelings, the Protector was as difficult to ignore as the loss of the Civil War. Many of Denham's Royalist contemporaries were already concluding that 'twas madness to resist or blame the force of angry Heaven's flame. Probably as early as 1653 Waller wrote his *Panegyric to my Lord Protector*, and the following year he published *Of a War with Spain, and Fight at Sea*, calling for the coronation of the Protector as king. Signs that Denham ever turned his coat are faint and indecisive; most likely he never went beyond the limited temporizing of everyone in England. It would nonetheless be strange if no sort of allusion whatsoever to the Lord Protector were to be found in the new *Coopers Hill*.

Structurally, the most instantly apparent difference between the new *Coopers Hill* and the old is the one that J. B., the editor of the 1655 first printing of the "B" text, pointed to. That is the vast expansion of the stag hunt in section 7 of the poem from the thirty-eight lines it had occupied in the "A" text to eighty-two lines — more than double its former length. Such a change cannot help but be reflected throughout the poem, especially since the overall length of the poem remained approximately the same. Expanding the share of one episode from about 10.7 percent of the text of the poem to about 22.9 percent can be accomplished only by reducing elsewhere, and in fact three whole sections and one additional subsection were heavily pruned in the revision. The alteration in the conclusion of the poem also readily strikes the eye of the beholder, but changes are all-pervasive, and even the larger ones must be approached in detail.

The opening of *Coopers Hill*, Draft IV, appears to be the opening of a poem very similar in structure to the *Coopers Hill* of Draft III, although a few small details serve notice that changes have been made. Line 1, for instance, has been rewritten, although it is rather difficult to be precise as to the merits of the rewriting. The "B" text even offers two versions of this line—the earlier in J. B.'s 1655 edition, the later in Denham's own 1668 version. The ultimate difference consists of the relative generalizing of the line: "there are Poets" instead of "we have poets." A similar change in line 3 alters the subjective and positive "therefore I suppose" to the more general and tentative "we therefore may suppose." But except as they set a tone of greater generality these two alterations scarcely affect the interpretation of the poem. And Draft IV, like Draft III, otherwise retains the twelve-line opening: the invocation of Cooper's Hill as Parnassus, and the statement of the greater boundlessness of the fancy than the eye positioned on its "auspicious height." It is in section 2, on Paul's and London, immediately following, that change on a large scale begins to be noticeable. The Draft III couplet about looking down on Paul's, a much-revised survivor from Draft I, is canceled outright and replaced by six lines in which Denham for the first time discourses independently of Waller's poem on the emblematic significance of the cathedral:

My eye, which swift as thought contracts the space
That lies between, and first salutes the place
Crown'd with that sacred pile, so vast, so high,
That whether 'tis a part of Earth, or sky,
Uncertain seems, and may be thought a proud
Aspiring mountain, or descending cloud . . .

(IV, 13–18)

Here the rivalry between mind and eye is for the moment reconciled. Whether or not Denham can actually see St. Paul's adequately from this distance is beside the point. For the first time in any version

230

of *Coopers Hill* the cathedral is also seen as a cloud (like London);
but if it is a cloud it is one descending — a condescension from
Heaven. If it is a mountain it is one aspiring — an attempt from earth
to reach Heaven. In either case the cathedral signifies an attempted
harmony between earth and Heaven, although it is in fact neither
cloud nor mountain. Yet it is the eye, not the fancy, that has so construed the building, performing an act that, when performed by the
mind, is emblemizing. The eye therefore is not deceived, since the
mind can extract meaning from both apparent illusions. These lines
are then fittingly concluded by the six-line allusion to Waller's poem
which first entered *Coopers Hill* in Draft II.

Perhaps because he had to some extent lost sight of the georgic
relevance of the next Draft III lines, on weather prognostication, or
because he felt their function was better performed by the dis-
covery of a "descending cloud" at St. Paul's, they are now all canceled, to be replaced by a couplet that associates city and cathedral
in a single view. This is followed by a revised version of the "crowd/
cloud" couplet, which has had a different form in every draft of
Coopers Hill, and then by another new couplet on the relationship
between the emblemizing, or emblem-interpreting, faculties of the
eye and of the mind:

Under his proud survey the City lies,
And like a mist beneath a hill doth rise;
Whose state and wealth the business and the crowd,
Seems at this distance but a darker cloud:
And is to him who rightly things esteems,
No other in effect than what it seems.

(IV, 25–30)

This passage has the effect, among others, of resolving the ambivalence of St. Paul's. For the purpose of further discourse it has been
definitively identified as a hill (mountain) rather than a cloud. As
such it can take its place more distinctly in the vast tableau of the
Thames Valley as one of the hills: not merely a locus coequal in sig-

231

nificance with St. Anne's Hill and Windsor, but as unequivocally a hill. As part of the same equalizing process, culminating what had begun fumblingly in Draft II, Denham has already specified that the hill of St. Paul's is "Crown'd with that sacred pile" (line 15). Each of three symbolic hills in Draft IV of *Coopers Hill*, for the first time, is carefully and explicitly provided with a crown. In his retirement at Wilton in 1653 Denham was apparently able to take a synoptic view of his twelve-year-old poem such as he had never been in a position to take before, and the results are apparent in the product.

The next six lines of the poem, on the self-confounding busyness of the Londoners, are retained relatively intact from Draft III, which had inherited them from Draft II. The following six-line excursus in Draft III, on plots and plotting, is, however, dropped. In 1653 the lines retained hardly any of the relevance they had had in 1641 or 1642, which even then was slight. By 1653 any plots being made or unmade were likely to be Royalist plots against the Protector, and Denham would have felt little compulsion to denounce them if he gave them any thought at all. Since by 1655 he began to be involved himself in such plots, it may have been a wise prescience that advised him to drop these lines, although indeed they were at best excrescent. Certainly they can hardly be regarded as expressive of a general truth, and on that ground alone would have been liable for excision from Draft IV.

Like a faint reminiscence of unsophisticated youth the end of section 2 of the "B" text retains the couplet on the happiness of sweet retired contentment, which had first served a quite different purpose in Draft I.

This section, then, on St. Paul's and London, although shorter in length than the equivalent section of Draft III (twenty-six as against thirty-six lines) is much more fully developed and organized. The cathedral has become one of the sequence of hills examined in turn in the poem and visually connected by the flowing of the Thames. As such it is recognized to be the hieroglyphic of an attempt harmoniously to unite Heaven and earth. Despite the Civil War (and even despite the desecrations chronicled by Dugdale and others), the renovated cathedral still stood and was still preserved in Waller's poem. It is also an emblem of religious harmonizing attempted by a king, and so, by anticipation, a contrast with the religious dis-harmonizing effected by Henry VIII at St. Anne's. It is also, how-ever, now surrounded by a low mist rising up — the Puritan zealotry that wished to obliterate it entirely; the City mercantilism that did obliterate the King.

Section 3 opens with the Mars and Venus couplet unchanged, for, although the royal iconography can no longer apply, the castle on the hill still displays the chorographic unity of beauty with strength. The next eight lines, however (III, 51–58), are condensed into and replaced by four (IV, 41–44). Chiefly eliminated is the simile of the hill as a pregnant woman. The result is to sharpen recognition of Windsor as an example of harmonized opposites: "such a Rise, as doth at once invite/A pleasure, and a reverence from the sight." The next four lines are also condensed into two. Both texts recognize Windsor Castle as an emblem of its master, Charles I. But where the "A" text had dwelt for three lines upon the opposites harmoniously combined in the person of the King, the "B" text curtly, and in the preterite tense, states the relevance of the emblem to the King in a single line that closes the couplet opened by the announcement of the emblem:

Thy mighty Masters Embleme, in whose face
Sate meekness, heightned with Majestick Grace.[38]

(IV, 47–48)

The next twelve lines are fundamentally the same in both texts, but so rewritten for Draft IV that although the rhyming words are changed for only one couplet, in others ostensibly identical words

---

38. The "A" text had employed a preterite verb also, but to quite other effect: "I *saw*" (sweetness and awe) refers only to the time of the seeing; in the King's face majesty and love "appear" in 1641–42.

233

assume quite different syntactical functions. One important change is the specification that Windsor Castle *crowns* its hill, formerly only implied:

A Crown of such Majestick towrs doth Grace
The Gods great Mother . . .

(IV, 59–60)

Taken all in all, this new subsection describing the castle as an emblem of the King's harmony occupies twenty-six lines of the poem as against thirty-two in the "A" text, but the reduction is almost entirely a matter of greater succinctness and increased generality.

The subsequent subsection, on Edward III, is likewise altered in the direction of succinctness. The first thirteen lines of the sequence remain unaltered, but the remaining seven lines are much improved, weeded of verbiage, and condensed into five. And the last subsection, on the Order of the Garter, has been revised in a similar manner.

The first four lines on the Garter, somewhat rewritten, are retained from Draft III to Draft IV. The next couplet, however, was canceled. This had remarked on the ornaments afforded to the order by "The King, the Cause, the Patron, and the place." In 1653 the Garter had been discontinued, there was no king, St. George was discredited, and Windsor Castle was falling into disrepair. The following fourteen lines, however, on Edward III as a prototype of both Charles I and Henrietta Maria, are allowed to stand, although one might question the continued appropriateness of referring to that couple's "better Fate" (line 95). Four lines thereafter, however, on potential conquests that Edward never made, are properly dropped. Then eight lines, on Edward's prophetic selection of St. George as patron, and his choice of the device of the Garter — both adumbrations of Charles I — are compressed into six:

When he that Patron chose, in whom are joyn'd
Souldier and Martyr, and his arms confin'd
Within the Azure Circle, he did seem
But to foretell, and prophesie of him,

234

Who to his Realme that Azure round hath joyn'd,
Which Nature for their bound at first design'd.

(IV, 101–106)

This is much improved over the "A" text original, eliminating repetitions, and above all making at last a kind of consistent sense out of the relationship of the King to the sea. But the ironies of fate had made Edward's prophecy even more exact than Denham had originally imagined. After an intervening couplet (which is retained in the "B" text), Denham had spent six lines in the "A" text trying to demonstrate the parallels between King Charles and St. George. The developments of history since 1642 now spared him the effort and allowed him to state in a single pithy couplet what had become already established in the English popular mind:

Nor doth he need those Emblemes which we paint,
But is himself the Souldier and the Saint.

(IV, 109–110)

The nominal leader of armies engaged in active warfare for more than four years had culminated his soldiership in January 1649, when he laid down his corruptible crown to become St. Charles the Martyr. Not merely Heylyn's formula of "Soldier and Saint" for St. George, but Denham's own formula of "Soldier and Martyr" fitted King Charles with awful exactitude.

The pruning of this last subsection reduced its length from forty to twenty-eight lines, and the whole section on Windsor in the "B" text was reduced to seventy-two lines in place of ninety-two in the "A" text. The references were all, or almost all, either brought up to date or universalized and made atemporal, but essentially the meaning of the section remained the same. In contrast with the crowned hill of St. Paul's, representing royal religious harmony threatened by the popular "mist," the crowned hill of Windsor represented unthreatened royal harmony. Its presentation is largely political, but the reminder that the King is also a saint connects back to the religious significance of St. Paul's. The fact that the saintly King is also a soldier betokens a harmonious balance of the two sides of his nature, and points forward by implication to St. Anne's Hill, where King Henry demonstrated how the military and religious aspects of a king can be dissevered and work at cross-purposes, when they do not indeed unite in destruction.

The opening of section 4, on St. Anne's Hill, was also radically changed by the "B" text revision. Seven lines by one means and another were reduced to three. Chiefly a rather flaccid transitional simile was eliminated, and the switch from consideration of Windsor to consideration of St. Anne's Hill made with a minimum of wasted motion:

Here should my wonder dwell, & here my praise,
But my fixt thoughts my wandring eye betrays,
Viewing a neighbouring hill . . .

(IV, 111–113)

St. Anne's is no longer characterized as an "emulous" hill, and here, consistently with the way the examination of St. Paul's had been conducted, it is the poet's eye, moving over the expansed hieroglyphs, which leads the movement of his mind.

Except for minor verbal changes, some clear improvements and some merely variants, the next thirteen lines remain the same between Draft III and Draft IV. The next four lines of Draft III are successfully compressed into a couplet. What is lost in the compression is the suggestion that Henry VIII might have had some basis for self-deception in cloaking his desecration of the church with the language of reform. In general the "B" text tends to eliminate all the faint half-excuses for ill acts which had been reluctantly conceded in the "A" text, and Henry's despoliation, though commented on in a statement of universal rather than particular applicability, becomes finally characterized as one of brazen hypocrisy:

No Crime so bold, but would be understood
A real, or at least a seeming good.

(IV, 127–128)

Denham at this point, however, indulges in a further generality occupying two of the lines he has saved, as a transition to his revised
formulation of the discordance between Henry's pen and his sword:

Who fears not to do ill, yet fears the Name,
And free from Conscience, is a slave to Fame.

(IV, 129–130)

This generalization is a prelude to the specific formulation of the
paradox of Henry's acts. Of the four lines devoted to it in the "A"
text, the first two, on the contrast between Henry's "learned Pen"
and his "much more learned sword," are replaced by a wittier couplet.
Here Denham plays on the two meanings of the word "style": a
pen, and a *title*. Primarily, therefore, he is concentrating in the one
word references to the pen with which Henry wrote *Assertio Septem
Sacramentorum* and to the title "Defender of the Faith" he won from
Pope Leo X as a reward for the book. The second couplet remained
unchanged:

Thus he the Church at once protects, & spoils:
But Princes swords are sharper than their stiles.
And thus to th'ages past he makes amends,
Their Charity destroys, their Faith defends.

(IV, 131–134)

Even in these lines the generalizing typical of the "B" text is
evident: the second line is less a specific remark about Henry VIII
than a generalization about princes for which Henry furnishes only
one out of any number of possible examples. But further consideration of the first couplet prompts other thoughts. If Denham were
eager to pun at the expense of Henry VIII, would he not have
done better to write "Thus he the Church at once *defends*, & spoils"?
True, this would leave a repetition of "defends" in line 134, but Denham often repeats key words. And certainly the wordplay on Henry's
"stile" would have been very much more pointed.

But Denham wrote what he wrote, and "the cause, and time /
Considered well" suggest he may have had another motive for doing

so. On December 16, 1653, the *Instrument of Government* was promulgated, establishing the Protectorate by which Oliver Cromwell, thitherto "Captain-General of the forces," ruled King Charles's former realms from the empty seat of the English kings. The first article of the *Instrument* is worth considering by Denham's reader (italics added): "I. That the supreme legislative authority of the Commonwealth of England, Scotland, and Ireland, and the dominions thereunto belonging, shall be and reside in one person, and the people assembled in Parliament: the *style* of which person shall be the Lord *Protector* of the Commonwealth of England, Scotland, and Ireland." [39] Of perhaps slightly less relevance is the specific provision in Article XXXVII "That such as profess faith in God by Jesus Christ . . . shall be *protected* in, the profession of the faith and exercise of their religion."

To see Denham as thus attributing to Cromwell the same sort of gross religious hypocrisy he finds in Henry VIII requires some sort of explanation and defense. Whether Denham is to be construed as intransigent or merely sardonic, some justification for either attitude can be found in the circumstances of Cromwell's rule. For one thing, the guarantee of protection in Article XXXVII of the *Instrument* for "such as profess faith in God by Jesus Christ" specifically excepts all those who do so under the forms of "Popery or Prelacy," intending by the latter the Anglican establishment for which the Cavaliers had fought. For another, Denham seems to have had his eye in 1653 on the desecration of other churches than St. Anne's Chapel. The lines on princely hypocrisy are followed by fourteen lines retained intact from the "A" text on the medieval lethargy of the church, in contrast with the modern calenture. But in the "B" text these are followed by eight new lines, of strikingly little relevance to Henry VIII or St. Anne's Hill:

39. Reproduced in S. R. Gardiner, *The Constitutional Documents of the Puritan Revolution 1625–1660* (3d ed.; Oxford, 1906), p. 405.

Who sees these dismal heaps, but would demand
What barbarous Invader sackt the land?
But when he hears, no Goth, no Turk did bring
This desolation, but a Christian King;
When nothing, but the Name of Zeal, appears
'Twixt our best actions and the worst of theirs,
What does he think our Sacriledge would spare,
When such th'effects of our devotions are?

(IV, 149–156)

England no doubt contained many ecclesiastical ruins as a result of Henry VIII's seizure and suppression of the monasteries, but by 1653 it contained many fresher churchly ruins as well. To the depredations of a "Christian King" had been added many more, committed more recently in "the Name of Zeal." The shibboleth word "zeal," first included in Draft II of *Coopers Hill*, occurs earlier in the "B" text in conjunction with St. Paul's. There it refers to Puritan fanaticism. And Puritan fanaticism had indeed desecrated and destroyed many churches throughout England during and after the Civil War. Iconoclasts had zealously "rattled down" the centuries-old, stained-glass windows of Canterbury; they had confiscated church ornaments and plate and jewelry from altar services; they had rifled and defaced tombs; they had shattered altars and statuary; they had stripped the lead from roofs for bullets. Even St. Paul's, which Denham continued to regard as "preserved," had been converted into a cavalry depot and sawpits had been dug in the floors for sawing up the scaffolding used in King Charles's renovation. Catalogues of these desecrations abound in Royalist complaints and elegies of the period, and they continued to be instanced long after the Restoration. Bishop Henry King, for instance, in a long rambling *Elegy Upon the most Incomparable K. Charls the I*, expends dozens of lines upon description of the Puritan pillaging of English churches, which he compares freely with the historical activities of all the noted heretics, persecutors, and vandals who at

239

various times have harassed the Church. In what became stock terminology he wrote:

Your over-active Zelots so promote,
That neither Tomb nor Temple could escape
Nor Dead nor Living your Licentious Rape.

This language was not foreign to Denham, and closely resembles
that of his addition to the "B" text of *Coopers Hill*, ostensibly inspired by the contemplation of the ruined chapel on top of St.
Anne's Hill.

St. Anne's Hill, unlike St. Paul's and Windsor, has been deprived
of its crown, the chapel. Uncrowning had by 1653, however, an
immediate political and religious relevance as well as a symbolic
significance. When Denham carefully emphasizes the crowns worn
by his first two hills, therefore — for the first time in this "B" text —
he thereby emphasizes the contrast with St. Anne's. It allows him to
compound into one terrible image of disharmony and violent alternation of opposites the despoliation of the church carried out by Henry
VIII and that carried out in the name of zeal by his antimonarchist
Puritan successors. Henry's monarchic tyranny becomes identified
with its extreme opposite, and so in its ultimate paradoxical effect,
a blow not only against harmony but against monarchy as well.
By reverse implication, therefore, Denham once again identifies
harmony with regulated monarchy.

The next section of *Coopers Hill* — the fifth, on the Thames —
despite many internal changes is not greatly different in essence in
Draft IV from what it had been in Draft III. The first eighteen
lines of the "A" text version are converted into twenty lines in the
"B" text by the dropping of one couplet and the addition of two,
but the changes thereby effected are stylistic rather than notional.
The replacement of the next twelve lines by six, however, involves the
cancellation of one of the two former "king" similes ("As a wise
King . . .") which may be felt, especially since the retained "king"
simile is a negative one, effectively to obliterate the identification

of the Thames with the kingly power in the state. Since the kingly power in England had been obliterated by the act of 1649 abolishing the monarchy, and since the new conclusion of *Coopers Hill* seems to reflect the destruction of the kingship, perhaps the obliteration here is a considered one. Further changes, however, involving the next six lines, though complicated appear to be essentially stylistic.

A major change in the "Thames" section cannot be ignored, however, whatever its significance. The "A" text had contained four lines (219–222) invoking the Thames as a model for the poet's verses and promising immortal fame as a reward. In J. B.'s 1655 edition of the "B" text these lines had been replaced by the two "Thames couplets" which later became so celebrated, and in Denham's 1668 reissue of *Coopers Hill* the replacement was effected by eight lines in all (IV, 189–196). Thereafter Denham preceded the "Thames couplets" by a further six-line addition, essentially expanding and universalizing the celebration of the river as a medium for commerce. Since Dryden published his challenge to discover the reason for the sweetness of the "deep yet clear" couplet many attempts at its metrical and ideational analysis have been made, the most recent by Wasserman (*The Subtler Language*, pp. 82–85). Of present concern, however, is the significance of these lines in the full meaning of the poem. Since Draft I Denham had been striving to formulate the hieroglyphic meaning he senses in the stream, and if he has not now achieved that goal he has at least accomplished a formulation so memorable as to impress itself on the interpretation of *Coopers Hill*:

O could I flow like thee, and make thy stream
My great example, as it is my theme!
Though deep, yet clear, though gentle, yet not dull,
Strong without rage, without ore-flowing full.

(IV, 189–192)

Since the river can no longer convincingly be regarded as an emblem of the specifically kingly power (which has been abolished in England and deleted from the poem), it must be an emblem of something somewhat different.

At first that something might be construed as harmony — *concors discordia*, the equable balance of opposites. But further consideration reveals that it must be something else: harmonious *power* — the power in the state (or in the universe), whatever its particular locus, which guarantees our peace, happiness, and prosperity as long as it remains within bounds, but which can destroy us if it runs wildly over its banks.

The sixth section of *Coopers Hill*, on Windsor Forest, begins in the "B" text with what appears as an anomaly — twenty lines of verse carried over almost unaltered from the "A" text. It is the longest single sequence of verses to be unaffected by the great revision. These twenty lines present an anomaly of another sort as well, however. They are the lines that present the vision of contrast between the gentle stream and the wooded hillside as an emblem of the harmony of balanced opposites. If the newly added "Thames couplets" in the preceding section be regarded as also emblematic of harmony, the consequence is not merely an impression that Denham is repeating himself, presenting in succession two separate emblems of harmony, but also that he is contradicting himself or at least shifting his symbolic terms. For in the earlier image the water of the stream had alone constituted the emblem, and now the water is but half an emblem composed of the confrontation of water and hill.[40] But if the water emblem is regarded in its separate appearance as signifying power rather than harmony, as has been proposed above, the anomaly vanishes.

In the remainder of the "Windsor Forest" section the clumsy and inexplicable images of the "A" text are now deleted. Diana and Mars, whose presence had never been assimilated into the development of the poem, are both excluded, together with the puzzling compari-

---

40. Wasserman complains of "an abrupt and apparently unmotivated redefinition of the images" at this point of the poem (*The Subtler Language*, p. 70).

son of Cooper's Hill with "our surly supercilious Lords." Instead the
mountain is presented in a much more favorable light, though still
as the emblem of political lordliness; perhaps the remarks are a
tribute to the sufferings of Charles I, although they could as well
be applied, by anyone who cared to do so, to the situation of Oliver
Cromwell:

But his proud head the aery Mountain hides
Among the Clouds; his shoulders, and his sides
A shady mantle cloaths; his curled brows
Frown on the gentle stream, which calmly flows,
While winds and storms his lofty forehead beat:
The common fate of all that's high or great.

(IV, 217–222)

The following section of the poem, "Egham Mead," is immediately connected to the foregoing, in an emblematic development
of the scene of harmony presented at Windsor Forest. Here the
meadow between hill and stream becomes the arena of their composed opposition, while the presentation of the hill as ruler and the
stream as power confers on the meadow the status of a political
emblem, the middle ground upon which civic prosperity flourishes:

Low at his foot a spacious plain is plac't,
Between the mountain and the stream embrac't:
Which shade and shelter from the Hill derives,
While the kind river wealth and beauty gives;
And in the mixture of all these appears
Variety, which all the rest indears.[41]

(IV, 223–228)

This section has no real equivalent in the "A" text, but in his alteration of four lines of the "A" text (lines 251–254) into the next six
lines of the "B" (lines 223–228) Denham has made, one cannot escape
feeling, an artistic mistake. Perhaps he might have legitimately de-

---

41. "Variety": see "B" text, note to line 228, for the use of this word to signify "contrast."

sired to rid his poem of the dryads and naiads with which he had formerly personified the woods and stream and incidentally explained something of his mode of poetic vision in creating *Coopers Hill*, but he has lost that and gained nothing discernible in return by the six lines he has substituted. The new lines in fact are tautological and silly, insisting ultimately only that Egham Mead still looks the same as it would have looked in the past to "some bold Greek, or Brittish Bard," although none such chanced to look at it. The "quick Poetick sight" can still see what they would have seen there, but now apparently does not choose to do so. Perhaps Denham failed to remember or recognize the point of his previous lines, but it seems impossible to justify what he put in their place. The dropping of one couplet out of the remaining eight lines of this part of the poem, however, reducing the number to six, may without cavil be regarded as a stylistic improvement.

With line 241 of the "B" text commences the description of the stag hunt, the most prominent feature of this version of *Coopers Hill*. The first line does not differ much from its antecedent of the "A" text, except in the important detail that the name of "our Charles" is suppressed, replaced by "the King." Every conceivable reason calls for this change. Charles I was dead, and so could no longer be spoken of in this familiar affectionate manner. To Parliamentarian and Cromwellite readers moreover, including those newly converted, the reference would seem needlessly intransigent. For faithful Royalists, on the other hand, a reference that could apply only to Charles I would seem to exclude Charles II from acceptance as "our Charles." Last, "the King" is generic, "our Charles" particular, and the whole endeavor of the "B" text revision has been to convert the particular into the general and universal.

After this first line the changes in the stag hunt are immense, far greater than those made in any other section of *Coopers Hill*, and these great changes require explanation. If the stag hunt as originally composed and as modified for publication in 1642 was organized as a parallel series of references to the trial and death of the

Earl of Strafford, what is to be made of a version of the hunt more than twice as long as the original, elaborated at a time when Strafford's fate was obscured by all the lurid events of the interim? Wasserman saw this problem, but failed to solve it: "Artistically considered, what is especially bothersome about the description of the hunt in the later version is that it constitutes so large a fraction of the poem. By its disproportion it seems to upset the structure and the sustained political reading of the poem. It would appear, therefore, that by 1655, when the execution of Strafford had lost much of its pointed political significance in the public mind, Denham chose, at the expense of structure, to blur the political reference by greatly multiplying the purely descriptive features of the chase." [42] Wasserman's explanation of the change, Denham's desire to blur the reference to Strafford, amounts to hardly more than a restatement of the problem. To blur the significance of the stag hunt by expanding the proportion of the poem it occupies from a tenth to more than a fifth of the whole seems a highly perverse process. It seems all the more unlikely in view of the additional fact, which Wasserman also notices, that J. B., the editor of the 1655 "B" text, not only calls deliberate attention to the expanded stag hunt as the prime distinguishing mark of his "authentic" text, but also specifically characterizes it as "that excellent Allegory of the Royall Stag."

When the eighty-two lines of the "B" text stag hunt are compared with the thirty-eight lines of the original, it will be found that essentially only six of the original lines are dropped in the course of the revision. These six lines are replaced by, or expanded into, twenty-six lines. This means that thirty-two lines of the old stag hunt survive relatively unchanged into the new stag hunt, and that the remaining increment of thirty lines largely takes the form of straightforward addition to the text, rather than of revision and rewriting. It is among the lines of this increment, as well as the lines of the twenty-six-line expansion, that Wasserman's thesis — that the dif-

---

42. *The Subtler Language*, pp. 75–76.

ference between the shorter and the longer stag hunt resides in the multiplying of "purely descriptive features of the chase" — may be tested.

The six lines of the "A" text which are obscured by revision (III, 265–270) relate briefly, in a personifying manner, the anxiety and indecision of the suddenly roused stag. The twenty-six lines that replace them (IV, 243–268) begin with some four unprecedented lines on the "flower of youth" who accompany the king on his hunt. Thereafter the lines narrate the stag's slothful sylvan retirement, his shocked surprise at the noise of the hunt, his attempt to persuade himself that it is an illusion, his panic, his indecision, his flight, his self-congratulation at escape, and his dejection at discovering the hounds still in pursuit. These details may constitute "purely descriptive" features of the chase, but the stag throughout is credited with human motives, emotions and reactions. Far more, in fact, than the original six lines, these twelve invite us to regard the stag as a person. When, therefore, six lines retained intact from the "A" text follow, in which the stag approaches his friends and is rejected by them and abandoned like a declining statesman, there is no sense of shifting values, nothing not absolutely consonant with what has gone before.

But then follow fourteen new lines, the first couplet attaching immediately to the simile of the statesman. Eight of these lines, in conjunction with the statesman couplet, will repay analysis here:

Like a declining States-man, left forlorn
To his friends pity, and pursuers scorn,
With shame remembers, while himself was one
Of the same herd, himself the same had done.
Thence to the coverts, & the conscious Groves,
The scenes of his past triumphs, and his loves;
Sadly surveying where he rang'd alone
Prince of the soyl, and all the herd his own;
And like a bold Knight Errant did proclaim
Combat to all, and bore away the Dame.

(IV, 273–282)

This passage has all the coloration of a pastoral masque, the same transparent allegorizing. Considering first the proposition that the stag hunt originally represented in some way the trial and execution of Strafford, it is evident that it no longer does so. The details here added can hardly be described as very convincing purely descriptive features of the chase, but they certainly do not contribute to an allegorical depiction of Strafford. Yet they seem very strongly to be describing somebody, somebody other than Strafford. Strafford was hunted down to his death, but he never had cause to remember with shame his own guilt in allowing another person to be so hunted down. The "A" text stag did not suffer from the remorse of conscience which afflicts the "B" text stag; but it may be in a peculiar way that the guilt of the "B" text stag arises out of his part in the death of the "A" text stag. To desist from riddles, King Charles I was to say more than once, toward the lonely and fearful end of his own life, that all his sufferings had come upon him as a just punishment for his sin in letting Strafford die. According to Dr. George Bates, successively principal physician to Charles I, Cromwell, and Charles II, even on the scaffold the King alluded finally to Strafford: "Yet for all this, God forbid that I should be so ill a Christian, as not to say, that Gods Judgments are just upon me; many times he doth pay injustice by an unjust Sentence, that is ordinary; I will say this, That unjust Sentence that I suffered to take effect, is punished by an unjust Sentence upon me. . . ."[43]

If a stag hunt had once proved a sufficient vehicle to carry a series of references to the trial and execution of a prominent statesman, it could equally carry a burden of reference to the trial and execution of a king. By 1653 in England any suggestion of a great and awe-inspiring trial and execution would surely have called first to mind the fate of Charles, not that of his minister dead eight years before him. The bulk of new material added to the stag hunt of *Coopers Hill* before its republication in 1655 does not in fact consist of descrip-

---

43. *Elenchus Motuum Nuperorum in Anglia*, p. 154.

tion of the hunt, but of allegorizing detail of precisely the nature dear to the heart of Charles himself, the "royal actor" who perhaps scarcely ever perceived the distinctions that divide allegory from life. In the lines reproduced above the stag is called "Prince of the soyl," a far from descriptive detail, and so also with the contents of the other lines.

To commence with the last couplet: the stag who was prince of the soil is also compared to a knight-errant, a further humanizing touch. But in *Coopers Hill* King Charles has already been compared to, and identified with, a knight-errant — St. George. In his own right, too, the King was a knight — a member (though sovereign) of the Order of the Garter, the Order of the Knights of St. George. And even separately, in the allegorical world of his own creation or inspiration, the King was the knight St. George who "bore away the Dame." In a portrait that still survives (now in Buckingham Palace; see frontispiece) Rubens had painted Charles in the guise of St. George slaying the dragon, with Queen Henrietta Maria in the background as the rescued Princess Agnes. The setting of the painting is precisely the setting of the stag hunt in *Coopers Hill*, the Thames Valley. In countless masques at court the King had enacted similar roles, though the capacity for effective action in politics eluded his symbol-bewitched mind.

This hunted stag also finds himself sadly surveying "The scenes of his past triumphs, and his loves." Most of Charles's triumphs had been symbolic or allegorical, but preeminently their scene had been the rebuilt banqueting hall at Whitehall. In 1629 or 1630 Charles had commissioned Rubens to paint a series of allegorical canvases on the general theme of Stuart government to decorate the ceiling of the hall. In 1635 these were mounted into place, where they remain. They consist of three large central canvases, narrating respectively "The Apotheosis of James I," the "Benevolent Government of James I," and "England and Scotland Crowning the Infant Charles I," together with six smaller canvases on such allegorical subjects as

"Chastity Destroying Lust," and other benefits of the Stuart reigns.[44] The same hall was the scene, at Christmas 1639, of the last royal masque of Charles's reign, or indeed of any English reign, Davenant's *Salmacida Spolia.* In this masque the King himself, dressed in silvery blue as the wise prince Philogenes, lover of his people, and the Queen, in the guise of an Amazon, descended from the clouds to vanquish the furies of discord and rebellion. Yet it was through the banqueting hall, to a scaffold set up outside one of its windows, that Charles was conducted to his execution. The significance of this was also not lost on Dr. Bates: "At length they agree it will suffice, that he lose his head upon a Scaffold to be erected before the Banquetting-House of *White-Hall,* that from the same place where he used to mount the Throne, and appear in the sacred pomp of *Majesty,* he might pass to the Block, and cast off the Ornaments of *Royalty,* where he commonly put them on."[45]

Twelve of the remaining sixteen lines of increment to the stag hunt serve in various ways to characterize the doubts and indecisions of the hunted stag, and, although none can be tied down to a one-to-one correspondence with details of the King's last days (or years), as a whole the lines are strongly reminiscent of the tale of broken promises, double-dealing, faithless negotiations from positions of weakness rather than strength, and ever more certain doom, which is the history of King Charles from the end of the first Civil War in 1646 until his death in 1649. Nor is the notion of presenting the King's end as the hunting down or death of a beast unusual or unique to Denham. Bishop King's *Elegy,* earlier mentioned, consistently treats of the hounding down of the King as a hunt, a "King-catching Sport," and says of the King that "The *Mountain-Partridge* or the *Chased Roe* / Might now for Emblemes of His Fortune go."

---

44. See Oliver Millar, *Rubens: The Whitehall Ceiling* (London, 1958), for discussion of these allegorical paintings, with reproductions.
45. *Elenchus Motuum Nuperorum in Anglia,* p. 151.

Denham himself had compared the dead king to a fallen stag in 1649, in his "Elegie Upon the Death of the Lord Hastings":

But as the Leader of the Herd fell first,
. . . so none
But this white fatted Youngling could atone,
By his untimely Fate, that impious Stroke . . .

(lines 27–31)

The remaining four lines are a revival from drafts I and II of the ship simile that had been abandoned with Draft III. The simile is much altered, and used for the first time in conjunction with the hero simile, which is retained almost unchanged from Draft III. The effect is to increase the power of the stag's death. Like the stag of the earliest drafts, he goes down fighting to the last; like the Draft III stag, he begs his fate from "Some nobler foe" and dies proud of the wound. But just as he was hunted by "the King" rather than by "our Charles," so he receives his deathblow from "the King" rather than from "Charles." This ending comports equally well with the end of Charles I as does the end of the earlier stag with that of Strafford. The apparent difficulty involved in regarding Charles as receiving his death wound from "the King" is fairly easily resolved. In the first place it can be recalled that the stag hunt is not a point-for-point allegory: in the earlier versions there was no insinuation that Charles had hunted Strafford to death. Second, it can be pointed out that the generic "king" need not be identified with any individual monarch. Charles *did* accept his end gracefully when it came, and saw in it God's dispensation for him. Perhaps it may suffice to identify "the King" who slays Charles as God, though other identifications might be conjectured, but really no identification whatsoever is required. Charles fought a war to the end with his enemies, first on the battlefield, later in negotiations, and last by his dignified refusal to acknowledge the authority of those who killed him. At his death he conducted himself flawlessly, wearing a double shirt on that January morning, lest he tremble and be thought afraid: "I would have no such imputation. Death is not terrible to me; I bless my God I am prepared."

The following subsection of *Coopers Hill*, on Magna Charta, is reduced in the "B" text from twenty lines to fourteen. The six lines removed were those debating the justification of armed subjects who act against their princes. The original referent of these lines had been the action of the barons against King John, but now, when armed subjects have taken action to the last extreme against King Charles, Denham will not allow justification of such acts to be even moot. He had been dubious about approving the act of the barons; the more recent act was to him "that impious Stroke / That sullied Earth, and did Heaven's pity choke." In the surviving lines one verbal change also deserves note. In the "A" text "Faire Liberty" had been meant a prey to "tyranny," that is, the excess of monarchy. In the "B" text the hunter is identified as "lawless power." This phrase has an extraordinary family of associations with the death of King Charles which originates with Charles himself. At his trial President Bradshaw told the King he was before a court of justice, to which Charles responded, "I find I am before a *power*." Andrew Marvell, in his memorable description of the King's execution, asserted that "This was that memorable Hour / Which first assur'd the *forced Pow'r*" and he concluded the same *Horatian Ode* by reminding Cromwell that "The same Arts that did gain / A *Pow'r* must it maintain." And William Godolphin's 1654 plagiarism of *Coopers Hill*, a panegyric on Cromwell, not merely speaks of "that *Power*, which now informs our Age," but glosses the word itself, by a marginal note, as "The Lord Protector." [46]

The conclusion of *Coopers Hill* in the "B" text is shorter than that in the "A" by twelve lines, and is also rearranged so as to achieve an entirely different emphasis. The first six lines, a synopsis of English history after Magna Charta, remains the same. That history, of increasing popular demands and decreasing royal strength, had already

46. See App. C, below.

been enacted by 1641 and 1642, and further events had only seen the pattern carried to its ultimate possible extent. The next six lines of the "A" text had been those that predicted the Antaeus-like reassertion of kingly strength; to have continued them in the *Coopers Hill* published in 1655 could have been only indecent mockery or deliriously fantastic illusion. Denham could follow no sensible course with them other than the one he did: to cancel them completely. But having removed these lines he did not continue directly to those that had followed them in Draft III, the image of a calm river rising into flood. Instead he brought forward from a later point the six lines on kings and subjects running respectively to successive extremes of oppression and anarchy, which now take on the aspect of a continuation of the remarks on post–Magna Charta history, as well as of a generalized summation, in terms of the laws of opposites, of the lessons of that history. After this, the final six lines of the "A" text are dropped entirely, and their place is taken by the detached image of the river in flood.

The effect is dramatic. In the "A" text the flooding river had constituted a simile, describing the overflowing by kings of the bounds of law, and warning by implication of the dire effects of kingly rage aroused. Its purpose was to caution his subjects against provoking King Charles to extremes, lest they be inundated in the deluge of his power. Now the image is absolute and unattached. The river itself in the poem, the Thames, had been revalued. No longer the emblem of kingly power, it had been changed to the emblem of sheer power, the energy contained within a state. Within the banks and shores of law that power is beneficial, as it had potentially been in the reign of Charles I. Overflowing its banks it is uncontrolled, chaotic, destructive. The end of the final version of *Coopers Hill* is an awesome image of sheer power unrestrained:

When a calm River rais'd with sudden rains,
Or Snows dissolv'd, oreflows th'adjoyning Plains,
The Husbandmen with high-rais'd banks secure
Their greedy hopes, and this he can endure.

But if with Bays and Dams they strive to force
His channel to a new, or narrow course:
No longer then within his banks he dwells,
First to a Torrent, then a Deluge swells:
Stronger, and fiercer by restraint he roars,
And knows no bound, but makes his power his shores.

(IV, 349–358)

Denham had been mistaken, it appears, when in 1641 and 1642
he predicted that tampering with the king's prerogative would result
in an overflow of kingly power that would drown the people's free-
dom. The event had been even more dire than he had predicted.
While a majority of the nation had stared aghast, a determined minority, Cromwell and his ironclad, new-model soldiers, had cut off
the head of the King, and in time had even turned out the Rump
Parliament, the remnant of those who had pretended to have begun
the contention for the liberties of the subject and for the ancient rights
of Englishmen. Cromwell ruled by the sword, not by any legitimate right, despite the various desperate efforts from time to time
to ground his rule on some kind of constitutionality, some kind of
ancient precedent, some color of universal assent. Whether Cromwell could or could not continue to control indefinitely the power
he had seized, that power was loose in England, unfettered, unlimited by anything but the extent to which it could be enforced. For
all Cromwell's strength, the constitutional position of England during his regime could be summed up in the word chaos. Such at least
seems to be Denham's final statement in *Coopers Hill*.

When the final version of *Coopers Hill* is looked over as a whole,
what does its shape appear to be? It is not the poem Wasserman
takes it to be, for he tries to read the text created in 1653 and 1654
as if it had been written in 1642. But there is a continuity of design
from the earlier *Coopers Hill* to the later; if there were not, the
separate drafts would have to be regarded as separate poems. The
final *Coopers Hill* devotes somewhat under half its total extent to
setting up in the landscape discernible from Cooper's Hill three

emblematic hills: St. Paul's in London, Windsor, and St. Anne's Hill. The first hill exists as part of a complex hieroglyph that adumbrates the significances of the later two hills: royally instituted religious harmony is threatened by the low mist of Puritan zealotry. The second hill is Windsor, which has been at least, as an unmixed royal locus, a perfect emblem of its harmonious master, who combined not only the complementary attributes of meekness and majesty, but also, verging on religious considerations, soldiership and saintliness. But, whereas in the "A" text Denham had dwelt lovingly on the series of opposites harmoniously balanced at Windsor and in the King, he seems now rather hasty, blunt, or even perfunctory. History has taken flattery out of his hands, and Charles had realized his identity with St. George in a way more terrible, and therefore more embarrassing, than Denham had earlier dared contemplate.

In contrast with the harmony of Windsor is the disharmony of St. Anne's — direct product of the sacrilege of Henry VIII, but now also, as reality overtakes poetry, emblem of Puritan desecrations all over England. Henry VIII has become fused with the Lord Protector, the "defense" offered by the one and the "protection" offered by the other being not easily distinguished from each other, nor from spoliation. Ultimately the prospect of all three hills is dispiriting, and Denham turns to contemplate the Thames. What may also be noticed about the examination of the three hills in the "B" text is that it lacks all immediacy. Draft I of *Coopers Hill* was ostensibly a view of the Thames Valley from the summit of Cooper's Hill, and Draft IV is ostensibly the same thing. But Draft I was written by a man with a lively sense of what could actually be seen from the top of the hill, Draft IV by one whose sense of the actuality of the scene had long since been dulled. Draft IV is almost entirely a conceptual poem rather than a visual one, and that fact accounts both for its relative strengths and weaknesses.

The Thames, which provides the conceptual unity of the poem as it does the visual unity of the landscape, flowing past Windsor Castle, Windsor Forest, Egham Mead, Cooper's Hill, St. Anne's Hill, and

London, is examined separately at the exact physical center of the poem. As an actual river it is seen as the chief source of England's prosperity and a uniter of the world's opposites in harmonious union. As a hieroglyph therefore it can now be recognized as expressive of both harmony and power. It is the power in a state, specifically in England, and the source of wealth as long as it also remains harmonious. The "Thames couplets," therefore, in the new *Coopers Hill* are more than a metrical tour de force, or the happy objective correlative of the doctrine of harmonized opposites which they became for the Augustans, but the key to the poem. The river is also the thematic catalyst by which the static symbolism of the three hills is converted into the kinetic symbolism of the hunt and England's recent plunge into political chaos.

At Windsor Forest the power symbol of the river, image in England's landscape of what should be true in the English state, is entered into juxtaposition with the ruler symbol of the mountain. The whole presents an ideal image of orderly government. History has shown Denham that the ruler is not necessarily the repository of the nation's power. But when the power is harmonized within laws the ruler can serve as a buffer to shelter the commonwealth from the storms of fate, while the power of the state serves to enrich both.

Into this landscape, which is a perfect icon of a prosperous commonwealth, ride "the King" and his followers in pursuit of a stag. Because the stag hunt is ostensibly no more than that, and because stag hunting is by its nature an innocent occupation, this activity can be regarded as not disturbing the harmony of the scene, and as being "more innocent" than a different sort of hunt which had taken place at the same spot. But the very contrast of the two hunts is a kind of equation, and therefore the stag hunt has an underlying quality hostile to harmony. Although hitherto in the poem kings have often been the object of attention, and although the stag hunt is conducted by "the King," it is interesting that between the beginning and the end of the hunt the King is not visible at all. The subject of the poem for seventy-nine lines of verse is the hunted stag, not the hunter, and

for the stag the scene is far from one of harmony, tranquillity, or prosperity. So in England's temperate isle, which God designed as itself
an emblem of and an inducement toward harmony, men have nonetheless been engaging themselves in the bloody king-catching sport,
as earlier they had hunted down the Earl of Strafford.

Despite the lesson of harmony inscribed in the field of Runnymede,
men have not learned to harmonize their own lives. At the signing of
Magna Charta a chance had been opened to Englishmen to achieve a
harmony in their commonwealth, but the opportunity had been cast
away. The kinetic violence that underlay the stag hunt has been a
constant of English history, and the river of power in the state, unlike
the gently flowing Thames, has been forced to burst its banks. As
a topical and contemporary reference, the end of *Coopers Hill* in
1655 states that, controlled by the usurper Cromwell or not, mere
anarchy is let loose upon England. When Denham republished his
poem in 1668, at a time when by his lights order and legitimacy had
been restored to England by the national submission to the rightful
government of Charles II, descended to him "by inherent Birthright,
and lawful undoubted Succession," he found no need to alter his poem
again. By the careful conversion of particularities into generalities
effected in the revision of 1653–54, even the depiction of chaos at the
end could be retained. In the poem's own generic statement, such
chaos is what inevitably ensues striving to force the stream of national
power into "a new, or narrow course." Although the English monarchical system had returned to its old channel, to flow at least
for a while longer as equably as the Thames, Denham could believe
that the lesson embodied in his hieroglyphical poem would remain
relevant even in a future when Englishmen might have forgotten
the lessons of their civil war.

Appendix A

COOPERS HILL
LATINE REDDITUM

The fact that a Latin translation of *Coopers Hill* was published in the seventeenth century is a testimony to the high esteem in which Denham's poem was held in its own time. The fact that the translation was issued from the Sheldonian Theatre at Oxford only seven years after Denham's death seems to testify that the poem had already come to be considered in some sense a classic. The potential interest of the translation for modern students of the poem, moreover, is also high, for, in the paucity of explicit and detailed explication of their own poetry and that of their contemporaries by the English Augustans, a translation of a poem must necessarily reveal something of how the translator viewed and interpreted it. It is only one of the several paradoxes surrounding *Coopers Hill Latine Redditum* that its maker should have been relatively blind to most of Denham's subtler nuances of art. Matters of contestable interpretation need not be instanced in this regard; it is quite apparent, for example, that the translator was all but blind and deaf to the charms of the famous "Thames couplets" which certainly did not escape the notice of most later Augustans.

The translation is based on the "B" text of *Coopers Hill* — that is, a text that contains the famous lines — and it does translate the "Thames couplets." But another paradox of the translation is that it is based on J. B.'s 1655 first edition of the "B" text, although by 1676, when the translation was printed, not only had the revised and more complete final "B" text appeared in the *Poems and Translations* volume of 1668, but also in the second edition of 1671. One consequence of this anomaly is that the translation has no equivalent for the

257

final "B" text lines 193–196, which did not appear in J. B.'s edition. In a few places, which are indicated below in the notes, *Coopers Hill Latine Redditum* also faintly suggests some acquaintance on the translator's part with the "A" text of *Coopers Hill*, although the instances may perhaps also be explained as readily by some of the translator's special poetic habits. Among these habits is that of being specific where Denham is general, and personal where Denham is impersonal. To a certain extent this fact appears to be a function of the translator's concept of the nature of Latin as distinguished from English poetry: the view that Latin poetic propriety calls for "Phoebus" where Denham speaks of "heavens eye" may also require the naming of "Henricus" where Denham more allusively mentions a "Christian King." On one aspect of translation, at any rate, the translator sees eye to eye with Denham: that is, by a remarkable feat, *Coopers Hill Latine Redditum* comes to be couched in exactly 354 hexameters, precisely the number of lines contained in J. B.'s version of *Coopers Hill*. This feat is accomplished despite a certain lack of synchrony within the poem which, for instance, causes the gap occasioned by the absence of lines 193–196 of the final "B" text to fall between lines 190 and 191 of the translation; by the end of the poem, however, the line discrepancy, which seldom grows very large, has been entirely eliminated.

Another paradox of *Coopers Hill Latine Redditum* is that, although the translator was a relatively obscure man and the work was published anonymously, the edition itself is by far the most splendid that any version of *Coopers Hill* has ever appeared in. The volume is a large handsome quarto of twenty-one pages in three sheets (pp. [2 (1, title)] + 21 (1–21, the poem) + [3, blank], signn. [π]¹, A-C⁴). The type is large (great primer italic, leaded), clear, and well set. The margins are wide, and the pages (with the exception of the shorter pp. 1 and 21) carry only eighteen lines of text each. Of this elaborate edition 1,025 copies were printed, and Anthony Wood seems to have contributed the sum of £5 12s. toward the cost of printing (the information is derived from Falconer Madan's *Oxford Books* [Oxford, 1931], III, 332, but the note on *Coopers Hill Latine Redditum* is somewhat garbled and full of errors and mistranscriptions). The motivation of this care and expense has not come to light.

The translation, as remarked above, was published anonymously, but Anthony Wood, in *The Life and Times of Anthony Wood, Vol. II*, ed. A. Clark, Oxford Historical Society Publications No. 21 (Oxford, 1892), p. 349, and in the *Fasti Oxonienses*, in *Athenae Oxonienses*, II, 332 as well as on the title page of his own copy of the work, reveals that the translator was Moses Pengry, chaplain to the Earl of Devon, to whose son, Lord William Cavendish, the translation is dedicated. On the title page of his copy of *Coopers Hill Latine Redditum*, now in the Bodleian Library (pressmark Wood 383 [51]), Wood wrote this note:

Anthony à Wood Oxon, given to me by Moses Pengry.
Bac. Div. & Fellow Brasenose Coll. who translated
this poem from Engl. into Latine, June 15. 1676.
    Chapl. to yᵉ Earl of Devon.

(The transcript of this note I owe to the courtesy of D. G. Neill, assistant librarian, Department of Printed Books, Bodleian Library. Madan's transcript of the same note contains at least three misprints.)

The text here reproduced of *Coopers Hill Latine Redditum* is taken from the copy of the work now in the William Andrews Clark Memorial Library, Los Angeles, where its call number is *PR3409/ D2C7/1676. Two manuscript transcripts of the translation have been compared with the printed text. The variant readings below the Latin text in this Appendix are drawn from these two manuscript transcripts, which appear to be independent of the 1676 edition. One is a transcript interleaved with a copy of the 1709 separate edition of *Coopers Hill* now in the Henry E. Huntington Library, San Marino, California (call no. 280856). In the present listing this transcript is designated *HEH*. The second is a manuscript of the translation, in fifteen pages on eight sheets, now in the collection of Mr. James M. Osborn of Yale University, through whose generosity it has been made available for this edition. This manuscript, designated *Osborn* in the present listing, appears from its handwriting to have been transcribed at some time close to the date of the original translation. In the apparatus the designation *MSS* indicates agreement of both manuscripts.

Wing's *Short-Title Catalogue* assigns *Coopers Hill Latine Redditum* the number D997. The title page of the edition is as follows (the first two words in black letter):

COOPERS HILL / LATINE REDDITUM. / AD / NOBILISSIMUM D^{num} /

GULIELMUM D^{num} CAVENDISH, / Honoratissimi Domini /

GULIELMI / COMITIS DEVONIAE / Filium Unicum. /

[*cut*: *Sheldonian Theatre*] /

OXONII, / E THEATRO SHELDONIANO, M D C LXXVI.

The Text

COOPERS HILL / LATINE REDDITUM. / AD / NOBILISSIMUM DOMINUM, / GULIELMUM / D^{num} CAVENDISH, &c. [half title].

Si fuerint Vates, Parnassi nulla bicollis
Somnia qui norint, Heliconis pocula nulla;
Quid loca crediderim quicquam tribuisse Poetis?
Parnassum faciunt, faciunt Helicona Poetae.
Qua residet Rex cunque sita est ibi Regia; & omnis   5
Qua Musae posuere domos, Parnassus haberi
Vult locus; & si quid valeant mea carmina, Tu Te
Parnassum praestas, & das in carmina vires.
Neu mirere, tuo si fretus vertice campos
Tollar in aerios, & nullo tramite notos;   10
Mens ubi discurrit sine fine, oculoque vel ipso
Liberior, primo spatium qui corripit ictu,
Atque locum dicto citius se sistit ad istum,
Quem sancta atque ingens, & caelo proxima moles
Consecrat; incertum visu terraene sit Illa,   15
An pars aetheri caeli, juxtaque videtur
Mons sursum tendens, ac nubes lapsa deorsum.
Paulo sacra Domus, cujus fastigia cantu

---

3 Poetis] Poetae *Os-*   4 Poetae] Poetis *Os-*   13 istum] ipsum *HEH*
 born   *born*   15 terraene] terrenae *Os-*
                                born

 1. Si fuerint Vates] A translation of *1655*'s "If there be Poets," in contrast with *1668*'s "Sure there are Poets."

 17. nubes lapsa deorsum] Translates *1655*'s "a falling cloud" in contrast with *1668*'s "descending cloud" (line 18).

Nupera Musa petit, facilique supervolat ala.
Quin stabis, ferrum quamvis extrema minetur, 20
Tempusque, ignisque, zelusque nocentior illis;
Optimus & Regum dum Te donaverit aevo, Carolus I.
Optimus & vatum longo sacraverit aevo. Edm. Waller Armig.
Surgentem late circum se despicit urbem,
Ceu nebulam, sensim quae nititur ad juga montis. 25
Urbem, cujus opes & pompa, negotia, turba
Nubes apparent procul aspicientibus atra;
(Idque quod apparent tibi sunt, si rite putas rem:)
Per quam festinant huc illuc ordine nullo
Caeci mortales, hic perdere, & ille perire. 30
His luxu truduntur opes, opibusque vicissim
Luxus, uti pax est materque & filia belli;
Qualiter in pelago fluvius se perdit, & arctos
Per ductus remeat rursum perdendus in illo.
O laris angusti requies, O munera nondum 35
Nota satis, secura & nescia fallere vita!
    Proxima (Martis amor, Venerisq haud infirma cura)
Perpulchre munita meos Winsora gradatim
Ima e valle tumens oculos incurrit, in altum
Tam modice surgens, tam lente, nullus ut horror, 40
Nulla jugipraeceps feritas oculosve pedesve
Arceat; in clivios faciles ascendit, & idem
Delectatque oculum locus, & castigat eundem.
Talem se placido Dominus Tuus ore ferebat;
Talis in Augusta sedit Clementia fronte. 45

---

22 *Shoulder*] *not in MSS*	34 rursum] cursum	*HEH*	in cliuos *Os-*
23 longo] dum te *HEH*	*HEH*	*born*	
Shoulder] *not in MSS*	42 in clivios] inclivos		

23. *Shoulder*: Armig[er]] I.e., "Esquire."

30. Caeci mortales] One of Pengry's own frequent additions to Denham's text; these are not all noted.

37. Martis amor, Venerisque haud infima cura] May be an attempt to achieve an effect similar to that of the original's transverse chiastic structure (lines 39–40), but weakened by the referential vagueness of Venus's "haud infima cura."

Is tuus est fastus dignatae pondere tanto;
Sic caput attollis sola sub mole superba,
Qua vix majorem fert Atlas, maximus Atlas
Caelumque aethereosque humero qui sustinet orbes.
Utprimum Natura parens hac prole tumebat,   50
Hunc illam bene gnara operis formabat in usum;
Et tacite, saeclis olim volventibus, inquit,
Has auras feriat centeno vertice Castrum.
Dixerat, & quisquam non captus mente oculisque
Abnuat, aut Divae jussis parere recuset?   55
Tale decua capitis gestat turrita Cybele,
Caelica cum proles maternum Numen adorat:
Nomina non majora tamen, nec plura, tot inter
Heroas, tot Semideos, Superosque frequentes,
Atria quam possunt Winsorae ostendere, monstrant   60
Divorum Fasti, aut Famae monumenta recondunt.
Neu repetam cui natales Arx debeat ista,
Nominis Angliaci Decus & Tutela; Tibine
Albianax, an Brute Tibi; an fundamina Caesar
Fecerit, Arthurusque Brito, Cimberne Canutus.   65
Nec minor est prisco de Te lis tempore mota,
Quam cum Maeonides septem committeret urbes:
Huic ortu similis Tu par & honore fuisses,
Huic si qualis erat talis mihi Musa fuisset.
Utcunque eximius (quisquis fuit Ille Virorum)   70
Est Locus, eximioque accessit digna loco Mens.
Singula quid referam Regum cunabula, Regum
Sponsales thalamos, Regum veneranda sepulchra?

---

65 Fecerit] Gesserit (can-   Jecerit *Osborn*   usne *MSS*
   celed, replaced by)   Arthurusque] Arthur-

56. turrita Cybele] An instance of Pengry's insistence on personalizing carrying him
back, perhaps unwittingly, from the "B" text's "The God's great Mother" (line 60) to the
"A" text's "Cibele."
65. Arthurusque] "Arthurusne" of the *MSS* is more probably correct.
72–73. Regum / Sponsales thalamos] A gratuitous addition by Pengry.

Sed tacuisse nefas Te Magne Edoarde, Tuumque

Te Patre majorem Gnatum, qui Lilia carpsit

Victrici dextra, atque Tibi gestanda ferebat;

Bellonamque Tuae Sociam famaeque torique,

Uno quae capto peperit Tibi Rege triumphos,

Atque Illum peperit, cui captus paruit Alter.

Tum demum Titulos condebas Auctor Equestres,

Sive Amor elatum, Tibi seu Victoria pectus

Accendit, certe causa haec sat honesta, sat illa est;

Nec dispar caeptis aluit successus Honores,

Utpote quos Reges longe lateque potentes

Affectent, studio sacra post Diademata summo.

Quod si Fata Tibi tantum praescire dedissent

Venturas, quantum rebus praesentibus uti;

Si nosses fore, captivis ubi Regibus istis

Orti miscerent thalamos Neptisque Neposque,

Qui, quicquid tenuit Tua vasta potentia, quicquid

Vastior ulta animus voluit tenuisse, tenerent;

(Queis melior Fortuna dedit quodcunq; vel unquam

Victrix causa solet sperare, aut victa timere;)

Si quod manaret proprio de vulnere sanguis

Nosses, quo maduere diu confinia Regna,

Nec tua sic, nec Avi saevisset nobilis ira,

Nec consanguinea tepuissent caede nepotes.

Cum Tibi Patronum fortem, sanctumque legebas,

Armaque Cyaneo cingebas Regia Balteo;

His praemonstrabes Insignibus Arma, Virumque

Edv. 3

Princip. 75
Cognom.
Nigrum.

Phillipam
Reginam.
Joannes
Gallorum.
Davide Scotorum.

80

85

Car. Jac. 6. F.
Maria Hen.
Mag. F. 90

95

Divum Georg.
Cappad.

100

74 *Shoulder*] *not in MSS*   77 *Shoulder*] *not in MSS*   95 Regna] Regum *HEH*
75 *Shoulder*] *not in MSS*   79 *Shoulder*] *not in MSS*   98 *Shoulder*] *not in MSS*

75. *Shoulder*] Princip[em] Cognom[inatum] Nigrum — i.e., the Prince surnamed Black, the Black Prince.
89. *Shoulder*] Car[olus] Jac[obi] 6[ti] F[ilius] Maria Hen[rici] Mag[ni] F[ilia.]
98. *Shoulder*] Divum Georg[um] Cappad[ociae] — St. George of Cappadocia.
100. Arma, Virumque] Probably a deliberate reminiscence of *Aeneid* I.1: "Arma virumque cano . . ."

Qui patriis Regnis adjecit Caerula ponti,
Fecitque Imperii partem, quae Terminus ante
Talis erat, qui fine carens sua brachia pandit
Qua patet orbis, & isto gaudet limite claudi;
Nempe Virum pietas quem vera, & bellica virtus   105
Concelebrant, citra fragiles pictasque tabellas.
  Mirari haec juvat usq; atq; hic juvat usq; morari,
Ni traherent alio fixam vaga lumina mentem,
Vicinum ad collem, cujus venerabile culmen
Ornarant quondam longaevi tecta Sacelli;   110
Jussa reformari donec vicinior Aedes
(Cognita verticibus rasis, & caclibc vita)
Corrueret, passim grassanti clade; sed absit.
Absit ut excidio Templorum Ecclesia surgat!
Musa mihi causas memora, quo crimine laesus,   115
Quidve dolens tantas Henricus volverit iras.
Nonquid erat luxus Fratrum, atque insana libido?
Ergone tam castus fuit Ille, piusque probusque?
Haecne illis, haec Ille opprobria, quae Sibi dici
Conscit posse magis? Satis est pro crimine Census,   120
Solus apud Reguem pro crimine Census egenum,
Cui steterat reparare exhausti Commoda Fisci
Fraude pia, & luxu damnato pascere luxum.
Ipse autem sceleris summo molimine gestit
Sanctus censeri, laudemque a crimine captat.   125
Nec sceleri licet armato fiducia tanta est,
Quin recti speciem, & fictum sibi poscat honestum.
Cujust mens (ita fit) jamdudum obsurduit, auris

---

104 limite] limine *HEH*	Henricus in *HEH*	125 laudemque] *lau-
116 tantas Henricus vol-	121 Reguem] Regem	demque *HEH* (*in*
verit] arsit, tantas	*MSS*	*margin*: *laudes)

116. Henricus] Although Denham's reference is certainly to Henry VIII, his original of this line asks, "What crime could *any Christian King* incense / To such a rage?" ("B" text, lines 118–119).

123. Fraude pia] Another contribution from Pengry alone.

Impatiens famae est, tituloque laborat in uno.
Scilicet aedificat simul, & Sacra diruit Idem;   130
Quam Regum Stylus est Regum sed acutior Ensis.
Quaeque piis dederat proavis, sic damna resarcit,
Eversorque Operum prodit Fidei Defensor.
Tunc illas habuit cellas ignobilis oti
Vana Superstitio, & mendax pietatis imago,   135
Trabs & pondus iners: sed nostra, Ciconia facta,
Relligio contra nimis est animosa voraxque.
Nullane Zonarum est medias quae temperat auras?
Omnia quin frigus, vel saevior ignis aduret?
Haeccine visa salus membris torpentibus una est,   140
Conjicere adversam in Febrim? Ratione medendi
Nulla est, ni Somnum excipiat manifesta phrenesis?
Usque adeone nihil scire est, nisi eo usque sciamus,
Dum magis optandum fuerit nescire, manuque
Per noctem palpare vias, quam luce diurna   145
Fidere Ductori falso, & per devia ferri?
Quis vero haec cernens dubitet quin exterus hostis
Terram omnem ferro fuerit populatus, & igni?
At postquam audierit, quod tantis stragibus Auctor
Nec durus Scytha sit, gelida nec Gotthus ab Arcto,   150

---

142 excipiat] accipiat
     HEH

130. aedificat . . . diruit] Pengry's rendition of "protects . . . spoils" (line 131).
131. Regum] Used to translate "Princes'"; illustrates Pengry's narrowing and particularization of Denham's generalization.
     Stylus] It is difficult to say if Pengry recognized or intended the pun in the original. *Stilus*, "title," is not classical Latin, although it does occur in medieval and post-medieval writing; *stilus*, "pen," is classical.
134. A line that independently achieves a Denham-like tension, and produces neatly "Fidei Defensor" — Henry VIII's style — with an effect like that of punning.
135. Entirely Pengry's own contribution to *Coopers Hill*, seeming to reflect a harsher Protestant rejection of Popish idolatry and superstition than Denham ever committed himself to.
148. ferro . . . & igni] Another original contribution by Pengry, perhaps reflecting the earlier "sword, or time, or fire" ("B," line 21, Latin, lines 20–21).

Sed Rex Indigena, & Christi de nomine dictus;
Cum nihil intersit, sed solo nomine distent
Optima nostra, atque Illorum turpissima facta;
Talia cum fuerint pietatis vulnera, quid jam
Sacrilega restare manu inviolabile credat? 155
   Hinc variis animi turbatus motibus (ira
Propter quae tulimus, propterque ferenda timore)
Ex alto demitto oculum, qua Thamesis imas
Convalles secat, & lascivis gressibus errat,
Thamesis Oceano patri charissima proles; 160
Cujus in amplexus gestit properare, marinum
Et liquida in Fiscum sua vectigalia pendit,
Ut fluit in vitam mortalis vita perennem.
Quod si non aureas sub gurgite volvat arenas,
Nec vomat electrum sicut Tagus Eridanusque; 165
Ecce tibi genuina, magisque innoxia dona,
Quae, misso fundo, ripa spectabis utraque,
Quam super extendit se, atque almis incubat alis,
Infundens gremio venturi veris honores;
Quos mora non perdit nimis importuna, tenellum 170
Opprimit ut partum quandoque improvida mater:
Impete nec fluctu, tanquam Rex prodigus, aufert
Quas donarat, opes; viridis nec munera prati

---

153 Illorum] Heroum   160 charissima] *gratis-   *gin:* *charissima)*
  HEH   sima *HEH (in mar-* 164 volvat] volvit *Os-*
                                                       born

151. Rex . . . & Christi de nomine dictus] Pengry's own qualification of Denham's "a Christian King" (line 152).
152. nihil . . . sed solo nomine] "nothing but a name alone," Pengry's rendition of "nothing, but the Name of Zeal" (line 153) suppresses Denham's "Zeal," contrary to Pengry's usual practice of increasing specificity.
165. Tagus Eridanusque] Translates Denham's "streams . . . Whose foam is Amber, and their Gravel Gold" (lines 165–166), another instance of Pengry's particularization. The Tagus was famous in antiquity for its golden sands; on the banks of the Eridanus (or Po), according to Ovid (*Metamorphoses* I) the sisters of Phaethon, transformed to poplars, weep tears of amber.

Corruit, aut sata laeta, hominumque boumque labores.
Sed bonus it felixque, & jugi fonte; Deoque   175
Adsimilis gaudente animo sua dona revolvit.
Nec sat habet vicina sibi sic rura beare,
Sed vento & pelago communior omnia visit;
Et non ingratae ditissima faemora ripae
Ostentat, largusque oras dispergit in omnes,   180
Divitiasque refert gemino sub Sole jacentes
Velivolo curru, & nostram facit Indiam utramque.
Quaerit opes ubi sunt, ubi desunt Ipse ministrat;
Urbibus & sylvas, & sylvis conserit urbes.
Usque adeo nulla est Regio non cognita Nobis,   185
Illius in gremio cum totus veneat Orbis.
O si sic fluerem, & grandi decurrere possem
Par Argumento, ad fundum pellucidus imum,
Lentus, at haud segnis, validus sine vortice, plenus
Alveo, sed propriae contentus margine ripae!   190
    Explicat hic rerum varias Natura figuras,

---

174 hominumque boum-
    que] boumque ho-
    minumque *HEH*
175 felixque] foelixq *Os-*
    born
    & jugi fonte] et
    [*blank*] fonte *HEH*
179 faemora] foemora

Osborn munera
HEH
183 desunt] non sunt
HEH
187 possem] possim *Os-*
born
188 pellucidus] perluci-
dus *HEH*

Between 190 and 191
HEH leaves gap, cor-
responding to four
lines of 1668 Coop-
ers Hill (*193–196*)
not in 1655 and
therefore not trans-
lated.

    174. sata laeta . . . boumque labores] A reminiscence of *Georgic* I.325–326: "sata laeta boumque labores / diluit" and *Aeneid* II.306: "sternit sata laeta boumque labores." In a reverse process, when Denham had occasion to translate the *Aeneid* line (*The Destruction of Troy* [1656], line 295) he used a version ("mocks the Plough-mans toil") of the *Coopers Hill* original of the present phrase: "mock the plowmans toyl" (line 176). Perhaps this coincidence shows Pengry's recognition of the claim of *Coopers Hill* to be regarded as in some sense a georgic (see B. O Hehir, "Vergil's First *Georgic* and Denham's *Coopers Hill*," *PQ*, XLII [1963], 542–547).
    187–190. Pengry's version of the "though deep, yet clear" couplets (lines 189–193). Denham's antithetical effect and balance of structure are almost wholly lost, except insofar as they must necessarily be reflected in almost any translation, even a prose retranslation into English: "O might I thus flow, and run on with greatness equal to the theme, clear to the bottommost depth, slow but not sluggish, strong without turbulence — channel full, yet contented within the bounds of proper shores."

Incertum studio Nobisne Sibine placendi.
(Nec minor Artifici, quam Spectatoribus ipsis
Esse solet, quanquam causis diversa, voluptas;
Ut spectat natos amor unus, & alter amicos.)   195
Haud Illam latuit, quod quae rebusque sonisque
Convenit, Harmoniam pariat Discordia mater.
Talis erat quae prima dabat Discordia pacem,
Formamque, & mundo pulchros afflabat amores.
Frigida dum pugnant calidis, humentia siccis,   200
Summae certa fides, & constant foedera mundi.
Aspera dum late, & dumetis horrida Sylva
Stat lymphas juxta, & tranquillo opponitur Amni;
Talia dum coeunt tam longe dispare forma,
Mirabundum animum oblectat non una voluptas.   205
Has si Narcissus quondam inspexisset in undas
Illimes, puroque fluentes agmine; blando
Haud ita reflexae periisset vulnere formae,
Nec Se, sed nitidam in fundo vidisset arenam.
Interea celsus Mons inter nubila condit   210
Aerium caput; ex humeris Toga frondea longe
Pendet, & ad talos densis demittitur umbris:

---

208 periisset] periissent 212 demittitur] immiti-
    Osborn   tur *HEH*

Between 191 and 192] As noted above, four lines of the fully developed "B" text of
1668 (lines 193–196) are not represented in Pengry's translation as they are not represented
in J. B.'s edition of 1655, providing evidence that it was that edition Pengry used as his
original.

197. Harmoniam pariat Discordia mater] Pengry's rendition of "the harmony of
things . . . from discords springs" (lines 203–204; *1655*, lines 199–200). Here Pengry's
penchant for personalization has misled him into faulty mythologizing, for according to
Hesiod Aphrodite was the mother of Harmonia, her father Ares. The conjunction of Ares
and Aphrodite, or Mars and Venus, constituted the "Discordia" from which Harmonia
springs. Denham at this point does not seem to be thinking of mythology, however, but
of Heraclitean cosmology, specifically the remark of Heraclitus recorded by Aristotle: "That
which is in opposition is in concert, and from things that differ comes the most beautiful
harmony."

206. Narcissus] Another example of Pengry's specification, this time of Denham's "the
self-enamour'd youth" (line 214; *1655*, line 210). But all editions of *Coopers Hill* had carried the name "Narcissus" in a shoulder note.

Dumque Supercilia, in rugas contracta minaces,
Torve prospiciunt labentem leniter Amnem;
Ardua Frons (ea sunt Summorum fata) procellis   215
Crebris objicitur, ventoque rigescit, & imbri.
Ante hirtos depressa pede provolvitur ampla
Planities, ulnis circundata Montis & Amnis:
Illi alter ventos dedit, & contemnere Soles;
Frugibus illam alter ditatque, & floribus ornat.   220
Denique (quae reliquis accedit gratia) passim
Singula commendat cunctorum discolor ordo.
Graeculus hanc siquis Vates, Bardusve Britannus
Vidisset Scenam, qualis venisset ad aures
Fama, quod hic tenerae Nymphae, Satyrique petulci   225
Lusissent connubia, nocturnasque choreas?
Sunt & adhuc vestigia acutis visa Poetis
Tenuia, sed crassi fugiunt commercia vulgi.
His cum Sylvano Faunus dat jura viretis;
Huc venit, & pingues per campos pascitur agmen   230
Cornibus arboreis, & onusta fronte superbum;
In quibus exhibuit quid summe daedala possit
Natura, atque uno monstravit munere, quam sit
Res summas facilis dare, difficilisque tueri.

---

221 accedit] accedat *Os-*   225 quod] quot *Osborn*
born

   213. Supercilia . . . minaces] Technically close to the original: "his curled brows /
Frown" (lines 219–220; *1655*, lines 215–216), but perhaps inadvertently reminiscent of
the "A" text: "our surly supercilious Lords, / Bigge in their frownes" (lines 245–246).
Here, as in the case of "Cybele" (line 56, above), Pengry at the very least is reversing the
process by which Denham converted the "A" to the "B" text, and thereby is shedding some
incidental light on the nature of the process.
   225. Nymphae, Satyrique] Denham's "Fairies" have been eliminated, perhaps as lacking classical credentials. By accident Pengry has thus restored the conjunction of water and
woods represented by the naiads and dryads of the "A" text.
   226. nocturnasque choreas] Perhaps a reminiscence of the "soft dances" of the "A"
text; the "B" text here has only "feasts" and "revels," which might, of course, independently have given rise to "choreas."
   234. difficilisque tueri] Reverses the sense of the original: "Great things are made, but
sooner are undone" (line 240; *1655*, line 236).

Hic Regem, cum sat patriae populoque dedisset,   235
Prolatis paulum rebus, curisque remissis,
Accinctum vidi ad praedam, cui plurima pubes
Nobilium stipat latus, & delecta juventus;
Ardua qui poscunt, interque pericula laudem,
Audacemque hostem exoptant, minimeque fugacem.   240
   Jam Cervus formae, & maturi conscius aevi
(Pigritia partim, partim suadente timore)
Abdiderat sese in latebras, quas nec tua, Phoebe,
Nec tua, Venator, percurrere lumina possent.
Vix cubat, arrectas cum longe verberat aures   245
Improvisa canum rabies clamorque virorum.
Exilit attonitus, sed adhuc incredulus, istos
Persuadere volens sibi se lusisse timores;
Dum sonus ingruat, atque oculis testantibus adsint
Majora auditis jam visa pericla periclis.   250
Dumque videt varia saltus indagine cinctos,
Praeclususque aditus, atque artes mille nocendi;
Olli multa pedum virtus, multusque recursat
Frontis honos, seu terga dabit, seu pectora bello.
Stabitne an fugiet? Pudor hoc, metus impedit illud;   255
Praepollet metus, & pedibus confidere monstrat.
Tum fugit, & sese cursu miratur in ipso,
Praevertisse sonum exultans, & signa sequentum;
Donec turba frequens mox instet nare sagaci,
Vimque minus celerem compenset odora canum vis.   260
Jamque pedum falsamque salutem, & perfidum odorem

---

257   sese cursu] cursu sese
      HEH

235. Regem]   Translates "the King." For once Pengry fails to particularize.
243–244. nec tua, Phoebe, / Nec tua, Venator]   Pengry's personalization of "nor mans eye, nor heavens" (line 250; *1655*, line 246).
255. This entire line is Pengry's. Cp. Sir Robert Howard, *The Duel of the Stags*: "Asham'd to flie, and yet afraid to fight" (line 88).

271

Incusat, causasque sui vestigia fati.
Exin amicitias veteres pertentat, & infert
Se socium vulgo, cui nutu olim imperitarat.
Agmen non aeque cautum transversa tuetur   265
Suppliciter venientem, illumque fugitve fugatve.
Qualis, ubi summo Regni detrusus honore
Hostibus objicitur ridendus, flendus amicis
Aulicus, invitus recolit, quando esset eodem
De grege, Sese alios itidem sprevisse jacentes.   270
Hinc nemorum secreta petit, saltusque per omnes
Migrat, & agnoscit veterum loca conscia amorum;
Metiturque oculo tristis quos ante per agros
Errabat rerum Dominus, rurisque gregisque,
Audebatque unus cunctis indicere bellum,   275
Opponens sese, Victorque potitus amata est;
Horrendum insonuere ingentia Tela, minaeque
Frontis, & ad fluvium Sylvae retulere Triumphos.
Nunc languet primum, & pugna se subtrahit; Ipsi
Tanti Amor ante fuit, vel Vita charior ipsa.   280
Nunc omnes terrent aurae, fronde hostis in omni est;
Quotque hostes subeunt, mortes tot adesse videntur.
Dein lassus, depulsus ab his, atque actus ab illis
Hanc unam cernit, nullam sperare, salutem.
Inde animos iterum sumit, vanumque timorem   285
Ponit; & incursus omnes stat tendere contra.
Jamque illum taedet fugisse; fugaque pudenda
Amissas optat, serasque ad praelia vires.
Verum ubi multiplici sentit deprensus ab hoste,

---

278 fluvium] Fluvios
     HEH

   270. alios]   The explicit object, and the plural, effectively obviate any possibility of viewing this line as an allusion to Charles I's remorse over his part in the death of Strafford.
   274. Dominus]   Translates "Prince."

Obsessusque canum venantum, hominumque corona;   290
Valdius incoeptum, temerariaque improbat ausa,
Quam, quem non multo damnaverat ante, timorem:
Caeca loca esse malae fidei, majoraque pensat
Quam desperatis, dubiis discrimina rebus.
Tunc cum nil socii prosint, viresque dolique,   295
Et desit quasi terra fugae, se mittit in undas:
Et secum, certe non hic quoque ab hoste lacessar;
Altum est quod teneo, Canibusque voracius ipsis.
Sed frustra, intrepide sequitur malesana caterva;
Nec levat Unda sitim, sitis ista levanda Cruore est.   300
Ceu Navim exagitant, cui vel negat Æolus auras,
Vel Neptunus aquas, parvae celeresque Biremes:
Stat mole ingenti, pereat ne prorsus inulta,
Prospectans, ecquae numerosa e classe supremas
Ausint ferre minas, desperantemque furorem.   305
Sic Canibus pugnat Cervus, vim vique repellit
Hastato capite, & compensat vulnere vulnus.
Ac veluti, circum quem densi cominus hostes
Adglomerant, Heros nunc hos, nunc demetit illos;
Utque est contemptor lucis, certusque cadendi,   310
Haud tam vile sui pretium vult sanguinis esse,
Plebeia ut dextra cadat; at si forte virum quem
Conspicit insignem Natalibus, Hunc vocat, orat
Hunc mortem, mortisque Illustri Auctore levatur:
Sic ubi lethiferum relum dimittit ab arcu   315

---

291 incoeptum] incaep-   309 Adglomerant] *Con-   314–316 *Left margin*]
    tum *Osborn*   currunt *HEH* (*in*   L M W *Osborn*
300 Nec] Non *HEH*   margin*: *Agglomer-   315 lethiferum] letifer-
301 Navim] navem   ant)   um *HEH*
    HEH   314 mortem] *orat *HEH*   arcu] *ictu *HEH* (*in*
306 vique] vimque *Os-   (*in margin*: *mor-   margin*: *arcu)
    born*   tem)

301. Æolus] Pengry's personification of Denham's "wind."
302. Neptunus] Pengry's personification of Denham's "Sea."

Carolus; haud dubium Cervus consentit ad ictum,
Undantemque lubens animam vomit, atque fluenta
Purpureo moriens ringit crystallina rivo.
    Pulchrum certamen, culpaeque immunior iste est
Venatus, quam quo per eosdem pristina campos,   Runny   320
                                           Meade.
Ceu Fera, Libertas Dominis agitata superbis
Constiterat primum, & sua Se collegit in arma;
Qui conatus erat, vel saltem debuit esse
Ultimus, oppressi populi postrema medela.
Hic Illae primum Tabulae caluere Sigillo,   Magna   325
                                           Charta.
Per quas Arbitrium dominandi tollitur, & Vis:
Fit Civis, qui Servus erat, nomenque Tyranni
Invisum in Regis mollescit amabile nomen.
O Regnum felix, ubi Plebs cum Principe certat
Officiis, & amat quoniam se sentit amari!   330
Hinc neque sic Pax ista fuit diuturna: Sigillum
Deerat adhuc aliud; sanciri sanguine poscit.
Armatus Populus, quo plus de Regibus aequis
Rettulit, hoc usque est ausus sibi plura rogare;
Dum Reges dando tandem Regalia prodant,   335
Et concedendo decedant Jure negandi.
"Invitus qui dat, sese arguit Ipse timoris;
"Gratiaque ingrata est, sunt indonataque Dona.

---

318   crystallina] Chrystal-   325   *Shoulder*] *not in*   336   decedant] concedant
     lina *Osborn*   *HEH*   *HEH*
320   *Shoulder*] *not in*   329   felix] foelix *Osborn*
     HEH

    316. Carolus]   Translates "the King." Once more Pengry reverts, perhaps by accident, to the "A" text "*Charles*."
    321. Dominis]   Pengry's interpolation; presumably he refers to the Norman kings, rather than to the barons gathered at Runnymede.
    322. sua Se collegit in arma]   Pengry abandons the stag or deer simile; perhaps here he is thinking of the barons in arms.
    327. Civis]   Translates "Subject."
    329. Plebs . . . Principe]   Translate respectively "Subjects" and "Kings."
    333. Regibus]   Translates "Princes."
    338. Gratiaque ingrata . . . indonataque Dona]   A wordplay Denham would have approved of, but not contained in his original.

Dum prensare manu, quae non retinere valerent,
Tendebant Reges, primos fecere Rebelles: 340
Dum Populus contra, Legum munimine rupto,
Irruit in vetita, & plusquam popularia jura,
Excessu parili demens peccavit; Uterque
Fit minor, in quantum male certat major haberi.
Cum Fluvius subita pluvia, nivibusve solutis   345
Augetur, victorque tenet contermina prata,
Molibus a latere objectis, atque aggere crebro
Tutatur messes Vicinia cauta futuras.
Hactenus haec aegre fert, fert tamen; attamen ultra
Si quid tentatur, veteremve arctare canalem,   350
Seu mutare novo, notumque avertere cursum;
Nescius ista pati tumet, intonat, obice ab ipso
Diluvium factus, quod erat Torrens modo, nullasque
Agnoscit ripas; Qua vult Se sistere, Ripa est.

FINIS

---

339 valerent] valeret [?]   340–344 *Right margin*]
     Osborn   L M W *Osborn*

341–342. Legum munimine rupto, / Irruit in vetita] Here Pengry makes explicit, in an admirable formulation, the concept of civic disorder as a flood, which had lain implicit in the "deep yet clear" lines, and which Denham brings to the surface only with the specific image of the flooding river which concludes the poem. The present lines are chiefly Pengry's own.

343–344. Approximately translate lines 347–348, or *1655*, lines 343–344, thus bringing the Latin and English once more into synchrony.

345–354. The river in flood: a direct translation of *1655*, lines 345–354, or *1668*, lines 349–358.

Appendix B

WALLER'S POEM *UPON HIS MAJESTIES REPAIRING OF PAULS*

Old St. Paul's Cathedral, completed in 1240 and subsequently re-modeled and enlarged, with its great spire, loftier even than Salisbury, was the glory of medieval London. But the lofty spire, when lightning conductors were unknown, was also the cathedral's greatest peril. In 1444 a fire in the timberwork of the steeple, occasioned by lightning, effected such damage that it was not sufficiently repaired until 1462. In 1561 a far greater disaster struck the cathedral, for lightning "which by natural order smiteth the highest" struck the steeple on the 4th of June, causing a fire that consumed the whole spire of the steeple down to the battlements at its base, and also totally destroyed the roof of the entire church, the rafters, and the interior timbers. At the instigation of Queen Elizabeth money was raised and repairs set on foot, so that by the end of the year the nave was reroofed, and within three years the transepts also. But the steeple was never re-erected, and for the remaining century of its existence the crossing of St. Paul's was crowned with a square battlemented tower, the stub of the ancient steeple.

The Reformation had deprived the church of most of its former sources of revenue, and successive bishops of London and deans of Paul's, after the fire of 1561, found it necessary to expend annually double the funds they received for the maintenance of the entire fabric of the cathedral on the roofs alone. At the beginning of his reign, and again in 1620 and 1621, James I was inspired to project national subscriptions for the complete renovation of the cathedral, but each time his interest cooled, and at his death little had been accomplished. In 1628, under Charles I, William Laud became bishop of London, and with his typical energy undertook the complete restoration of the cathedral as an integral part of his larger plans to strengthen and invigorate the Ecclesia Anglicana as by law established. Under Laud's influence Charles I issued a royal commission, dated April 10, 1631, which provided seriously for the raising of money and rebuilding of the cathedral. During the space of eleven years following, according to Sir William Dugdale, historian of St. Paul's, "through the powerful Solicitation of the said Bishop of London," thousands of pounds were contributed to the work. Donations came from the King, the bishops, the nobility, aldermen, private gentlemen, colleges in both universities, legacies of private persons, from collections from the clergy and from the counties, cities, and boroughs of the realm. In the sentiments of many, Laud's "powerful Solicitation" was not readily to be distinguished from blackmail or coercion. England was during the same period grumbling under the impositions of tonnage and poundage and ship money, and the contribution of further wealth to the cathedral, widely resented, was in the eyes of antiprelatical Puritans equivalent to enforced sacrifice to Baal or Dagon. Laud's interest in the cathedral did not diminish with his elevation to Canterbury in 1633, and his new position as primate merely strengthened the force of his solicitations. His ecclesiastical policies were bitterly resisted, and his desire to reedify the cathedral church of London was recognized as freely by his enemies as by himself as merely one important part of his grand design to reinforce episcopacy throughout the King's dominions.

Despite such opposition as that exemplified by Lord Brooke "passing by Water, upon the *Thames, March* 13. *Anno MDCXL.* with three other Lords, [who] said concerning this famous Cathedral; *viz. That he hoped, that one of them should live to see no one Stone left upon another of that Building*," collections proceeded apace from 1631 until 1643. In April 1633 the work itself was begun, the houses near and adjoining the church being compounded for (in the total amount of £11,080 16*s.* 8*d.*) and pulled down, and the churchyard fenced in so the masons might work in it. Reconstruction was carried on for about nine years until stopped forever, the task still unfinished, by the outbreak of civil war. In March 1643 the houses and revenues belonging to the dean and chapter of Paul's, together with all money, goods and materials for repairing or furnishing the church, were seized by order of Parliament, and for much of the time until the Restoration the building was used as a cavalry depot.

Altogether some £101,330 4s. 8d. was collected for the repair of St. Paul's, whereof £10,295 5s. 6d., derived from ecclesiastical fines, was donated by King Charles for the express purpose of renovating the west end. Particularly this involved erection of a covered portico with Corinthian pillars, the design of Inigo Jones, to serve as an ambulatory for those who had been long in the custom of transacting business within the nave, even during times of divine service. The largest contributions to the cathedral came in 1635 and 1638, in which years, respectively, donations amounted to £15,927 11s. 9d. and £15,931 11s. 10d.; in 1643 the total receipts amounted to exactly £15. It is known that the nave was largely restored before the King's portico was built, and the additional fact that the King's own largest contribution in a single year (£2,860) came during 1637 taken together with that knowledge suggests that the portico was built about 1637 or 1638. By inference, therefore, also (see lines 51–54), Waller's poem on St. Paul's was probably written in or about those same years.

Not a great deal need be said here about Waller's poem. It is briefly discussed and related to the career of John Denham in my life of Denham, *Harmony from Discords*, pp. 19–27, and here and there in the present volume incidentally to discussion of *Coopers Hill* (see pp. 213–214). Additionally, a few relevant notes are attached to the text below. Yet perhaps worth some notice is the apparent inversion of the predictable with regard to the subject of this poem. The Puritan Lord Brooke prays for the destruction of the cathedral in words deliberately recalling Christ's prediction of the downfall of Herod's Temple in Jerusalem, whereas Waller, the Anglican defender, chooses to view St. Paul's in the Old Testament light of Solomon's Temple and the second temple constructed after the Babylonian captivity, and selects his language from the scriptural ambience of Kings, Chronicles, Ezekiel, Haggai, and Zechariah.

By 1641, in any event, Denham had echoed this poem in *Coopers*

Hill, and by 1642 at latest had openly alluded to it, and had echoed it also in the original version of his poem on the "The Earl of Strafford's Tryal and Death." Obviously, then, Waller's poem was in manuscript circulation by that time, for it was not printed earlier than its appearance in Waller's *Poems* of 1645. The editions of that year are bibliographically complicated and three in number:

1) *The Workes of* . . .
2) *Poems, &c. Written by* . . . Printed by I. N. for Hu. Mosley.
3) *Poems, &c. Written by.* . . Printed by T. W. for Humphrey Mosley.

The second and third of these denounce the first as surreptitious, yet the third consists of sheets of the first bound up with additions, and a new title. The present text is drawn from that in a copy of the third of these editions (*Poems, &c. Written by Mr. Ed. Waller of Beckonsfield, Esquire*) now in the Henry E. Huntington Library. A few readings have been corrected in the light of later editions; on the whole the corrections correspond to those made by G. Thorn-Drury in his edition of *The Poems of Edmund Waller* (London, 1905). All corrections are listed in the textual notes subjoined immediately below the text. The designation *ed.* stands for the 1645 edition used as the basic text.

Upon His MAjESTIES *repairing of* PAULS

That shipwrackt vessel which th'Apostle bore
Scarce suffer'd more upon *Melitas* shore,
Then did his Temple in the sea of time
(Our Nations glory, and our Nations crime)

---

4 crime)] crime.) *ed.*

Title] Later editions of Waller's complete *Poems* add "in the Year 1631."
1. th'Apostle] St. Paul; see Acts 27 for details of his shipwreck.
2. *Melita*] The ancient name for Malta, site of Paul's shipwreck; see Acts 28:1.
4. glory] St. Paul's had been for long the most imposing building in Europe; it remained "the goodliest Monument and most eminent Church of [these] Dominions; and also . . . the principal Ornament of the City of London, the Imperial Seat of this . . . Realm" (Commission of Charles I, April 10, 1631).
    crime] That the fabric was far gone in decay. Cp. Denham's "On the Earl of Strafford's Tryal and Death," manuscript version: "Our nations glory and our nations hate."

When the first Monarch of this happy Isle   5
Mov'd with the ruine of so brave a pile,
This work of cost and piety begun
To be accomplish'd by his glorious Son;
Who all that came within the ample thought
Of his wise sire, has to perfection brought.   10
He like *Amphion* makes those quarries leap
Into fair figures from a confus'd heap:
For in his art of Regiment is found
A power like that of harmony in sound.

    Those antique minstrels sure were *Charles*-like Kings,   15
Cities their lutes, and subjects hearts their strings;
On which with so divine a hand they strook

---

13 Regiment] Regiments   15 *Charles*-like] *Charles*
   ed.   like *ed.*

5. I.e., James I.
5–6. Cp. *Coopers Hill*, "A," 81–82 ("B," 65–66):

> Not to looke backe so farre, to whom this Ile
> Must owe the glory of so brave a Pile.

7. Cp. William Dugdale, *History of St. Paul's* (2d ed; 1716), pp. 137–139: "[King James's] princely Heart was moved with such Compassion to this decayed Fabrick, that . . . [he] issued out his Royal Commission . . . [and] himself, to give Example unto others, began the Subscription. . . . But the Collection of Monies went so slowly forward, as that . . . the Prosecution of the Work became wholly neglected."

8. his glorious Son]   Charles I.

8–10. Cp. Dugdale, *History of St. Paul's*, pp. 140–142: "Doctor Laud became Bishop of London [1628] . . . and within a few Years after, procured another Commission from King *CHARLES* for that Purpose [1631] . . . By which Commission the said King . . . resolving to go on therewith effectually, declared . . . that there should be Letters Patent issued out for the receiving of Publick Contributions from all People throughout the whole Kingdom. After which it was not long, but that Monies were brought in to the said Chamber of London accordingly. . . . And in *April* [1633] the Work itself was begun."

11. *Amphion*]   Legendary builder of Thebes, son of Zeus and Antiope. The stones for the walls of Thebes moved into their places of their own accord under the influence of his lyre.

13. Regiment]   Rule; government.

14. Cp. *Coopers Hill*, "A," 229–230 ("B," 203–204):

> Wisely she knew the harmony of things,
> Aswell as that of sounds, from discords springs.

15. Those antique minstrels]   Amphion, and presumably Orpheus, and others.

Consent of motion from their breath they took.
So all our mindes with his conspire to grace
The Gentiles great Apostle, and deface   20
Those State-obscuring sheds, that like a chain
Seem'd to confine and fetter him againe;
Which the glad Saint shakes off at his command
As once the viper from his sacred hand:
So joyes the aged Oake when we divide   25
The creeping Ivy from his injur'd side.

  Ambition rather would affect the fame
Of some new structure, to have borne her name;
Two distant vertues in one act we finde
The modesty, and greatnesse of his minde;   30
Which not content to be above the rage
And injury of all impairing age,
In its owne worth secure, doth higher clime,
And things halfswallow'd from the jaws of time
Reduce; an earnest of his grand design   35
To frame no new Church, but the old refine:

---

21 State-obscuring] State observing *ed.*
27 affect] effect *ed.*
28 structure,] structure; *ed.*
name;] name *ed.*
35 Reduce;] Reduce *ed.*
36 Church] Chuch *ed.*

16–18. Cp. Bacon, "Of Empire": "The Answer of *Apollonius* to *Vespasian*, is full of Excellent Instruction; *Vespasian* asked him: *What was Neroes overthrow?* He answered; *Nero could touch and tune the Harpe well; But in Government, sometimes he used to winde the pins too high, sometimes to let them downe too low.*"

21. State-obscuring sheds] Shops and houses that had sprung up within the precincts, and close to the west end of the cathedral, were, at Laud's instigation, compounded for and pulled down.

24. As once the viper] See Acts 28:3–5.

29–30. Cp. *Coopers Hill,* "A," 61–64:

> Thy Masters Embleme, in whose face I saw
> A friend-like sweetnesse, and a King-like aw;
> Where Majestie and love so mixt appeare,
> Both gently kind, both royally severe.

36. The renovation of the ancient cathedral is made to serve as an emblematic rebuttal of the Puritan contention that Charles I's Laudian church policies (of which this recon-

Which Spouse-like may with comly grace command
More then by force of argument or hand.
For doubtfull reason few can apprehend,
And war brings ruine, where it should amend.   40
But beauty with a bloodlesse conquest findes
A welcome sovereignty in rudest minds.

  Not ought which *Shebas* wondring Queen beheld
Amongst the works of *Solomon* excell'd
His ships and building; emblems of a heart   45
Large both in magnanimity and art:
While the propitious heavens this worke attend,
Long wanted showres they forget to send;
As if they meant to make it understood
Of more importance then our vitall food.   50

---

44 excell'd] excell'd, *ed.*

struction formed part) were "innovations" in religion; at the same time the *refining* of the
old edifice showed that Charles was not reverting to Popery, but erecting the "true Protestant religion."

  40–41. war . . . beauty] I.e., Mars and Venus. In Renaissance cosmic-allegorical astrol-
ogy, Venus always "curbs and moderates" Mars and "checks his destructive influence" (see,
e.g., Pico della Mirandola, commentary on Benivieni's sonnet in explication of Botticelli's
"Mars and Venus").

  43. The Queen of Sheba's visit to Solomon is recorded in I Kings 10 and in II Chronicles 9.

  45. ships and building] Solomon's ships are mentioned several times, e.g., I Kings 9:26:
"And king Solomon made a navy of ships in Ezion-geber." His buildings are chiefly his
Temple and his own palace, at Jerusalem. The pertinence of Waller's allusion is to Charles I's
shipbuilding program, for which the unpopular "ship-money" was levied: the "Sovereign
of the Seas," 254 feet long and armed with 144 guns — the pride of Charles's heart — was
launched in 1637. The reedification of St. Paul's, the most expensive of the King's building
projects, was equally dear to his heart and equally onerous to his subjects.

  47–50. Although there were frequent bad harvests in England during the 1630's they
were occasioned more by excessive rain and flooding, with resultant smutting of grains, than
by drought. Waller's reference is perhaps to Haggai 1:9–11, the Lord's reproval of the
Hebrews returned from Babylon for their desultoriness in rebuilding the Temple: "Because
of mine house that is waste, and ye run every man unto his own house. Therefore the heaven
over you is stayed from dew, and the earth is stayed from her fruit. And I called for a drought
upon the land, and upon the mountains, and upon the corn, and upon the new wine, and
upon the oil, and upon that which the ground bringeth forth." The application to the opponents of St. Paul's is clear enough.

The Sun which riseth to salute the quire,
Already finish'd, setting shall admire
How private bounty could so far extend;
The King built all, but *Charles* the *Westerne* end:
So proud a fabrick to devotion given,   55
At once it threatneth and obligeth heaven.

Laomedon that had the gods in pay,
Neptune, with him that rules the sacred day,
Could no such structure raise, Troy wall'd so high,
Th'Atrides might as well have forc'd the sky.   60

Glad, though amazed, are our neighbour Kings
To see such power employ'd in peacefull things.
They list not urge it to the dreadfull field,
The taske is easier to destroy, then build.

> . . . *Sic gratia regum*
> *Pieriis tentata modis* . . .—Horat.

---

54 *Charles*] Charles *ed.*   56 threatneth . . . oblig-   *sions read*: threatens
                                 eth] *sic ed.*; *most ver-*   . . . obliges

51–52. Inigo Jones, the architect of the renovation, first renewed the nave, making the fabric secure from weather, and repairing the decayed Gothic work in a plain utilitarian style.

54. The King built all]   The entire reconstruction took place under the King's commission of 1631.

Charles the *Westerne* end]   See Dugdale, *History of St. Paul's*, p. 143: "the most magnificent and stately *Portico*, with *Corinthian Pillars* . . . at his own Charge [the King] erected at the West-End thereof; where he placed the Statues of his Royal Father (King *James*) and himself . . . Which *Portico* was intended to be an Ambulatory for such, as usually by walking in the Body of the Church, disturbed the solemn Service." This Roman portico, however incongruous with the Gothic style of the building as a whole, was Jones's chef d'oeuvre in the renovation. Under Cromwell it was converted into shops for seamstresses.

57. *Laomedon*]   Son of Ilus and Eurydice, father of Priam; the founder of Troy. His refusal to pay Poseidon for his work in building the walls of Troy led ultimately to the fall of the city.

61–64. At the same time a justification of Charles's unpopular pacific policy toward the Spanish and a hint of his latent destructive power (cp. the warning at the end of *Coopers Hill*, "A" text).

Afternote]   "Thus the favor of kings was sought in Pierian measures" (Pieria: birthplace of the Muses). The source is *Ars Poetica*, 404–405, where Horace actually wrote "*et gratia regum*. . . ."

Appendix C

THE FIRST PLAGIARISM
OF *COOPERS HILL*

On January 1, 1650/1, Royalist Oxford having been subdued and purged, the Lord General Oliver Cromwell was elected chancellor of the university. A few years later, in June 1654, the chancellor, who had meanwhile become His Highness Oliver, Lord Protector of the Commonwealth of England, Scotland, and Ireland, having concluded on favorable terms a naval peace between his dominions and the Dutch, the university celebrated the event by publishing a volume of laudatory poems. This volume, called *Musarum Oxoniensium* Ἐλαιοφορία: *Sive, Ob Faedera, Auspiciis Serenissimi Oliveri Reipub. Ang. Scot. & Hiber. Domini Protectoris, Inter Rempub. Britannicam & Ordines Faederatos Belgii Faeliciter Stabilita, Gentis Togatae ad vada Isidis Celeusma Metricum*, contained 134 poems, of which 95 were in Latin, 5 in Greek, 2 in Hebrew, 27 in English, 3 in French, 1 in Welsh, and 1 in Anglo-Saxon. Among the Latin poems, one was contributed by Gulielmus Godolphin, a student of Christ Church. The same person, under the name of Will. Godolphin, also wrote one of the English tributes. Godolphin's set of English verses — to call them even a poor poem would be to grossly overesteem them — in intention flatters the Protector, in matter flatters John Denham. For a very considerable portion of the substance of Godolphin's fifty lines is fetched, with only the flimsiest disguise, from *Coopers Hill*. It is of course the "A" text that Godolphin mines; at least three editions of that had seen print since 1642, and the "B" text was not to be printed until the year following Godolphin's borrowings.

William Godolphin (1634–1696) had been elected to a studentship at Christ Church in 1651. He remained at Oxford until after the Restoration, receiving the M.A. in 1660/1. In a few extremely tangential ways his life touched Denham's apart from the plagiarism of

1654. His sister Ruth, for instance, married Valentine Greatrakes, the Irish "stroaker" whose rough ministrations to Denham's lameness were blamed by some for provoking Denham's attack of insanity in 1666 (see my *Harmony from Discords*, chap. vii). In 1665 Godolphin became M.P. for Camelford in Cornwall, and so joined Denham in the Commons. In 1667 when the Earl of Sandwich was sent as ambassador to Spain (see *Harmony from Discords*, chap. viii), Godolphin was sent as his deputy. Godolphin was knighted in 1668, became himself ambassador to Spain in 1671, was accused of Roman Catholicism at the time of the "Popish Plot" and ordered home. He remained in Spain, openly professed Catholicism, and died there in 1696, leaving a fortune of £80,000.

The following text of Godolphin's English verses from *Musarum Oxoniensium* is taken from *Several Poems in Praise of Oliver Cromwel*, printed in *State-Poems Continued From the time of O. Cromwel, to the Year 1697*, I (London, 1709), 13–15.

Affinities between Godolphin's verses and *Coopers Hill*, "A" text, are subjoined immediately below the text.

As when two Streams divided gently glide
The lofty Banks their humble Bowers deride;
The Husbandmen divert them where they list,
Nor can those weaker Floods their Dams resist.
But if they join, and to one Torrent grow,   5
Swelling they rage, and no Restraint will know;
O'er the adjoining Fields dilate their Wings,

1–6. *Coopers Hill*, lines 333–342:

> When a calme River rais'd with sudden raines,
> Or Snowes dissolv'd o'reflowes th'adjoyning Plaines,
> The Husbandmen with high rais'd bankes secure
> Their greedy hopes, and this he can endure.
> But if with Bays, and Dammes they strive to force,
> His channell to a new, or narrow course,
> No longer then within his bankes he dwels,
> First to a Torrent, then a Deluge swels;
> Stronger, and fiercer by restraint, he roares,
> And knowes no bound, but makes his powers his shores.

7. *Coopers Hill*, line 334:

> . . . o'reflowes th'adjoyning Plaines

Hatching that Plenty which the Summer brings.

Such the Events have been, and such the Fates
Of our disjoin'd and reunited States: 10
Who, while asunder from each other torn
By cruel War, became their Neighbours Scorn.
But since that *_Power_, which now informs our Age,   *The Lord
Hath reconcil'd the Strength, and quell'd the Rage   Protector
Of the disturbed Sea, the Fire, the Wind,   15
And (what is more) the Tempests of our Mind;
Far now our Ships their Canvas Wings shall stretch,
And the World's Wealth to richer _England_ fetch,
Till greater Treasures over-spread our Coast,
Than _Tagus_ or _Pactolus_ Sands can boast.   20

With this Design our busy Vessels range
About, to make our Isle the World's Exchange.
Others in times of Brass and Iron live,
Naught but our Pines the Golden Age can give:
Which fell'd, bear better Fruit than when they stood   25

7–8. _Coopers Hill_, lines 195–196:

> O're which he kindly spreads his spacious wing,
> And hatches plenty for th'ensuing Spring

14–16. Cp. _Coopers Hill_, lines 17–18:

> Now shalt thou stand, though Time, or Sword, or Fire,
> Or Zeale (more fierce then they) thy fall conspire

17–18. _Coopers Hill_, lines 209–216:

> So Thames to _London_ doth at first present
> Those tributes, which the neighbouring countries sent;
> But at his second visit from the East,
> Spices he brings, and treasures from the West;
> Findes wealth where 'tis, and gives it where it wants,
> Cities in Desarts, woods in Cities plants,
> Rounds the whole Globe, and with his flying towers
> Brings home to us, and makes both Indies ours.

19–20. _Coopers Hill_, lines 191–192:

> And though his clearer sand no golden veynes,
> Like _Tagus_ and _Pactolus_ streames containes . . .

21–22. _Coopers Hill_, lines 217–218:

> So that to us no thing, no place is strange
> Whilst thy faire bosome is the worlds Exchange.

The branching Glories of the fruitful Wood.
 No foreign Navy shall impede their Course,
Circling the Globe with uncontroled Force.
While, with the Sun, they round the World, their Might
Becomes as Universal as his Light; 30
Making those Bounds which bind the farthest Land,
The Limits, *Cromwel*, of thy large Command,
Cromwel! the Name which made a greater Noise
Among his Foes than Waves or Cannon's Voice.
'Tis he that conquers when he please, and he 35
That makes *Greek Fables English History*.
 Tell me, *Astrologers*, th'Event; and make
From this Conjunction a new *Almanack*.
 Storms oft enrich the Soil; and since our *Peace*
Proceeds from *War*, we hope for more Increase. 40
So Bones which have been broke become more sound,
And *Hydra* stronger from its fruitful *Wound*.
Than *War* naught could our States have closer tied,

28–30. *Coopers Hill*, lines 215–216:

> Rounds the whole Globe, and with his flying towers
> Brings home to us, and makes both Indies ours.

31–32. *Coopers Hill*, lines 131–134:

> Who has within that Azure round confin'd
> These Realmes, which Nature for their bound design'd.
> That bound which to the worlds extreamest ends,
> Endlesse her selfe, her liquid armes extends.

36. Cp. *Coopers Hill*, lines 251–254:

> Where from the woods, the *Dryades* oft meet
> The *Nayades*, and with their nimble feet
> Soft dances lead, although their airie shap
> All but a quickie Poëticke sight escape.

39–40. *Coopers Hill*, lines 37–38:

> While Luxurie, and wealth, like Warre and Peace,
> Are each the others ruine, and increase.

(The *Storms* of Godolphin's lines 39 are not unlikely those forecast by Denham in *Coopers Hill*: in either case they represent the civil wars.)
 41–42. Cp. *Coopers Hill*, lines 331–332:

> Till Kings like old *Antaeus* by their fall,
> Being forc't, their courage from despaire recall.

They're *join'd by Kind* who are *by Blood ally'd.*
Such our Agreement is, as when one Flame   45
Meeting another, both become the same.
Hermaphroditus so and *Salmacis*
(Whose Bodies join'd in a perpetual Kiss)
With our two *States* receiv'd like Union;
Went *Two* into the *Stream*, return'd but *One.*   50

W. Godolphin, St. Ch. Ch.

Appendix D

MECHANICAL INSPIRATION: *COOPERS HILL* IN POOLE'S *ENGLISH PARNASSUS*[1]

When John Denham propounded to Cooper's Hill, "if I can be to thee / A Poet, thou *Parnassus* art to mee," he had in mind a more elevated view of poetic inspiration than that which motivated Joshua Poole to compile his *English Parnassus: Or, a Helpe to English Poesie.* The fact did not deter Poole from listing, among the sixty "Books principally made use of" in the construction of his plagiarist's handbook, the name of "Cowpers Hill."

The English Parnassus: Or, a Helpe to English Poesie. Containing A Short Institution of that Art; A Collection of all . . . The choicest Epithets, and Phrases . . . Alphabetically digested — to give the title in fuller form — was issued in London in 1657, and was exactly what it claims to be. The *Short Institution to English Poesie* is a separate discourse written by one J. D. — who may very well have been John Dryden. J. D. incidentally informs the reader that Poole himself was already dead at the time. The *Parnassus* itself occupies 396 pages, and consists of gobbets of unattributed quotations from the works of various poets, collected under alphabetically arranged headings consisting of rubrics designed to cover every poetical situation that Poole could conceive of. In a sense it was a book of "familiar quotations," designed not for the toastmaster or journalist, however, but for the aspiring poet. Perhaps to diminish inhibitions in his readers against making full use of the glittering treasure trove of poetic gems he spreads before them, Poole is a perfect libertarian in the transcription of his sources, and has no hesitation in running together any

---

1. I have touched on the matter of this Appendix previously in "Denham's *Coopers Hill* and Poole's *English Parnassus*," MP, LXI (1964), 253–260.

number of "choicest Epithets, and Phrases," from any number of poets, under the same heading. His nearest approach to documentation of his sources is the single initial list of sixty "Books principally made use of." *Coopers Hill*, the author of which is not named, is in very mixed company in this list. Its companions include Milton's *Poems* of 1645, collections like *Justa Edouardo King naufrago* and *Johnsonus Virbius*, and such unspecified sources as "Comedies and Tragedies, many."

Coopers Hill appears to have been levied on for twelve contributions, but since only the "A" text was made use of by Poole (he may have been already dead when the "B" text was first published in 1655, and certainly did not live long enough thereafter to have made any use of that text), the *English Parnassus* was untouched by the splendor of "though deep, yet clear." Exactly how many later poets or poetasters may have been unknowingly inspired by one of Poole's fragments of *Coopers Hill* there is no way of estimating. The fragments he selected can, however, be isolated, and the employments he subjected them to exposed. It will be noticed that the rubric under which Poole places a snippet is often fantastically unrelated to the context from which he derived it.

The places from which Poole derived his twelve samplings of *Coopers Hill* are not distributed evenly or randomly through the text of the poem. Five of his twelve selections are drawn from the single thirty-two-line sequence 49–80, one from the isolated couplet lines 133–134, one from the four lines 187–190, and the remaining five from the twenty-three-line sequence 239–261. In Poole's *Parnassus* pages 289–624 are misnumbered 239–572, so in the following examples the printed page number is followed by the real page number in square brackets whenever the two differ.

The relevant lines of the *Coopers Hill* sequence 49–80 are these:
Windsor the next (where *Mars* with *Venus* dwels,
Beauty with strength) above the valley swels   50
Into my eie, as the late married Dame,
(Who proud, yet seemes to make that pride her shame)
When Nature quickens in her pregnant wombe
Her wishes past, and now her hopes to come:

290

With such an easie, and unforc'd Ascent,   55
Windsor her gentle bosome doth present:
Where no stupendious Cliffe, no threatning heights
Accesse deny, no horrid steepe affrights,
But such a Rise, as doth at once invite
A pleasure, and a reverence from the sight.   60

. . . .

So *Windsor*, humble in it selfe, seemes proud   65
To be the Base of that Majesticke load.
Than which no hill a nobler burthen beares,
But *Atlas* onely, that supports the spheres.

. . . .

. . . she cannot boast
Amongst that Numerous, and Celestiall hoast
More *Heroës*, then can *Windsore*, nor doth Fames
Immortall booke record more noble Names.   80

From these lines the epithets and phrases that Poole culls are as
follows:

1. (From lines 49–50) page 270, heading BUILDING *v*. CASTLE:
       Where Mars with Venus dwells,
       Beutie with strength.
2. (From lines 53–54) page 281, heading WITH CHILD:
       When nature quickens in the pregnant womb
       Her wishes past, and now her hope, to come.
3. (From lines 59–60) page 447 [497], heading PLACE
   PLEASANT:
       With such a rise as doth at once invite
       A pleasure, and a reverence from the sight.
4. (From lines 67–68) page 244, heading ATLAS:
       He that the noble burthen bears,
       And on his back supports the spheares.
5. (From lines 79–80) page 297 [347], heading FAMOUS:
                                       Fames
       Immortal books record no nobler names.

Coopers Hill lines 133–134 read thus:

That bound which to the worlds extreamest ends,
Endlesse her selfe, her liquid armes extends . . .

   6. In Poole's *Parnassus*, page 476 [526], they recur, under the heading SEA:

That bound which to the worlds extreamest ends,
Endlesse her self, her liquid arms extends.

For *Coopers Hill* lines 187–190 what Denham wrote was this:

Thames the most lov'd of all the Oceans sonnes,
By his old sire to his imbraces runnes,
Hasting to pay his tribute to the Sea,
Like mortall life to meet Eternity.

   7. In the *Parnassus* on page 468 [518], under the heading RIVER, appears this:

The Oceans sons,
That to their old sires strict embraces run,
Hasting to pay their tribute to the sea,
Like mortal life to meet eternity.

   The final five of Poole's selections to be noted all come from within the twenty-three-line sequence of *Coopers Hill* lines 239–261. In Denham's poem the relevant portions of that sequence are these:

The streame is so transparent, pure, and cleare,
That had the selfe-enamour'd youth gaz'd here,   240
So fatally deceiv'd he had not beene,
While he the bottome, not his face had seene.
  . . . .
Where from the woods, the *Dryades* oft meet
The *Nayades*, and with their nimble feet
Soft dances lead, although their airie shap
All but a quicke Poëticke sight escape;
There *Faunus* and *Sylvanus* keepe their Courts,   255
And thither all the horrid hoast resorts,
(When like the Elixar, with his evening beames,
The Sunne has turn'd to gold the silver streames)
To graze the ranker Meade, that noble Herd,
On whose sublime, and shady fronts is rear'd   260
Natures greater Master-peice . . .

Poole's excerpts from this passage follow:

8. (From lines 239–242) page 494 [544], heading A SPRING *or* FOUNTAIN:

> The water so transparent, pure, and clear,
> That had the self enamour'd boy gaz'd here,
> So fatally deceiv'd he had not been,
> While he the bottome, not his face had seen.

9. (From line 240) page 412 [462], heading NARCISSUS:

> The selfe enamour'd boy.

10. (From lines 251–256) page 563 [613], heading WOOD *v*. ARBOUR, SHADE:

> Where Dryades oft meet
> The Naiade, and with their nimble feet
> Soft dances lead, although their aierie shape,
> All but a quick poetick sight escape.
> There Faunus and Sylvanus keep their court,
> And thither all the horrid hosts resort.

11. (From lines 257–258) page 286 [336], heading EVENING:

> When like Elinar [*sic*] with his evening beames
> The sun hath turn'd to gold the silver streams.

12. (From line 261) page 273 [323], heading ELEPHANT:

> Natures great Master-piece.

Perhaps a few other shards of "Cowpers Hill' lie still uncovered in the immense midden heap of Poole's *English Parnassus*, but there is no easy or logical way to identify and retrieve them. The headings under which these twelve samples are dispersed show how impossible the task would be of recovering them through consultation of topic headings. Meanwhile an advance toward a study of the indirect influence of *Coopers Hill* on subsequent poetry through the medium of the *English Parnassus* might be commenced if someone would undertake, for instance, a census of later poetical elephants who are described as "Natures great Masterpiece."

Appendix E

IMITATIONS AND PRAISES
OF *COOPERS HILL*

It would be supererogatory to reproduce here the contents of the two similar appendixes attached by T. H. Banks to his edition of *The Poetical Works of Sir John Denham*: Appendix D, "References to Cooper's Hill," and Appendix E, "References to the 'Thames couplets.'" Of more value is the remarking of a number of early references or imitations not noticed by Banks, and a placing of some imitations and praises in chronological relationship with *Coopers Hill*.

1. Apparently the first of all poetic ventures to be influenced by *Coopers Hill* was a poem by Abraham Cowley, only some fragments of which survive. In later life Cowley asserted that he had once written a poem in "three Books of the Civil War" reaching as far as the first battle of Newbury in September 1643. The fragments that remain of this poem seem to owe occasional sparks to *Coopers Hill*. For example:

> . . . Edward prov'd his Cause,
> By a Sword stronger than the *Salique* Laws . . .
> Two Kings at once we brought sad Captives home,
> A Triumph scarcely known to ancient *Rome* . . .

> To her great *Neptune* Homag'd all his Streams,
> And all the wide stretch'd Ocean was her *Thames* . . .

> And then, with desperate Boldness, they endeavour
> Th'Ague to cure, by bringing in a Feaver.

These are scarcely conclusive, but if real reflections of *Coopers Hill* they are astoundingly early. The general parallel in tone, method, and conception of Cowley's poem to Denham's has been noticed by

Ruth Nevo (*The Dial of Virtue* [Princeton, 1963], p. 37); these parallels were not noted by Banks.

2. In Herrick's collected poems of 1648 occurs what is the earliest certifiable allusion to *Coopers Hill*, a congratulatory poem "To M. Denham, on his Prospective Poem." There is no clue as to the date at which Herrick composed it, nor any clear evidence in the poem itself of what specific merits he saw in *Coopers Hill*. (The text of this poem is reproduced in my *Harmony from Discords*, pp. 87–88.)

3. William Godolphin and Joshua Poole vie for the credit of earlier ransacking of *Coopers Hill*. Godolphin's plagiarism was published in 1654, which accords him some degree of precedence. See Appendix C, above, for his poem.

4. Joshua Poole had died sometime before the publication of his *English Parnassus* in 1657, and he had undoubtedly begun work on his vast untidy magpie's nest many years before, so that he may well have preceded Godolphin in excerpting from *Coopers Hill*. Like Godolphin, Poole used the "A" text exclusively. See Appendix D, above, for the evidence of his work.

5. An anonymous poem called *The Session of the Poets* (not to be confused with Suckling's *A Session of the Poets*) initiates the charge that Denham bought *Coopers Hill* from an obscure vicar, its true author, for forty pounds. This poem was written sometime between the Restoration and Denham's death, and therefore must be counted among the earlier praises of *Coopers Hill*. (Samuel Johnson characterizes the accusation as "the common artifice by which envy degrades excellence.")

6. In 1664 John Dryden dedicated his play *The Rival Ladies* to the Right Honourable Roger Earl of Orrery. In the dedication he wrote: "This sweetness of Mr. *Wallers* Lyrick Poesie was afterwards follow'd in the Epick by Sir *John Denham*, in his *Coopers-Hill*: a Poem which your Lordship knows for the Majesty of the Style, is, and ever will be the exact Standard of Good Writing." Banks fails to notice this famous remark, recording only from Wood, *Athenae Oxonienses*, this judgment: "A poem it is which for the majesty of the stile is, and ever will be the exact standard of good writing." Wood has obviously borrowed the sentence entire from Dryden.

7. In 1666 appeared in quarto a long rambling poem of 566 lines, by Robert Fage, in close though disjointed imitation of *Coopers Hill*. It was S^t. Leonards / Hill. A Poem. / Written by *R. F.* Gent. / Licensed, *May* the 14th. 1666 / *Roger L'Estrange*. / *London*, Printed for *John Simms*, at the / Cross-keyes in *Cornhil*, near the Royal / Exchange. 1666. The poem deals with such topics, marked by shoulder notes, as "London," "The Great Park," "Windsor Castle," "King John of France, & David King of Scotland," "Edward the 3d.," "Edward the black Prince," "The river Thames," and "The Hunting of the Stag," as well as with such less familiar matters as "Sir George Carterets Family" and "The harmony of the Birds." The extent of verbal imitation is nothing short of scandalous, but surprisingly for such a late date of publication, it is the "A" text that can be recognized in the imitation. For example:

[London's] great Ships, bring Spices from the East
To enrich our Land, and Ingots from the West.

Cp. *Coopers Hill*, Draft III ("A"), lines 211–212:

But at his second visit from the East,
Spices he brings, and treasures from the West.

Banks is quite unjustified in regarding a phrase in this poem — "not half as clear as Thames" —as an echo of the "B" text "Thames couplets"; the "A" text Thames was already "transparent, pure, and cleare."

8. Early in 1666 Denham went mad for a time, but he had recovered by September. Consequently it was either late in that year or in 1667 that Samuel Butler, in his vicious and unaccountable *A Panegyric upon Sir John Denham's Recovery from his Madness*, wrote:

And now expect far greater matters of ye
Than the bought Coopers-Hill or borrow'd Sophy.

It is not evident whether this continuation of the slur originated in *The Session of the Poets* refers to the "A" or the "B" text. It is hard to imagine Butler aware of both, for even a demented enemy would scarcely maintain that Denham had bought the revision as well as the original of his poem.

9. Publication at Oxford in 1676 of Moses Pengry's translation of *Coopers Hill — Coopers Hill Latine Redditum —* provides the first

unambivalent evidence that the reading public has become aware of the "B" text. Most puzzlingly, this translation was made from the 1655 "B" text published by J. B. rather than from Denham's *Poems and Translations* edition of 1668 (2d ed.; 1671). See Appendix A, above.

10. The first apparent English reflection of the "B" text occurs in Charles Montague's elegy *On the Death of Charles II* (1685). This clearly reflects the "B" text "Thames couplets" by calling the Thames the emblem of Charles's reign because its channel is "strong and easy, deep and clear." Attention has been called to this reflection by Professor Wasserman (*The Subtler Language*, p. 69 n. 30); it was not noticed by Banks.

11. In appropriate places in the present work the fact has been noticed that the opening of *Coopers Hill* was inspired by the Prologue to Persius' *Satire* I. The notes to the texts of *Coopers Hill* also indicate that Dryden in translating Persius (1692) allowed his wording to conform closely to Denham's. But in the translation of the *Satire* itself Dryden imitated the "Thames couplets" of *Coopers Hill* in a manner not entirely warranted by fidelity to Persius:

The verse in fashion is, when numbers flow,
Soft without sense, and without spirit slow:
So smooth and equal, that no sight can find
The rivet, where the polish'd piece was join'd.
(lines 120–123)
This imitation was not noticed by Banks.

From 1700 onward imitations of, and references or allusions to, *Coopers Hill*, as a whole or in its parts, multiply astronomically. A garner of them would scarcely reveal anything new.

Index

No attempt is made in this index to list topics mentioned within the texts of *Coopers Hill*, except insofar as such topics are discussed in the notes or general discourse of this book.

Banks, Theodore Howard, Jr., viii, ix, x, xxviii, 6n, 16, 26, 27, 28n, 29, 37, 44, 46, 51, 52, 54, 57, 58, 59, 70, 72, 100n, 294, 295, 296, 297
Banqueting Hall (Whitehall), 36, 156n, 248, 249
Barlow, Thomas, 63, 66
Barnes, Thomas G., xiv, 47n
Barons (opposed to King John), xxiv, 131n, 132n, 159n, 161n, 206, 207, 251, 274n
Basing Chapel, 148n
Bates, (Dr.) George, 156n, 225n, 247, 249
Bateson, F. W., 165n
Bath, Order of the, xx
Battle of the Books, The (Swift), 174
Battle of the Summer Islands, The (Waller), 149n
Bellona (deity), 116n, 143n
Benedictine Order, 120n, 145n
"Benevolent Government of James I" (Rubens), 248
Benivieni, Girolamo, 282n
Bereblock, John, 138n
Berkeley, George, bishop of Cloynes, 166
Berkeley, (Sir) John, 138n
Berkshire, xxiii, xxiv
Birkenhead, (Sir) John, 138n
Bishops (of England), 27, 277
Bishops' Wars, 190
Black Prince. See Edward, Prince of Wales
Bliss, Carey S., xiv
Boas, George, 18n
Bodleian Library, Oxford, xiii, 28n, 61, 62, 63, 73, 259
Boethius [Anicius Manlius Severinus Boethius], 171
Book of God's Words, 18
Book of God's Works, 18, 19, 186, 190, 196
Borgia, [Cesare?], 169
Botticelli, Alessandro, 282n
Bourbon (dynastic family), 144n, 187
Boyle, Roger, Earl of Orrery, 295
Bradshaw, John, 251
Brasenose College, Oxford, 73, 259
Bridgewater, Earl of. See Egerton, John
Bridgewater House Library, 43, 78, 108
Britain. See Great Britain
British Museum, xiii, 28n, 56, 59, 61, 63n, 78, 92, 108
Brooke, Lord. See Greville, Robert

Browne, (Sir) Thomas, 18, 19
Buckingham, Duke of. See Villiers, Robert
Buckingham Palace, 119n, 248
Buckinghamshire, xxiii
Bucolics (Vergil). See Eclogues
Busy, Zeal-of-the-Land (character), 214
Butler, Samuel, 296

Caesar, Julius [C. Julius Caesar], 11, 13, 169, 179
Calais (battle 1349), 116n
California, University of, Berkeley, 61, 135
Calvinism, Calvinists. See Puritanism, Puritans
Camden, William, 116n
Camelford, Cornwall, 285
Canterbury, archbishop of. See Laud, William
Canterbury Cathedral, 239
Carisbrook Castle, 157n
Carolus. See Charlemagne; Charles I, king
Carpenter, Kenneth E., xiv
Carteret, (Sir) George, 296
Cartwright, William, 37, 199
Cary, Lucius, Viscount Falkland, 182, 183
Catalogue of the Harleian Manuscripts, A, 44, 47, 53
Catchwords, 44, 45, 51, 53, 72
Catholicism, 194, 285
Catiline [Lucius Sergius Catalina], 169
Causeway (at Egham), xxv, 133n, 181, 208
Cavaliers. See Royalism, Royalists
Cavendish, William, third Earl of Devonshire, 39, 73, 259, 260
Cavendish, (Lord) William, later fourth Earl and first Duke of Devonshire, 73, 259, 260, 261
Champollion, Jean François, 20
Character (literary genre), 18n
Charlemagne, 39, 40
Charles I, king, xix, xx, xxvii, 8, 14, 20, 21, 22, 26, 29, 31, 32, 35, 36, 39, 43, 53, 64, 109n, 110n, 113n, 114n, 117n, 118n, 119n, 130n, 131n, 132n, 138n, 140n, 141n, 144n, 145n, 154n, 155n, 156n, 157n, 158n, 159n, 160n, 161n, 179, 185–190 passim, 194, 195, 198, 199, 201, 203–214 passim, 221, 223–229 passim, 233, 234, 235, 236, 238, 239, 243,

ham] (O Hehir), xiii, xxviii, 23n, 27n, 29n, 64n, 67n, 138n, 278, 285, 295

Haslerig, (Sir) Arthur, 212

Havens, Raymond D., 6n, 7

Hazen, Allen T., 62n

Hebrew language, 284

Hebrews (nation), 282n

Heliades, 149n

Helicon, 11, 109n

Henri IV, king of France, 117n, 144n, 187, 264n

Henrietta Maria, queen, 21, 43, 53, 113n, 117n, 119n, 144n, 156n, 185, 187, 221, 234, 248, 249, 264n

Henry III, king, xxv, 117n

Henry VIII, king, 120n, 121n, 122n, 132n, 146n, 147n, 148n, 161n, 191–197 *passim*, 201, 207, 208, 210, 211, 212, 213, 233, 236–240 *passim*, 254, 258, 265n, 266n

Hephaestus (deity), 172n

Heraclitus, 167, 269n

Heraclitus: The Cosmic Fragments (Kirk), 167n, 172n

Herbert, Philip, Earl of Pembroke, xx, 34, 228, 229

Hero simile (in *Coopers Hill*), 31, 33, 130n, 158n, 223, 224, 250

Herod, king of Judea, 278

Herrick, Robert, vii, 228, 295

Herringman, Henry, 38, 70, 71

Hesiod, 12, 21, 113n, 171, 172, 185, 269n

Heylyn, Peter, xxviii, 63, 109n, 115n, 116n, 117n, 118n, 119n, 187, 188, 235

Hieroglyphics, hieroglyphs, 17, 18, 19, 20, 21, 23, 114n, 151n, 185, 186, 190, 195, 196, 197, 198, 200, 203, 209, 210, 211, 213, 214, 217, 232, 236, 241, 254, 255, 256. *See also* Emblems, emblemizing

Hieroglyphics of Horapollo, The, 18

Hieroglyphics of the Life of Man (Quarles), 19

High Court of Parliament, 109n, 181, 183, 184. *See also* Court, courts; Parliament

Hill poems, 6, 7

Hindle, C. J., xiv

Hippocrene, 179

Historie of St. George, The (Heylyn), xxviii, 109n, 115n, 116n, 117n, 118n, 187

History of St. Pauls Cathedral in London (Dugdale), xxviii, 140n, 280n, 283n

Hobbes, Thomas, 166

Hoe, Robert, 56

Hoeniger, F. David, xiv, 49n

Holles, Denzil, 212

Homer, 171, 172n, 185

Hooker, Edward Niles, 5n

Horace [Quintus Horatius Flaccus], 179, 207n, 283

Horapollo, 21

Horatian Ode on Cromwell's Return, An (Marvell), 14, 157n, 251

Howard, (Sir) Robert, 7, 13, 112n, 154n, 271n

Hunting, hunts, 13, 126n, 129n, 138n, 156n, 159n, 201, 255, 296

Huntington, Henry E., Memorial Library, xiii, 27n, 42, 56, 66, 73, 78, 106, 107, 108, 135, 259, 279

Hutchinson, Lucy, 110n, 122n, 127n

Hutchinson, Michael, xiv

Hyde, Edward, later Earl of Clarendon, 183

"Hymne to God my God, in my Sicknesse" (Donne), 197

Iconography, iconology, 21, 179, 185, 201, 233, 255

Ilus, 283n

Indies, 124n, 222, 287n

Influence of Milton on English Poetry, The (Havens), 6n, 7n

In Memory of the most worthy Benjamin Johnson (Cartwright), 37

Instrument of Government, The, xx, 147n, 238

Interregnum, 200. *See also* Commonwealth

Ireland, 146n, 188, 203, 238, 284

Irish (nation), 9, 203, 285

Isabella, queen of England, 116n

J. B. *See* B., J.

J. D. *See* D., J.

Jackson, William A., xv

James I and VI, king, xxvii, 13, 17, 118n, 144n, 145n, 156n, 189, 190, 248, 264n, 276, 280n, 283n

Jaques (character), 129n

Jean le Bon. *See* John, king of France

Jephson, (Colonel) William, 140n

Pseudogenres, 7, 8
Puritanism, Puritans, 27, 29, 110n, 122n, 132n, 140n, 148n, 194, 195, 213, 214, 233, 239, 240, 254, 277, 278, 281n
Putney, Rufus, vii n
Puttenham, George [or Richard], 112n, 174
Pym, John, 203, 207, 212, 221
Pythagoras, Pythagoreanism, 22n, 167

Quarles, Francis, 19, 113n
Queen, 185, 221, 249

Rader, Ralph W., xv
Randall, M., xiv
Ray, John, 168
Red Cross Knight (character), 144n
Reformation, 193, 276
Register & Chronicle Ecclesiastical & Civil, A (Kennet), 61
Religio Medici (Browne), 18, 19
Renaissance, 10, 21, 113n, 121n, 123n, 133n, 141n, 165, 167, 168, 185, 193, 200, 201, 207, 282n
Restoration (of Charles II), xx, 14, 15, 49, 239, 278, 284, 295
Rhizomata (Empedoclean concept), 126n, 152n, 167
Rival Ladies, The (Dryden), 295
River, simile or emblem (in *Coopers Hill*), 36, 196, 197, 198, 200, 201, 207, 208, 209, 211, 212, 217, 241, 242, 252, 255, 275n
Rome, 39, 150n, 179, 193, 294
Round Table (of King Arthur), 115n, 117n, 186
Round Tower (at Windsor), 186
Royalism, Royalists, 26, 27, 28, 29, 30, 35, 61, 62, 63, 65, 66, 182, 187, 209, 210, 214, 221, 226, 227, 228, 229, 232, 238, 239, 244, 284
Rubens, Peter Paul, 21n, 36, 119n, 156n, 248
Rubens: The Whitehall Ceiling (Millar), 249n
Rump Parliament, xx, 51, 253
Rump Songs, 43, 51n
Runnymede, Egham, vii n, xxvi, xxvii, 20, 127n, 133n, 152n, 181, 202, 206, 211, 224, 256, 274n

St. Anne's Chapel, xxiv, 20, 148n, 181, 191, 195, 238, 240

St. Anne's Hill, Chertsey, xxiv, xxvii, 20, 120n, 139n, 145n, 148n, 181, 191, 192, 195, 196, 197, 201, 202, 210, 211, 213, 216, 217, 218, 222, 232, 233, 236, 238, 240, 254
"St. Anne's Hill" (section of *Coopers Hill*), 207, 217, 222, 236
St. Edward, 116n
"St. George and the Dragon" (Rubens), 119n, 156n, 248
St. George of Cappadocia, 20, 116n, 117n, 118n, 119n, 144n, 156n, 188, 189, 234, 235, 248, 254, 264n
St. James's Park, 8
St. Leonard's Hill (Fage), 6, 7, 296
St. Paul's, deans of, 276, 277
St. Paul's Cathedral, xxvi, xxvii, 8, 20, 32, 79n, 110n, 140n, 145n, 148n, 177, 178, 179, 213, 214, 216, 217, 218, 219, 221, 230, 231, 232, 233, 235, 236, 239, 240, 254, 276, 277, 278, 279, 281, 282n
Salisbury, Countess of [Katherine Montacute? Joan of Kent?], 116n, 187
Salisbury, Wiltshire, 34
Salisbury Cathedral, 276
Salisbury Plain, 15
Salmacida Spolia (Davenant), 156n, 249
Sandwich, Earl of. *See* Montague, Edward
Satire I, Prologue (Persius), 109n, 138n, 179, 297
Scotland, 17, 117n, 118n, 144n, 186, 187, 188, 189, 238, 248, 284, 296
Scots (nation), 43, 117n, 144n, 157n, 158n, 187, 190, 203
Scott, John, 144n
"Second Eglogue" (Mantuan), 133n
Second Part of the Institutes of the Laws of England, The (Coke), 206
Secular Masque, A (Dryden), 201n
Selden, John, 119n
Seneca [Lucius Annaeus Seneca], 179
Session of the Poets, A (Suckling), 295
Session of the Poets, The, 295, 296
Several Poems in Praise of Oliver Cromwell, 285
Shakespeare, William, 49, 129n, 207n
Sheba, Queen of, 282
Sheldonian Theatre, 39, 73, 257, 260
Ship simile (in *Coopers Hill*), 31, 32, 33, 130n, 158n, 205, 223, 224, 250
Shoreditch Teachers' Training College, xxvi